Daughter

of a PORN

KING

Doesn't matter who your daddy is,
it matters who YOU are...

CYNTHIA L. GLICKMAN, PH.D.

Daughter of a Porn King

Acknowledgements

To God, the Universe and All That Is, thank you for the guidance, the light that has led my way, and the divinity that I have been so blessed to be bathed in throughout my life.

I am deeply grateful to my parents, my family and the men who have given me the greatest challenges that have been the impetus for my growth and understanding. By experiencing all of these contrasts and living through some of my darkest hours, I have been given the great blessings of experiencing the fullness of Joy.

I have found my J-Spot and recognize that it is my gift and talent to share and help others to find theirs too. I could not have asked for a more divine purpose. I am in love with life and the inhabitants on this planet, thanks to the fine-tuning that resulted from the often rocky and ultimately amusing journey that I have traveled.

To the soulful guides along the way who have supported me and encouraged me to shine my light, including Dr. Don and Robert Moore, I am forever grateful. And I couldn't leave out Rob Manis, who gave me a place to stay in Santa Barbara, LOL (keep in mind, all Robs – not Bobs, although I am grateful to all the Bobs too!).

To Tom Bird who told me I was an author before I believed in myself enough to be one. Thanks to his opening that can of worms, I wrote multiple books. And, to all of the lovely people who have encouraged me to write this autobiography in the first place, including but not limited to my editors: Catherine Rourke, who deeply strengthened my internal voice by following her guidance as an "editorial intuitive" and sharing her soul to birth the final version, and Bryna Rene who helped me to develop my storyline.

I hope that this book touches a place in YOUR soul that brings a smile to your face and plants some seeds of truth and growth in your life. If, by sharing my story, I have succeeded in that mission, then I have accomplished what I came to this planet to do.

Contents

Preface

Some kids had Lucky Charms for breakfast; my brothers and I had porn stars. The day my brother came downstairs and saw Traci Lords, one of the most successful porn stars of the day, sitting at our breakfast table in a see-through, lace teddy, eating a bowl of Cap'n Crunch and guzzling a bottle of Jack Daniels, we realized that we weren't like other ordinary kids...

I am the daughter of a porn king, and this is my story.

When reading this memoir, you may judge me. You may be disgusted by my upbringing and condemn my parents. You may even condemn me for some of the things I have done in my life. You may wonder, "What makes her so special?" And you would be right. I am, after all, just another ordinary girl with an interesting story. You are free to think, feel, and experience what you choose. Whatever works for you—that is great.

But I think, in the end, you will discover an amazing message here for *everyone* after reading my unusual and often entertaining story, for there is far more here than meets the eye in the title alone. Amidst all the assorted childhood memories and eye-candy narratives of babes and booty lies a much greater treasure.

My intention, however, is to share my experiences so that you may, perhaps, see that—even though we all come from various backgrounds and paint the glorious colorful playground we live in with our own unique strokes—ultimately, we are all very much the same. I hope that you too may realize that, within our life circumstances, lay hidden the amazing seeds planted for our personal growth and opportunities to find the real treasure deep within ourselves and life.

All my life, I have been judged by what my father did for a living, or for my assumed religion, and even simply for being a woman. Through experience, foresight and plain hard work, I have learned to cultivate a higher perspective. I've come to realize that the manmade "rules" we set for ourselves, our families and our society have no real significance in the grander scheme of things. These rules make us into contortionists, trying to squeeze us into boxes and cages that get smaller all the time, squashing our joy while making us lose our childlike nature.

If I followed all of society's rules—like making wishes only on birthdays or having 2.3 children and living in a house with the white picket fence—I think I would need medication! But I know that I can choose to be whoever I wish and that what my family members do has no impact upon my contribution to the world.

In other words, who my daddy is matters far less than who I am.

And the same goes for you. As long as I continue to develop who I am as a human being and follow my soul's path, societal rules are ultimately meaningless.

Today, my life probably isn't all that different from yours—but my background has been a profound catalyst for growth. Despite all the perceived bad stuff, I am grateful that I grew up in such a liberal home, with few-to-no boundaries, and that my strong sense of self gave me ample opportunity to discover my worth.

Don't get me wrong. I don't condone anything my family did— but neither do I condemn it. I simply view my life from a place of non-judgment and recognize that it provided me with a unique opportunity for accelerated personal growth. And it was such a great blessing in personal and spiritual development. Rather than making myself a slave to everything that was "wrong" about my childhood, I have made the choice to be free and follow what is in my heart—not in spite of but *because* of it all.

In the process of living and growing, I've done some things I'm not totally proud of. I've made what others may deem as mistakes, yet I do not choose to look at them this way. I believe there are no mistakes—only lessons and opportunities to correct our blunders.

My motto for life is "No Regrets," and I choose to treat every setback as a learning experience. I hope that this book inspires you to live the same way: to appreciate the humor and absurdity in life and recognize that sitting in judgment of ourselves and others will never lead to happiness. We all make decisions based on what we know at the time and then, looking back, it's easy to see what we could have done better or differently. But we didn't have the information then that we have now, so the "if's" and "but's" don't matter. Life happens in the present moment—so, choose to learn and laugh instead!

Here and now, I declare that, with regard to any promises I didn't keep or any persons whose feelings I may have hurt—I was just doing the best I could in the moment. Take nothing personal; it never is. I have forgiven myself and ask that you forgive me as well. I release you, and I release me. Being human means we are perfectly imperfect and I'm okay with that. I hope that, in the end, my story will help you give yourself permission to feel fine about that too.

So this tale is not just about porn or the impact it can have on the mind, emotions and life of a young girl; it is about love and embracing one's own authentic self. And, in that, my story offers far greater richness for those willing to listen, read in between the lines, and embrace the higher message that awaits them.

We are all fallible because we are human. We all go through challenging times and make choices that, in retrospect, don't seem right or intelligent. But we do the best we can in the moment and so, at the time, it was "right."

The important thing is to maintain compassion in our hearts for the dramas that others create in their lives, as well as for ourselves, realizing that we're not alone. We may be of different colors, genders, sexual orientation, sizes and shapes, but we are all one. And, at the core of it, we just want to be loved.

Intro

The Porn Convention

Men would line up for days just to get an autograph from some of these "booty-licious" mamas. The sexy, well-known porn stars would strut their stuff and sign autographs all weekend long. My father and sometimes the whole family would go on these exciting outings, always a great time—a little business, a little pleasure—the perfect vacation.

Video conventions were all the rage in 1979. The Tropicana, the Flamingo and the Sands in Las Vegas provided the perfect setting for film companies from all around the country to display their steamy wares. Movie stars and Hollywood hopefuls would roam around, doing the meet-and-greet thing, while vendors peddled their erotic goodies to throngs of people roaming around the floor. Posters and life-size cardboard cutouts sprang everywhere with big boobs and sometimes even characters in their racy costumes.

My dad, the "Porn King of L.A."—as the neighborhood kids so fondly called him—would go to these conventions to promote related products. And sometimes my two brothers and I would all tag along even though I was just seven years old. I'd never seen anything so huge or so incredibly ornamented as these hotel casinos with their lights, bells, tropical pools and video games. To me, they were like fairytale castles, all glitter and glitz, as perfect a paradise as I'd ever seen—places where anything could happen.

Totally hidden, behind a dark, forbidding curtain somewhere well away from the family-friendly areas, was the secret section for "Adults Only." The most popular area of all, where the largest number of people always lined up every time—specifically men, waiting to meet their dreamboat porn star—was in a separate part of the convention center requiring special passes to gain access. The elite of the elite, it had all the glitz and glamour to go along with it. And I am sure it cost a high price tag to get in, unless you had a booth, which would include special vendor passes. This is, of course, where my dad, Bob, would always set up his booths.

My brothers, Brian and Tim, and I all had special VIP passes that gave us full access to the secret section behind the curtain. When Tim and I were left on our own to explore, I felt like Dorothy in the Wizard of Oz.

Lions and tigers and bears, oh my!

This was a strange and unfamiliar land. Behind the curtain, everything was bright and colorful. Only instead of munchkins and flying monkeys, there were voluptuous vixens and porn stars.

Timmy, I don't think we are in Valencia anymore.

Talk about a circus. "Booty-licious" babes appeared everywhere signing autographs, sashaying around on six-inch, see-through hooker heels, draping themselves over the arms of stammering men. Posters of these same women hung over the booths, only in the posters they were naked—or nearly so. Whips and chains hung from racks and special "toys" shimmered under neon lights.

My eyes felt like they were going to explode. Swiveling my head around, trying to take it all in, I slowly stuttered, "Is this … for *real?*"

"Uh-huh." And with that, Tim—only eight years old, but feeling like a big man, protecting me—took my hand and led me deeper into the Land of Oz.

Wandering up and down the lanes, we noticed a funny smell in the air—a mix of booze, bodies and leather. I felt insignificant, like an ant, with all these larger-than-life figures towering over me. Women decorated every booth, perched on high stools with their long legs stretched out and their tiny skirts riding up their thighs. Shirtless men, flexing their rippling muscles and running their hands over their oiled chests like they were giving themselves a massage, occupied only a few booths. The female form predominated and commanded its revered pedestal like a worshipped goddess.

In the center of the convention, the real action took place, with larger and nicer booths and gleaming Rolls Royce's and Lamborghini's parked on the carpet. Flashing neon lights highlighted giant posters announcing "Fabulous Giveaways!" while actors dressed as Tarzan and Jane swung over the heads of the crowd on ropes attached to the distant ceiling.

It was all I could do to hang on to Tim and follow his lead. A big lump grew in my throat, and my eyes started to water—feeling like the cowardly lion. Shocked, amazed and excited to be here in this strange new world, at the same time I felt very small and confused. I instinctually knew that there was more to this than I actually realized, but I didn't know enough at that age to put my finger on it. There was just too much to take in.

"Come on, Cindy," Tim said, tugging at me. "Isn't this place cool?"

Cool wasn't the word. The more we wandered, the more I saw. I was fascinated by the actresses who sat on their high-seated stools, signing autographs with their puffy red lips pursed in concentration and their size-F boobs on full display. Even to a seven-year-old, it was obvious that what they were flaunting wasn't what they were gifted with from birth. Blouses barely concealed their nipples and skirts hung only long enough to hide their little "chi-chi." High, six-inch heels or better and those short skirts just made men CRAAAAZY. These women were the total epitome of a sex kitten. Meeeowww!

These women had power; oh my gosh! Men everywhere—flushed, dazed and drooling all over themselves—staggered from booth to booth with their eyes as wide and glazed as my own. They looked like they were under some kind of spell.

"BOOTY-LICIOUS"

I had seen pictures of girls like these on my dad's video boxes, but being up close to them was another story entirely. They looked stunning. Perfect. Or, at least, in this reality. I quietly wondered in amazement why this place was so huge with so many of these enthralling women everywhere.

Some with tremendous boobs and low-cut tops would motion to Tim, saying, "Come on over, honey." They drowned him with hugs and signed photos for him. No standing in line for this cutie! I walked around with Tim, completely astonished at their response to men—whether a boy or a grown adult, it didn't matter. One can only imagine what I saw and the scenes they set up and played.

Automatically, I identified that the way to get men to adore you and appreciate you meant that you would have to be skinny, with a beautiful, perfect body and long hair; wear insanely high heels; and sport skimpy outfits to attract their attention. Everywhere they walked and when they stepped away from their table, men would just follow them like they were goddesses. What did they have that was so dizzying to these men and how could an insecure, young, pre-teen girl ever reach such desired status? I felt so inadequate.

Every vixen, no matter how remote her booth, had an entourage
of men crowded around her. When she left her booth, the men
would follow her obediently—like she was the rooster and they were
the hens. They bragged loudly about standing in line for hours to get
a single autograph—and maybe a kiss.

At one of the booths, a woman with tremendous breasts and a
skimpier-than-average top caught sight of Tim. "Come over here,
honey," she purred. "Aren't you a cute little thing?"

The women in the neighboring booths were interested now. I
mean, how often do you see an eight-year-old boy at a porn convention? They thought it was just *precious*. They left their autograph
stations and gathered around my brother, ruffling his hair, leaving
kiss-marks all over his face and hugging him so tightly that his face
was pressed between their gigantic boobs. Tim grinned from ear to
ear, blushing so hard you could barely see the red lipstick on his
cheeks.

Insecurity rose up within me like a flame, and the knot in my
belly started to close in around my heart. When Tim finally emerged
from the all the pressing attention, he carried a glossy eight-by-ten
photograph featuring one of the actresses.

"Look at this," he beamed, holding it out to me. In the picture,
she was on her knees, naked except for tiny thong panties, arching
her back like someone was pulling her hair from behind. Her mouth
was open, her eyes luminous. She looked like she was waiting for
something really, really exciting—like a new toy at Christmas.

In the corner of the picture, she'd written, "For Tim. Be a good
boy!" I couldn't read the looping signature.

Tim was on a roll now. We went to other booths, and he got
hugged and kissed by other actresses. Again, Timmy didn't have to
wait in line. Some of the men scowled when they saw him waltzing

up, jealous that he'd stolen the women's attention. After all, they'd waited in line for hours just to get a twenty-second smile—and here was this little kid, drenched in their perfume and clutching a fistful of photographs.

I stood on the sidelines, my anxiety growing by the minute. Part of me watched Tim in astonishment but another part of me felt sick. More than anything, I wanted to be adored like these women. Just by snapping their fingers, they could get whatever they wanted. We'd seen mainstream actresses in the bigger, less secretive convention hall, but these women were so much more alluring. It was like they had magical powers and I wanted them too.

But it was the underlying mystery that really made me uncomfortable. Despite all the beauty and glitz, there was something *off* about all this—like a bad smell in a pretty house. I had the vague sense that this was all an act, no different than the Wizard of Oz behind the curtain who was still just a man and not some supernatural creature. These women were all dolled up like it was Halloween, or like they were performing a special role in a play. They weren't themselves. And they weren't *real. Maybe*, I thought, *the magic comes from their costumes…*

I wasn't what you'd call a girly type. In fact, I was a total tomboy. I wanted to run around and play baseball with my brothers, not dress up in frilly tutus. Every Barbie doll my mom bought me ended up stuffed in an old suitcase in my closet, generally with its head pulled off. My mother, Carla, always wanted to put makeup on my face, too, like I was a little Barbie for her to paint, but I never let her.

I wondered if she knew something about the magic that I didn't.

Who was I in this mix? Little Cynthia Glickman, Cindy the crybaby. A fat, ugly little girl whose parents left her alone at a porn convention. Sure, I laughed a lot, and I could make people smile, but no one here saw me. They wouldn't hear me even if I screamed. The spell was too strong.

That day I identified that the best way to get men to adore you and appreciate you as a woman was to have a perfect thin body, grow your hair long, wear high heels, and sport skimpy outfits. After all, it seemed the magic was in the "look"—a concept that would haunt me for years.

After a while, even Tim got sick of the circus. We went back to the main area of the video convention where there were posters for regular movies, people wearing regular clothes and even a few regular kids running around. We got to see "Weird Al" Yankovic, Lou Ferrigno and other famous people promoting their latest films. Just like in the secret section, actors and actresses were signing autographs and taking pictures with conventioneers, but the action seemed much less blinding in its intensity. For a little while, I was able to forget about where we'd just been. That's one of the things Hollywood is good for: helping you forget.

Lying in bed that night, exhausted and wrung out while listening to Brian and Tim snore, I leafed through the piles of signed pictures on the bedside tables. Overcome by an unfamiliar, desperate emptiness, I wondered how I would ever be able to measure up. Yes, that's right; I was just a seven-year-old girl.

My dad went to these kinds of conventions often. Before the age of Internet marketing, they offered the best way to promote his products. While he was there, he networked and schmoozed, just like any salesman, keeping his finger on the pulse of the latest and greatest. To him, it was just another job.

That convention in Vegas wasn't the last my parents dragged us to and it never seemed to occur to them how such exposure to sexual icons might affect their kids. I came along for the ride—not that I had much choice in the matter. While the environment continued to make me uncomfortable, we weren't brought up with "normal" societal notions about sex and relationships. So it probably wasn't as bad for me as it might have been for someone else. Still, deep in my core, I knew that the sex, the drugs, the booze and the display were not in alignment with who I was. As much as I wanted the sex-kitten magic, I didn't want that kind of life. I wasn't sure what real love was—but I knew the difference between love and showmanship.

Looking back, I can see the humor in it all—the lifestyle, the industry, and the casual way my parents lugged us into that world. Now it's hilarious to me to think of a little kid observing that scene. But it took a long time for me to come to this point. The subconscious imprint of that first convention on my psyche influenced my relationships and self-esteem for years.

I wasn't the only one bruised by the porn business. As I grew up, I came to recognize that the actresses I'd admired were, in many cases, little more than slaves to the trade. My dad never spoke badly of them—after all, they were filling his pockets with cash—but they weren't regarded people, either. What they thought or said was irrelevant. Outwardly, they were in control. But, inwardly, they remained subservient to the men around them because the men were running the show. By the time these women realized that the industry wasn't as glamorous as it was cracked up to be, they were in too deep: dependent on the money, or the drugs, or the attention. Not to mention the underage girls who got reeled into the business early and didn't know that they had many choices. They stayed in until the business spat them out.

The male actors didn't have it much better. I remember conversing with a guy in the industry who wanted so badly to get out of the business but felt he couldn't leave because no one else would pay him the kind of money he was making as a stud. He said that no one cared about him—he was just a prop, expected to "pop" on command. What he really wanted was a normal life with a normal girlfriend, but he was fairly well-known in the business and his name followed him wherever he went. No woman wanted to date him seriously because of what he did for a living. He had gotten himself into a trap, and he was miserable.

But all that is neither here nor there. At seven years old, I didn't realize that the magic the actresses possessed represented a twisted and manipulative version of true feminine power and subservient to male desire. I didn't understand how money could put people in a cage. I just saw the attention the stars got and desperately wanted some of it for myself.

CHAPTER 1

The Journey Begins

Who would pick a big Jew for a father whose chosen profession is pornography and a mother with a borderline personality? Someone ready for the ride of a lifetime!

And what kind of parents would choose to support their family via the porn industry? To comprehend the full story, we must go back to the very beginning... when Bob and Carla were a struggling young couple... to a time before porn became a household staple of the Glickman family.

As the Glickmans rushed rushed to the hospital in the dark of night, this baby girl wasn't waiting to come. At 4 a.m. Carla's water broke, and she prepared to have her third child—the last one for sure. She and Bob already had two boys, both still babies, and here was the third one on the way. With the threat of Bob's unemployment looming over their heads, bringing another child into the world felt like anything but a blessing.

But I came anyway.

Carla, working two jobs and going to beauty school at night, wasn't happy when she realized she was pregnant again. She took out her frustration on Bob and especially on herself.

My mother told me later that she never wanted me. In fact, she did everything she could to abort me, short of going to a clinic (which her Catholic upbringing labeled a sin). She drank and

15

smoked, leaned on the backs of chairs, slept on her belly, and drank disgusting herbal concoctions that the old wives' tales recommended as the best way to induce a miscarriage.

Wanted or unwanted, I was going to get on with it, regardless.

So, to my parents' surprise, Carla gave birth to me outside the hospital doors, in the front passenger seat of their station wagon, under the sterile lights of the entrance. I didn't even wait for the nurses to come out and assist. Eight pounds and crying from the start (as my father always said), I made my presence known. A girl it was and they had no choice but to accept it.

So there I was, an innocent child, born to Carla and Bob Glickman—a young, twenty-something couple just trying to make their way in the world.

But what does one do with a girl? Carla wasn't sure. At the very least, I should have been a boy. Boys are easier. I could have worn Brian and Tim's old clothes and followed in their footsteps.

Once Carla reconciled herself to the fact that she had a girl, she wanted to dress me up and put bows in my hair. But true maternal affection always remained beyond her capability.

For my part, I wanted nothing to do with her. She reeked of cigarettes and booze and something darker—a sort of angry, scattered confusion—and I recoiled at her touch. My happiness and light-heartedness confused and irritated her. Sometimes I know she couldn't help but smile at my antics—but other times she tried as hard as she could to stamp out my spark.

I don't remember much about my dad at that very young age. He traveled a lot for work and each time he left we would drive him to the airport. This was back in the days when family and friends could walk to the gate with passengers. I would stand at the enormous plate glass window and watch the plane take off, with tears flowing down my cheeks, waving goodbye to my daddy.

For a guy who'd dropped out of college, my dad was making a pretty good living in the construction business in 1967. (Not as good a living as his brother, Al, who'd just finished his law degree, but good enough for the time being.) Interest rates stood at an all-time high and construction jobs were plentiful when Bob and Carla met until the market started to crash. By the time my brothers and I arrived on the scene, my father was being laid off and my parents were facing the reality of welfare.

Finances had become really tight for them when I came along as they faced the recession in the early Seventies. Bob felt he had to do something more to provide for his growing family.

In his early twenties, my pops had warm hazel eyes and wore his brown hair cut close to his head. He was a heavyset young man who played football during high school. After two years in college, he decided to join the military and then completed his tour of duty. And that's when he collided with Carla. Standing at five-foot-seven, usually wearing a white T-shirt and blue jeans, he was a real regular guy.

Having spent several months in an orphanage as a child, Bob's challenges began right from the start. His mother had died when he was only two and, unfortunately, when his father, Joseph, wasn't able to take care of Bob. Soon, though, Joseph remarried, and Bob was able to come home to his father and new stepmother, Mildred.

A Polish Jew, Joseph escaped to Canada from Krakow during the Nazi invasion. So, my dad was raised as a Jew, went to Sunday school and Hebrew school, and even attended some private military schools that were infiltrated with Judaism. But he grew up in a world still full of a lot of anti-Semitism and felt burned by the religion due to the teasing and prodding he faced as a young boy. My dad was determined not to force his children to suffer the same abuses that he had to endure

Mildred, who already had a son of her own named Albert, was polished and classy, sporting short, set white hair and standing at about five-foot-three. Generally, she would wear black, with a long chain. She spoke softly when other people were around but was harsh, controlling and downright mean to Bob.

I just about pooped my pants when I discovered the reason her hairstyle was so set. Once, while she stayed at our house, my parents gave her my bedroom to use. I walked into my room and found a mop of hair hanging over my light. Ohmigosh! I had no idea what it was and it looked like an evil monster. When I got over my fright, I moved closer to see what this ball of hair was: two gray-colored, old-lady-style wigs that Mildred had flung over my light at the end of my bedroom—one for her head and the other for back-up.

She constantly buried my dad in guilt and made him feel stupid, scathing him for his actions and judging him for everything; that was how my mother became his perfect fit. Carla vibrated at that same level and gave him the treatment he was accustomed to. Is it any wonder why Bob thought nothing of porn for a living with influences such as Mildred in his early life?

Now I don't claim that he was aware of this on any level, however; he did, in fact, attract it to himself subconsciously, or energetically, because he never recognized the pattern and healed it. Not only did Mildred scrutinize everything he ate and make him feel guilty and bad for wanting foods she didn't agree with, but she also burned all of Joseph's deceased wife's pictures, leaving Bob with no trace or connection to his biological mother.

"Darling," she would say to him in her bitter, high-class voice, "Don't you think... I don't see how... Can't you do *anything* right?"

And then there was Carla—the soon-to-be wife of the future porn king.

Carla worked as a waitress at the drugstore coffee shop. She was a plump, attractive young woman with a passionate nature. She wore her dark brown hair teased into a massive beehive that needed a can of hairspray a week to stay afloat. Though only nineteen, she'd already had one failed marriage and a pregnancy with a drug dealer who abused her.

This was part of her pattern, similar to the relationship she had with her father, whose name also just happened to be Robert, like my father. (Just make a mental note of that for later on in the story). Carla's father whipped her with tree branches when she didn't do as he said or sometimes he would just harm her for his own laughs. Her relationship with her mother wasn't exactly nurturing either. Doris didn't really do anything at all and left my mother to take care of her four other siblings by herself. She was an immigrant from Ireland while her husband, my grandfather, had come from Italy. They met at a very young age and neither of them finished junior high school. They did whatever they could to support their family of five children.

Bob and Carla met in the drugstore café. Bob noticed her, of course—it was hard not to notice Carla, with her dramatic dark hair and smoldering eyes. But he never spoke to her until the day he ordered a Diet Coke.

"Why do you want a Diet Coke?" Carla asked. "You're just fine the way you are."

It was an off-handed comment (actually, she was wondering where his cute friend, Tony, was that day) but Bob, used to Mildred's insults about his looks, beamed at her. When she asked about Tony,

Bob said he'd been sent to Vietnam. After a moment of vague disappointment, Carla shrugged. No sense in chasing a man who'd probably come back on a stretcher.

"Why don't you come over to my place?" Bob asked.

Carla just snickered and asked, "Why would I do that? I just met you."

He replied, "Well, I have a Harley on my fridge; don't you want to see that?"

Bursting out in laughter, Carla took the bait. When they arrived at his apartment, he showed her the Harley motor that he did, in fact, have perched on top of his fridge. And, at that moment, he had her.

And so began my parents' romance.

It was a crazy relationship right from the start, full of passion and drama, anger and frustration. Carla was demanding and controlling. Bob, probably thinking that all women behaved like his stepmother, became more submissive—and subversive—by the day. But they also made each other laugh and, beneath the dysfunction, I believe that they really did love one another.

Bob wanted to make it official right away, but Carla made him wait. Although she'd been living on her own for a while, she was still legally married to her soon-to-be ex-husband and was resisting signing the divorce papers. She was afraid to jump into a serious relationship with a guy she'd just met and staying married to someone else was a surefire way to prevent herself from diving in headfirst and making another mistake. About 18 months later, Carla finally relented and signed the divorce papers.

Bob bought a huge sombrero—one of those floppy monstrosities you only see in cartoons and on Halloween. Leading Carla by the hand out into the middle of the street, he began to serenade her.

"Carla, oh my Carla," he sang. "Carla, I love you, baby!"

Hundreds of people gathered around, giggling and pointing—including Carla's sister and brother-in-law.

Carla's cheeks flushed an angry pink and she tugged at Bob's hand. "What are you doing?"

"Carla," he chanted again. "Oh my Carla!" The more embarrassed she became, the more loudly Bob sang. Not until Carla, mortified and more than a little pissed off, was ready to storm off into the crowd did he get down on his knees and sweep off his sombrero. He asked in his loudest voice, "Will you marry me?"

She gasped. "Bob?" Her anger melted away. So there'd been a point to all this after all.

Bob grinned. "Oh, Carla, my Carla…"

"Yes, yes, I'll marry you! Will you stop singing now?" Her tone was impatient, but she was smiling. After such a spectacle, how could she say no?

They went down the aisle in the traditional type of wedding, with Carla in a long, white bridal dress and Bob in a tuxedo. At the time, Carla wore a size 18 and Bob was just starting to get a belly. She loved him before he had a thing, with almost nothing to his name and little-to-no income, but this was light-years better than the previous marriage she had. Yet she still had her pattern, so she needed to create drama with Bob in order to simulate this abusive scenario.

***

My parents' behavior toward one another and toward me wasn't intentionally cruel, even if it hurt me deeply; they were simply perpetuating the behaviors they'd learned from their parents.

If I really did choose my parents with the offbeat sense of humor that is my birthright, I certainly provided myself with the raw materials to make a shining pearl. And if not, well…

If not, then it was only the luck of the draw that I ended up with two crazy parents in the porn business.

CHAPTER 2

Breaking into the Industry

"**B**aby, we're going big-time!" Bob exclaimed, as he stepped through the front door.

Carla came out of the kitchen to greet him with a confused smile on her face. She dusted her hands on her checkered apron, making sure her hair was still shellacked into its usual towering beehive.

"Honey," Bob continued, kissing her on one imperfectly made-up cheek. "I've done some thinking, and I've decided that it's time for me to step up and do what's best for our family. I think I'm going to give up looking for construction work and start selling porn to adult shops."

"Oh, dear!" Carla exclaimed, clapping her hands together. "What a wonderful idea! Having a husband in the porn business is every wife's dream. My family will be so proud and my friends so jealous."

"And what a fabulous way to raise our children," Bob added with a smile. "They'll all benefit from seeing what really goes on in one of the world's biggest businesses. Sex everywhere, no holds barred. Our little Cindy needs good role models, and the actresses we'll meet will be just the ticket."

"Oh, yes, our little princess learning from pornography actresses. Why save your money when you can blow it up your nose?" Carla giggled. "You're brilliant, dear. Oh, this is going to be great!"

And so Bob took his first steps on the road to money, fame and fortune, and the Glickmans lived happily ever after. Amen.

Of course, that wasn't really the way it happened. First, my family members are *not* the Cleavers, and second of all... Well, let's just say that two semi-normal people don't just dive headlong into the porn industry without reason.

Here's what really happened.

Our next door neighbor, Steve, had a tree in his yard that needed to be taken down. A short Jewish man with a big attitude and a few connections in high places, Steve was, by all appearances, doing pretty well for himself.

Bob and Steve were talking over the fence one day when Steve mentioned the tree. "I can help you out with that," Bob said. "You don't want that thing falling down on your garage."

That weekend Bob borrowed some equipment from the construction site and recruited members of his team to help. What should have been a simple takedown turned into a six-hour job, but Bob didn't complain. He was just happy to help a neighbor.

Steve was so impressed by Bob's generosity that, when he heard that my dad was going to be laid off, he called Bob over to his house.

"You helped me out," he said in his thick Brooklyn accent. "Now, I'm gonna help you out."

The job was simple: Call or visit existing clients to sell new products, get new clients when possible, and travel to the clients' locations to pick up payments for the products. Pretty standard sales job, right? Sure. But Steve wasn't selling basketballs or bedroom furniture. He was selling porn on eight-millimeter reels.

Bob, looking unemployment in the eye, didn't care one way or the other what those boxes contained, or what was on the shelves of the stores he serviced. Steve paid him the same salary he'd been making as a construction superintendent. He still delivered for Pizza Man at night, but eventually he was able to quit there as well.

"Let's wait three days before we make this decision," Carla suggested. But, in the end, the fact that Bob needed a job superseded whatever reservations she had, and selling porn was the best option available at the moment. She didn't want to sink back into the kind of poverty she'd grown up in and, if porn was her way out... well, so be it.

Bob would travel around the country collecting cash payments from Steve's clients every month. Back at home, he'd spend his time "pounding the pavement," as they say, making sales calls and organizing the shipping of products to adult film stores nationwide. At the time, it was illegal to sell pornographic materials across state lines, so he would talk to the clients in code.

"How many tennis balls do you want this time, Joe?" Bob would ask. "Fifty? One hundred? I've got all different colors. I'll give you a prime selection."

"How much for seventy-five?"

"Seven hundred. And that's a sweet deal."

It sure was. For the first two years, Bob and Steve made money hand over fist for those "tennis balls," and the stores sold them like hotcakes. The problem was that the FBI became aware of Steve's game. Some operative in Hawaii started recording phone conversations on Steve's line and picked up on Bob talking to Steve's clients. Code words or not, the FBI knew that there was no way anyone would pay seven hundred bucks for seventy-five tennis balls.

When the FBI knocked on Steve's door, he put on his most innocent face and said, "I don't know anything about any porn sales. You're gonna have to talk to Bob. He's the one you got on the tapes, right?"

Steve played dumb so well that the feds left him alone and called Bob in for questioning instead. Once they played the tapes for him, Bob knew Steve had thrown him under the bus. "Do you hear that voice in the background of the recording?" he asked the interviewer. "That's Steve telling me what to say. I didn't even know what those tennis balls were, or why someone would want to pay seven hundred bucks for them!"

Round and round it went. No charges were ever brought against Bob but, for obvious reasons, his working relationship with Steve was pretty much over. If something didn't come up soon, he'd face unemployment and pizza delivery again. No way was Bob going to let that happen.

Not long after the incident with the feds, Bob went to a video convention in Las Vegas since he could always find some good business there. Norm Arnold was a member of one of the more powerful Italian families in the game, and he and Bob got along pretty well. Norm drove a Rolls Royce and had more money than Steve had ever dreamed of making. When Bob told him how Steve had ratted on him to the feds, Norm turned stone-faced with rage.

"Are you fucking kidding me?!" he exclaimed, clenching his fists on the table. "That's unacceptable. We're all in the same business here—we're family. No one does that to family."

"I guess I'm not family," Bob said.

"You work for us; you're family," Norm said, in that tone that meant it was final. "Now, take a look at these."

From a box under his table, Norm pulled out six brand new, clear, laminated reel covers. "I'm coming out with a new line," he said. "And I want you to sell it for me."

It was a great offer, and Bob couldn't refuse. Later he went back to his hotel room and dialed Steve's number.

"Steve, I need to talk to you. Can you spare me some time this afternoon?"

"I don't have time for this right now," Steve grumbled. "What the hell do you want?"

Who wants to work for a guy like that? So Bob didn't waste any more time.

"I wanted to tell you in person but, if you're too busy, I guess I'll do it now. *I quit.*"

Later, Bob went to see a show. In true Vegas spirit, he gave the usher a generous tip and scored himself a seat in the second row. When he turned around, he saw Steve sitting a few rows back, fuming. To Bob, this was not only ironic, but hilarious. He laughed to himself through the whole show.

Turns out that Steve was even more pissed off than he'd looked. Not long after the convention, he asked his bosses in New York to order a hit. But Norm's family—larger and more powerful—put out a protection order to override it. After that, it was understood that no one could touch Bob Glickman.

For his part, Bob wasn't about to put himself in another situation where he could become the fall guy. He negotiated a deal with Norm and became a partner in his distribution business. He and Norm also started a company called J&I (short for Jews & Italians, which they thought was a great joke) that focused on splitting sixteen-millimeter films into eight-millimeter reels, which were easier to transport and sell. Norm, Bob and a third partner, Tommy, all drew their salaries from J&I.

To my dad, Norm was like a godfather—*the* Godfather—a larger-than-life figure who took my dad under his wing and taught him everything he needed to know about the porn business. For years not a day would go by when he and Norm didn't eat a meal together, or talk on the phone for hours at a stretch.

I asked my dad later if he'd ever been worried in those days—about associating with Norm and his "family," about the hit Steve had ordered on his life, about the business he was engaged in—but he shook his head. "If I'd been worried, or scared, I would never have succeeded in the business," he said. "I kept out of trouble as much as I could. But, really, I was so focused on making money that I didn't care about any of that other stuff."

In his mind, Bob wasn't doing anything wrong: He was only selling videos of naked women. It was legal (well, mostly) and it paid really well. His office was full of reels—and later videos—with titles like "On Golden Blond," "Cockpit," and "Frisky Business." There were women of all shapes and sizes and colors on the covers, but they all had pouty lips and gigantic boobs.

I guess it could have been worse: He could have been selling drugs, or weapons, or some other awful thing. If that had been the case, I wonder if his attitude would have been the same—but that doesn't really matter. By the time the trouble with Steve went down, he and my mom were already more than two years into a lifestyle they'd never imagined. And, when it came to making money, the sky was the limit.

***

What an amazing gift!

Why would one choose parents who hadn't even found themselves, didn't know who they were, and who decided to go into the sex industry? My chosen path is the catalyst for who I have become.

It has provided me with great contrasts, giving me guideposts in navigating this trail.

Most of us do have some tainted, issue-ridden childhood and it us up to us to decide how to respond to that experience. These become the building blocks of our character and the golden treasures of our lives. Without the darkness, there is no light.

Thanks to this background, I have been motivated to be and do something more for myself. I wanted to prove to the world that women are more than objects for trade and that we all have within us some divine gift and value, which we just need to tap into. We are here to strip away these diseases and dysfunctions that have been passed down through the generations, overcome the negative influences, or what seems to be working against us, and become the gods and goddesses we are meant to be.

Through years of self-evaluation and development in every aspect of my life, I have come to the realization that my value and gift is to spread the word to the world that you can be, do and have anything you choose, and I am living proof of it. I may have had it easier than some and I may have had a life that is totally outside the imagination of others. All I know is that it is my life. And I am still here to talk about it, share it, and be the woman I am today because of it. Striving to be better every day, I too am imperfect, but at peace with who I am.

But now, there's a lot more to share with you about my journey...

CHAPTER 3

Getting Burned

C arla was at home with the kiddies while Bob was getting
his feet wet in the porn business.

Coming as she did from an Italian family, Carla had a
few good recipes up her sleeve. Back when my dad was still working
construction, he'd gotten her a gig making lasagna and other Italian
specialties for Pizza Man restaurants all the way down to San Diego.
It kept Carla busy and helped bring in some extra cash. With her
hair teased into its usual beehive and a cigarette hanging out of her
mouth, she cooked for hours at a stretch—and basically gave us the
run of the house.

My mom was never very present, but the day I got burned she
was really off in Carla land.

Just past learning to walk as a toddler, I would grab anything I
could to pull my chubby self up to standing position. Then, teetering
around for a while, I would check out whatever my brothers were
doing. On this particular day, I was crawling around on the kitchen
floor while my mom cooked.

Our kitchen in Panorama City was equipped with one of those
old-fashioned ovens with the see-through glass doors. Carla was
making lasagna, so the oven ran up to a steamy 350 degrees. While
my mom zoned out in some other room, I decided that it was time to
stand up. Needing leverage, I grabbed the handle on the oven door.

As I attempted to get my balance, the door flung open and slammed against my face. Melted to the door, the skin on my face and hand evaporated on the blistering hot glass. Literally fused to the door, I screamed.

My brother, Tim, who was only three, came running and tried to pull me off the door. But it was too late; the damage was done. I screeched and shrieked and, finally, my mother came over to see what all the fuss was about.

Rushing to the hospital for me again, they packed my face and hands in ice, but it didn't do much. At that point, I had third-degree burns. But more painful were the wounds on my heart and soul—the deep lacerations of neglect.

Where was my mother when this was happening? Where was she *really*? Why wasn't she protecting me and watching over such a young toddler? What took her so long to come when I screamed? Had she seen what happened and simply been unable to stop it—or did she deliberately ignore my cries because she was sick of listening to them day in and day out? For years I asked myself these questions every time I looked down at the thick scars on my palms, or glimpsed the bumpy whitish marks on my face in the mirror—a daily reminder.

There's an emptiness that comes with knowing that your mother doesn't know, or care, where you are and what you're doing. I know now that Carla was as scarred as I was, in her own way, marked and molded by her own traumatic childhood. But you can't explain a parent's experience to a two-year-old who's just been physically and emotionally burned.

My dad didn't witness any of this; he was off collecting money in another state. But he was furious when he got home, and (predictably) the event turned into another one of my parents' battlefields. Bob couldn't believe that Carla could have been that neglectful. For weeks he nagged her to buy a gate for the kitchen—but that was Carla, and the moment the dust settled she drifted off into her own world again. Thankfully, I'd learned my lesson about ovens by that point.

***

"All I want for Christmas is my two front teeth..."

Hmm… How does one fall out of a car at four years old?

My guess is that I was trying like hell to get away from my mother. I must give Carla some credit, I suppose; it wasn't her fault I fell. But when I did, I slammed my front teeth up against the curb. The pain was excruciating, and I started crying. Cindy the crybaby—always crying about something.

"Will you shut up?" Carla snapped. "You are such a spoiled brat."

So much for parental sympathy.

A few days later, my teeth turned black. They still hurt like crazy, and my mother couldn't stand the sight of them. So she took me to the dentist's office to have them pulled.

They gave me laughing gas to sedate me, which was hilarious. Apparently, I got up and danced on the dentist's chair, chattering at all the assistants in the room. It took a little extra gas to knock me out.

My adult teeth finally started to come in a whole year later, and I had a blast being toothless. I'd walk up to strangers in the grocery store and start singing, "All I want for Christmas is my two front teeth, my two front teeth…" and then burst forth into giggles. It was a hoot, and I got a charge every time I made someone smile. Even at four years old, I loved spreading joy. The sour lemon look that came over Carla's face every time a stranger beamed down at me and patted my head just made me laugh harder.

As an adult, I get to let go of grudges. I forgive others for what I may have judged as trespasses, and it certainly makes for a lighter load. Holding onto baggage is like carrying a bag of poop over your shoulder and then complaining about how it stinks. Put the *damn* bag down if you don't like the smell.

I can now look at these situations with gratitude that I wasn't more severely burned, or even killed falling out of a car, and realize it was simply my perception of this experience. Everyone has the right to interpret his or her life experiences as they see fit. All that is relevant is how you comprehend it and how you have not only coped, but also transmuted the scars in your life.

The questions I always ask myself in a challenging situation include: What have I learned? What was my part? And what was the good in this? This keeps you out of blame and victimhood and propels you on the path of evolution. And, if it involves other people, it helps to know: How are you going to see the divine within the other person regardless of what happened?

My mother may have been busy or done nothing wrong. She could have leaped to this quickly and responded faster than I know. And maybe, just maybe, she did see it happen and just wasn't able to stop it. Who knows or cares at this point in time? All that matters is that we all have scars and we all can heal them by facing the issues rather than burying them deep in our souls.

But I still had a lot more injuries to face, whether from parents, porn or my peers…

CHAPTER 4

Moving On Up

It's Not about the Naked Women;
It's All about the Money – Cha-Ching!

I often had the great pleasure to meet scantily clad actresses coming into the house, slurring their speech and stumbling up the walkway. Shoot, who wouldn't be honored—right? I was just a kid and didn't know that these were pornography actors. And my parents kept this world away from me and my brothers for the most part—well, at least until I was old enough to understand it.

So, by age ten, I would go with my brothers to our parents' office and assist them with their business. Yeah, it was a family affair; we really worked together, you know. Everyone pitched in—even Mom!

My father would be off at work, watching film productions and selling boxes of videos with all shapes and sizes of naked women. He would leave us behind when we were little and travel around the U.S., going to adult film conventions and so forth.

One of the most fun experiences for my parents had to be when they got the rights to the movie, "A Certain Sacrifice," starring Madonna before she became famous. And before she shaved her armpits. It was considered a soft porn movie and my dad cut rights to the deal on a paper napkin with the guy over lunch. There were supposed to be legal terms with this contract, so my father had the rights to sell it first to all video stores.

My mother always claimed she was the one who designed the box cover and that it was her idea to get the movie. Either way, however it happened, they got the rights and designed a box cover for it and it was all the news around the country that Madonna had been in a B-rated, soft porn movie.

Our family moved up to the big time. When I was four, we relocated to Valencia, about twenty minutes north of L.A., near Magic Mountain. My parents bought a big, four-bedroom house, but Brian and Tim had to share because my Uncle Kris, who was only 17, came to live with us. He, too, began working in the family business.

Our house had two stories, with a two-car garage and a tiny yard, in a typical tract-home neighborhood. Five hundred homes in the development but only four styles of houses. Nevertheless, Valencia was a real suburb and a big step up from Panorama City. Our house sat on a quiet, tree-lined cul-de-sac with about twenty other homes. With clean air and bright sunshine, we were out of the smog (which would have been great for my asthma, if my mom hadn't been a chain smoker, trailing her own personal smog) and a big back yard to play in.

All in all, it offered the perfect environment for the family of a budding porn king.

Aunt Diane, my mom's sister, and her husband, Bob (she also married a Bob after her father's name), and her daughter, Dawny, lived just two streets away from us until we moved to the big house on the hill—everybody's dream—and then they were a subdivision away.

My very best friend, Lucy, lived in this house down the street. A thin, pretty girl with long thick brown hair, she came from a Hispanic family and an entirely different culture. But she and I, at this age, were thick as thieves. We would do girly things but, more than anything, I remember hanging out with my brothers.

I was a tomboy, thanks to Timmy and Brian, who taught me how to be a boy in girl's clothes. Actually, I never really got into girly things; I would much rather hang out with the boys and dig up frogs and lizards—they were lots of fun, in my opinion. Timmy and I collected ants and put them in jars and scared up some lizards to watch them run and do their funny little push-ups. He let me hang out with him and his buddies. We played in the paseos—little pathways down the road from our house and remained gone for hours entertaining ourselves.

My parents weren't around most of the time. I knew my dad was working, but my mom…Well, who knew what she was doing? While my brothers were in school, she was supposed to be watching me at home. Carla set me in front of the TV with some crayons and a coloring book and I would color and color for hours. I was a bit of a perfectionist when it came to my pictures and would spend hours getting them right, tracing the drawings and coloring them in carefully. When they were done, at last, I felt such a sense of accomplishment.

While I colored, I watched art shows in which they showed you how to paint; totally captivated by the way they used nothing but dabs of colored oils to create something beautiful. It was almost mystical.

Soon, I'd graduated from coloring books to paint-by-number sets. Those were the bomb!

I found it irresistible to see the picture transform into something that came alive for me. It was magnificent to be able to take something dull and white and, even though I wasn't creating it from scratch, turn it into something beautiful. My parents were never as impressed with my artwork as I was, but I always had a new set when I wanted one.

My parents might have been liberal (to put it mildly) in their approach to raising us, but when the money started rolling in, they were generous with it. They showed us that they loved us by buying us stuff. Christmases in Valencia were amazing; they would buy us tons of presents. I'll never forget the excitement of walking down the front stairs and seeing the entire family room filled with gifts. One year Tim got a top-of-the-line drum kit *and* a metallic blue guitar, and all three of us got bicycles.

Our cream white baby grand piano would be surrounded by presents. We started off with one of those square pianos that my mother positioned in the entry hallway of the house. But, eventually, as I continued to take piano lessons and my parents started to make more money, they upgraded to this fabulous baby grand. What an awesome piano. I practiced my scales but never really mastered it. Sometimes we ended the lessons, but I still loved playing on that keyboard. It took me to another place I hadn't been before, filling something inside of me that seemed missing.

My dad was running as fast as he could to make a life for himself and for us. He needed to prove to the world that he was a good man and to Carla that he was a worthy husband and provider. Since she wanted more— new furniture, more trips—he continued to produce. It didn't really matter to him *how* he made his money; all that really mattered was that he *did* make money and as much of it as possible.

To my dad, succeeding in business meant making a shitload of money and dealing with the fallout later.

Once, an interviewer asked him if he enjoyed the "porn" aspect of his job. "What was it like, being surrounded by naked women, and pictures of naked women, and videos of naked women doing naked things all day long?" he asked.

My dad smiled a bit and said, "I'm a Jew. It was just about the money."

Daddy got a new pair of shoes, except these shoes were a new Mercedes. We'd come home from school to see a new car parked in the driveway, and we already had multiple models: a Camaro, a Firebird, a Corvette and always a Mercedes—just like right out of the set of "Casino." When my parents chose our next home, the house on a hill, I think it was, in part, because the place had a two-car garage and a driveway long enough to park four-to-six more vehicles end-to-end.

My parents agreed on one thing, at least: The things you have prove what you're worth. Desperately seeking wholeness—something to gratify the internal void—they searched outside themselves to fill themselves up. For them, that translated as, "If I can just have a new car, then I'll be happy."

Although it bothered Carla that my dad was always looking at hot naked babes—in fact, she beat the living crap out of him verbally for it nearly every day—she wasn't willing to leave him. And neither of them was willing to leave the industry because that would mean stopping the flow of money.

My mom was trapped in a cycle, not knowing how to live such a lifestyle any other way. Having tasted "the good life," she wasn't about to give up fancy cars, furs and limo rides to the airport. The two of them made a good team for each other's imbalances; their addictions were each other's dysfunctions, and their dysfunctions were each other's addictions.

Bob chased the money for his own reasons. He was out to prove something. In some ways, I think he was also trying to prove to

Mildred—the only mother he'd ever known—that he was as good a person as his stepbrother, Albert. The best way to do that, he believed, was to succeed in business—like Al, but only in a different way.

All his life, his stepmother, Mildred, had compared him to Albert. Imagine Mildred's surprise, then, when Second-Best Bob bought her and Joseph a brand new powder-blue Cadillac. "Every time they get in it," my dad said, "they'll remember who gave it to them."

I never found out how Joseph and Mildred responded when they found out where my dad got the money to pay for this beautiful specimen.

This competition wasn't Uncle Al's fault, really. Al was just one of those guys who had it all. He'd finished college, which my dad had not, and he'd gone on to law school. By the time my dad was getting his feet wet in the porn business, Uncle Al was building himself a successful business in L.A.

Uncle Al and Aunt Judy

Uncle Al and Aunt Judy's house in Beverly Hills was amazing to me, with a huge green yard that was probably five times the size of our postage-stamp lot in Valencia and ten times what we'd had in Panorama City. It had a rolling hill and a long driveway that led to the back of the house where there was a free-standing garage and a casita-style guesthouse.

They had it all: live-in maids, nannies for my cousins and even resident nurses who came to assist my grandfather when he started to become ill. But it was the house itself, more than anyone who lived there, that made an impression on me. It was massive, like a fairytale castle. The front stairway was awe-inspiring and there was another one off the kitchen; the rooms intertwined like a maze. Once, when I was exploring the upstairs, I literally got lost. I couldn't find my way back downstairs for an hour.

It was in this house that I first decided I was going to go to college. Maybe it had to do with the message the house projected about Uncle Al's success; after all, he'd finished college (and law school), and my dad hadn't. Or maybe it was something someone said around that massive dining room table. I don't remember exactly when my realization came, only that it happened there, in Uncle Al's castle. All four of my cousins also completed advanced degrees.

My mother, on the other hand, resented being in Al and Judy's home. Ever conscious of her childhood poverty and lack of education, she was acutely aware of the fact that she didn't fit in. After one dinner party, she was so upset that she started in on my dad the minute the car door slammed. Flinging her arms around, stinking of booze, she screeched like a banshee, calling him every name in the book because he'd neglected to tell her that jeans weren't appropriate attire for one of Al and Judy's soirees. Apparently, all of my uncle's guests were as rich and cultured as Al and Judy themselves and dressed the part.

Not that I'd noticed. Squished into the back seat, I didn't understand why she was so upset. But she went on and on and wouldn't relent.

You can put lipstick on a pig, but …

In reality, it wouldn't have mattered if she'd been wearing couture; she would have felt the same inadequacy. She'd been raised by two dysfunctional and damaged people who'd never even finished junior high school, who existed intermittently on welfare, and who made sure to tell her how worthless she was on a daily basis. That feeling didn't leave her when she left her family behind; rather, it buried itself, only to come roaring back to life when she found herself out of her element. If it hadn't been the jeans, it would have been something else, because she needed to create an external reason for the fact that she was no match for these people.

It was partially Al and Judy's unwitting influence that inspired her to demand the best in life. If she wore fancy fur coats and drove expensive cars, then she herself would somehow become more valuable. The concept of going within herself to find happiness and peace completely eluded her. If she had the same stuff as Al and Judy, she reasoned, she would become just like them. If you drench it in enough perfume, the smell will go away.

No matter how hard my father worked or how many nice things he bought her, she always found something wrong with him. He was at fault for her discontent and the biggest target for her venom. Carla loved to play the victim. Her life was so hard; she'd been through hell…blah, blah, blah. According to her, no part of her misery was her own fault, and nothing that happened to her was a consequence of her own actions. I'm pretty sure she walked to school in the snow every day, uphill both ways. In Southern California, no less.

Whenever they'd get into one of their fights, she'd tell me, "Your father's a real asshole." Never once did she step back and look at her own role in the equation.

My dad took a lot of abuse from her, but he wasn't exactly passive, either. Rather, he was subversive and a lot more subtle. He would take me with him on a drive to the store and say things like, "You know, your mother is crazy. She's got a few screws loose. You really shouldn't listen to anything she says." He'd go on to say how ridiculous she was and how ashamed he was of her behavior. According to my dad, he'd never so much as touched another woman—but Carla was convinced he was having affairs all over the place, and so she tried to keep him on a short leash. She threw all kinds of unjustified accusations at him. Sometimes, he told me, he thought Carla fought just for the sake of fighting.

He would constantly complain to me. Even though he was gone a lot, I think he saw how my mother treated me and so looked to me for confirmation that, yes, the bitch was crazy.

Many times I would agree with him simply to gain his acceptance—as if, by disagreeing with him, I would be validating my mother's arguments and, therefore, doing something wrong.

"How can you not hate her for the things she's done to you?" he'd ask me. As if, by me saying that I hated my mother, he'd be justified in hating her as well. Just like Carla, never once did he step back and look at his own role in the equation.

The destructive force of my parents' relationship impacted my brothers and me in hundreds of ways, big and small—but it affected Bob and Carla more. Their unhappiness was completely their own fault, but they were neither the first couple nor the last to go through life in this way.

As they say, it takes two to tango.

CHAPTER 5

Battle of the Bulge

S omething was shamefully wrong with me. With a deep sense
of self-loathing, I began to hate the way I looked; besides,
wasn't that *all* that really mattered for a woman? It wasn't all
roses, living the porn lifestyle while being a chubby little girl. Going
to the convention left me with the sense I was missing the "It" factor,
some secret ingredient essential to the magic. And, with this body, I
would never measure up.

My father had a *serious* weight issue himself. When my parents
got married, he had a bit of a belly. But, by the time I was five, he
tipped the scales at more than three hundred pounds— obese for a
man of his height. He tried everything—liquid diets, grapefruit diets,
you name it. None of them worked.

While my dad's weight skyrocketed, my mother's also fluctuated.
When she decided she wanted to lose weight, she would feed me the
carbs on her plate: pancakes, potatoes and bread. When she decided
she no longer cared, she ate piles of whatever she wanted. And I ate
what she ate.

By the time I was in kindergarten, I was plump, wearing Huskies
and Pretty Plus sizes for little fatties. In fact, I was *so* plump that my
teacher actually had a conference with my mom about putting me on
a diet. Remember, we lived in Southern California, a place where it is

absolutely unacceptable for a young girl to be pudgy. Fat doesn't fly so close to Hollywood.

Feelings of deep inadequacy surfaced inside. Suddenly, I was not only being judged by myself, but by the people who were most important to me. Before I started school, I was a naive little girl who would walk up to strangers and say "Hi!" with a big smile on my face. I would tug on people's pant legs, look up at them and just start giggling. "Hee, hee, heeeeee!" I didn't know any better; I only knew that I wanted to spread joy and make other people smile. But once I got to elementary school, things started to change.

I thought being happy and silly would make everyone like me. But, at recess, the older kids would poke my chubby sides and others would call out, "Here comes the blimp!"—haa, haa, haa. They all laughed and chucked it up while I fell deeper into my own despair and pit of low self-worth.

Timmy's friends, who I looked up to, especially loved to tell me how ugly I was. Every day I would come home crying and thinking, *Maybe this is just how I am. I'm fat and ugly; no one wants me, and I'm stuck this way—for now.* I was always joyful and bubbly when in public, with a personality even bigger than my belly, but that wasn't enough to overcome the darkness I felt within when I was alone in the silence of my own void.

Crying my eyes out, locked in my room, I prayed to God. "Please, please, God, when I grow up, make me thin, fabulous and beautiful. I want to wear lovely clothes and be adored. When I grow up, I want to show them all."

After witnessing all the "booty-licious" mamas in Vegas, I was determined to succeed with the diets. But I dreaded drinking the disgusting chocolate shakes the family doctor gave us and I hated grapefruit even more (and still do). In the end, of course, neither of these things worked. All the shakes and grapefruit in the world couldn't teach me about eating properly. And they couldn't touch the teasing, or the images of perfectly sculpted naked women saturating my world. And it certainly didn't address the actual problem of self-hatred and emptiness I couldn't fill with food.

"Suck in your belly!" my mother would remind me. Tainted by the impact of the porn imagery, she was conscious of appearances too. Thanks to her harping on me, I would wear oversized shirts, attempting to hide my bulk. But, when I would come home from school crying, she'd say, "Oh, no, honey, you're perfect just the way you are. Those kids don't know any better." At the same time, she was pushing these disparaging diets on me.

Even my dad looked at me disapprovingly when he noticed I'd put on a few extra pounds. Between my parents, the kids at school, my uncle Kris (who worked for my dad), the Southern California no-fat attitude and the fact that my parents sold sex for a living, somehow I managed to get the idea: If I wasn't thin, I wasn't lovable.

But I just couldn't stop eating.

Some people talk about "emotional eating" like it's an excuse—a flimsy explanation for a bad habit and a lack of willpower. But it's more than that. As harshly as other people judged me, I judged myself far more. All I had to do was step into my dad's office to be reminded of the fact that women were only good for what they could bring physically, sexually or visually to the world. Every glimpse of myself in a mirror was a reminder that there was something wrong with me. But my parents' disregard for the huge negative impact their world had on me left a deep hole in my heart and in my soul—an emptiness that nothing could fill.

Today, as an adult, I understand that the only thing that could have possibly satisfied me was love. Love from my family and love from myself. But the hunger for something more—for an understanding of life and of my role as a soon-to-be woman in it—translated, to my child's mind, simply as *hunger—a void that had to be filled.*

Rather than lash out, I internalized everything—stuffing my emotions. I became even more outgoing and boisterous, trying to use my joyful, bubbly exterior to make up for my physical appearance. People told me what a great personality I had, which made it even more important for me to hide my feelings when I was sad or angry. And so, when I needed to be distracted from those emotions, I would eat. I didn't have many friends to call when I was bored, so I would eat. My brothers' friends didn't want a chubber like me around, so I would eat. When my mother or father hurt me, I would eat. At least when I was eating, I was doing *something*, instead of sitting there like a lump, alone and unwanted. It was a downward spin, darker and darker into silence and sadness within.

Food was always there for me. It never talked back to me, or told me what was wrong with me. It became my friend and then my addiction—my drug of choice. I ate until the sunken, empty hole in my heart was numb and I couldn't feel anything anymore.

I learned from my father a lot of what I knew about eating. After a big fight with my mom, he would grab the car keys and take off, and then come home to scarf down an entire three-gallon canister of cookies. He had a drawer at his office filled with corn chips and snacks. Sometimes I would hear him get up in the middle of the night and head to the kitchen, where he would eat for hours. Hunched over his commission books in his bedroom, filling out those old carbon copy forms, he would munch on even more cookies from those industrial-sized canisters.

Like father, like daughter—both trying to fill the void. I followed his example. On the way home from school, I would stop at the S&S Donut Shop and buy as many donuts as I could afford. I would sneak food into my bedroom and eat it in hiding. Then, overcome by guilt—because lovable girls were supposed to be *thin*—I would lock myself in my room for hours. The images from my dad's video covers were in my face all the time, burned into my mind. Beautiful, desirable women wearing virtually nothing to cover their perfect bodies. Women who earned attention and love (or so I thought) simply by being gorgeous. How could I ever compare?

When I got a little older, I would sneak into Brian's bedroom when he wasn't around and stare at the Playboy calendar on his wall. Twelve months of perfect girls. I would study these women's bodies—not in a sexual way, but critically. Comparatively.

If my legs could just look like that... I would think. *If my belly was flat like hers...*

I tormented myself for hours. Locked in my room later, full of food and self-disgust, I would feel that sucking emptiness inside me grow even bigger.

The images in the magazines I started reading as a pre-teen weren't as haunting as the posters in my dad's office; they just added insult to injury. The mainstream media takes the blame for a lot of body image issues in young women, and certainly there's something to that. But what I saw was so much bigger, so much darker, that even the most provocative pictures in *Vogue* or *Cosmopolitan* seemed tame by comparison.

What I didn't notice until much later was that as those Hollywood starlets—and the other goddesses who paraded around in my dad's videos—reduced their caloric intake to get thinner and thinner, they also looked meeker and meeker. They were becoming the objects the world thought they were: animate sculptures of skin and bone rather than vibrant, alert, intelligent, *healthy* women.

My parents weren't exactly versed in helping me build my self-worth. In fact, my mother's every word seemed calculated to do the opposite. I couldn't do anything right. My brother would get C's on his report card, and my parents would throw him a party. "Congratulations, Timmy, you didn't fail!"

I, on the other hand, got straight H's in elementary school, which meant "Honors." The one time I came home with an "S" for "Satisfactory," my dad actually asked me, "What's wrong? What happened here?"

Sometimes Carla and my dad would go out for a night on the town. She'd wear the heels that made her tower over him and the black-and-white fur coat that, with her dyed-black hair and long cigarettes, made her look like Cruella De Vil. She'd buy me three or four family-size packages of Nutter Butters, my favorite cookies, and tell me to be good. Maybe this was her way of saying she loved me, or maybe she just felt guilty that she was leaving us alone.

Either way, I loved those Nutter Butters. I would split them apart, so carefully, and eat the peanut butter strip inside. Then, I'd crunch on the outsides and wash them down with an entire gallon of milk. When I ran out of my own cookies, I'd eat the ones my brothers had chosen—those chocolate logs that were all flaky in the middle, or maybe some new, mysterious cookie I'd never had before.

Stuffed full of sugar with no way to release it, I would lie awake in bed for hours, staring at the ceiling. When my parents got home, my mother would stagger into my room to say goodnight. Reeking of booze and smoke, she'd mutter a bunch of indistinguishable words and try to kiss me, and then get pissed off because I got all tense and couldn't stand to kiss her back. "Whass wrong with you?" she'd slur.

I couldn't answer. What *wasn't* wrong with me? With a few more choice words, she'd stumble off to bed—and I'd be left there, full of cookies, even more ashamed of myself and her.

My dad didn't nag me the way my mom did but he didn't spend a lot of time with me, either. Whenever he did pay attention to me, my mom would get insanely jealous, so I couldn't even enjoy those moments. I couldn't shine brightly, even when I felt bright enough to shine. If there *was* something special about me—which I was beginning to doubt—it was becoming more and more obvious that no one really cared anyway.

Fatties Unite!

"Why do the fat ones always stick together? You're like a fat squad or something," my Uncle Kris asked with a chuckle and snicker.

Because of people like you, I thought. But I just smiled brightly at him and walked away. For heaven's sake, this was my birthday party, after all; couldn't anyone lighten up?

Annie, my best friend at Wiley Canyon Elementary, was a Hispanic girl from a very religious family, with sisters named Charity and Hope and a mother named Faith. Her dad and her brother were both named John. I would sleep over Annie's house whenever I could, and we'd walk to school together in the mornings. Annie and I shared a weight problem in common. We befriended another chubby girl named Julie, and the three of us were inseparable for the first few years of elementary school.

Maybe it wasn't so bad. After all, the police had squads, and cheerleaders had squads. And having friends to be on a squad with was kind of cool… even if it was a fat squad.

Annie was a good friend, but I thought she had a better life than I did. Her brother was nice and never bothered us when I came over, and her mom always made sure that we had everything we needed. Faith was a loving woman, a real nurturer. Sometimes, I wished my mom could be more like her.

Faith was also an amazing cook. She made traditional dishes like mole and tamales and always made sure there were plenty of snacks for us. My mom had stopped making lasagna for Pizza Man ages ago and hadn't picked up a pan since. Except on the rare occasions when my dad felt inspired to whip something up, we lived on pre-packaged foods and whatever we cooked for ourselves. Later, my dad hired nannies to do the cooking for us, but it still wasn't the same.

One night when I was sleeping over at Annie's, her dad came home drunk. John was usually a quiet guy and seemed nice enough, although he didn't say a lot. But that night he was screaming and swearing in Spanish at little Johnny (who hadn't done anything as far as we could tell) and he was so mad that his tanned face looked like it would burst into flame. He went to the closet and pulled out a shotgun. Teeth gritted, he leveled it at the room—at all of us—and pulled the barrel back like he was going to start shooting.

Wow. And I'd thought *my* family was crazy! Suddenly, having a mom who didn't want me and a father who was a "Porn King" didn't seem all that unusual. After all, Bob and Carla never pulled shotguns on us.

Faith was horribly embarrassed. She told me over and over how bad she felt that I'd had to see that, and then she cooked for us—because food was the only means she had to make it better. I don't remember Annie saying much of anything at all; it was as if she wanted to just bury the whole thing and forget it. And that was fine with me, since I was getting really good at burying things too.

***

Feeling fat, ignored, unloved and unappreciated at such a young age, a masterpiece of victimhood started taking serious shape. And it resembled nothing like the desired shapes of the women on the screen, magazines and video boxes covers I gazed at enviously while wolfing down my cookies.

I don't blame the magazines, Hollywood or even my parents. I do not even think the pictures of the women are unrealistic, maybe just touched up. But real women are so much more beautiful and divine when we accept and step into our true power. When we allow our authentic selves to shine through, we emanate beauty in our own unique and glorious ways. It begins with self-acceptance and love, which naturally makes us irresistible. And men are impacted as well.

But, when we compare ourselves, we set ourselves up to lose.

No matter how much support I could have had from my family, that downward spin, which is all too familiar to many of us, remains one of our choosing. When we have better tools and greater aware-ness, we can begin to give ourselves better scripts. Mine were clearly negative and self-loathing.

But what if, when those kids started teasing me, I didn't take it so personally? What if I could peer into their lives and see that maybe they were hurting too and had emptiness in their own hearts like I did? Then maybe I could have felt compassion for them rather than hatred for myself. One of the greatest lessons I have learned from this experience is: *not to worry about what others think about you but, rather, focus on what you think about them.* That alone creates huge freedom.

Thanks to the life that I have experienced, I have no regrets. I have no anger—only love for my parents—for I think they gifted me far more than they know. Some of the adversity goes back to that little girl in a ruffled dress, wanting so desperately to get the attention of a father who was too busy for her.

Other issues stem from seeing that she was unwanted from birth and that her cuter cousin was more desired and favored. Nobody cared about her feelings or to hear what she had to say. This little girl grew up seeing that what men wanted was women on posters in provocative positions and that this was the only way in which we were going to get attention.

I learned to suck up my emotions—and be submissive to what the man wanted. Acquiesce to the dominant male energy and desires because you, as a woman, didn't get to speak, to be heard or be concerned about. It wasn't about you; the man was in control and he expected you to follow his command. Isn't that how most women grow up?

The natural human response is to want somebody to love us, and it is a normal need to be loved, wanted and touched. But, without filling our own tank first, we cannot totally allow the magic to flow in and the beauty of deep, unconditional love that God has for us.

CHAPTER 6

All in the Family

B efore we go on with this story, let me explain something. I was born with a defect that makes me incapable of love— or at least in the world according to Carla.

Do you find that strange? I do. But that's what I was told. My mother insisted that I was an unloving child since birth. Not only was I a spoiled brat and an unwanted mistake, but—to add insult to her injury—I was born with a basic inability to love.

What the heck is this world coming to when a baby can't love?

Perhaps (and I'm only speculating), this was a teensy bit of a projection on my oh-so-loving mother's part at that time. I don't know much about babies, but I don't believe they can feed themselves when they are first born, and I'm pretty sure they aren't potty-trained right out of the shoot. These things have to be demonstrated to them by someone in the know. So, I'm guessing that learning to love also requires some parental assistance, demonstration and facilitation—a service Carla, at that point, clearly had little knowledge of how to provide.

I started internalizing long before I realized I was doing it. Of course I shied away from my mother; even when she meant well, she could be so cruel. It was almost better when she *didn't* pay attention to me. This "defect" of mine also goes a long way toward explaining why she favored Timmy so strongly. Tim, apparently, knew how to love her and he was, according to Carla, the genius of the family.

53

The first year we lived in Valencia, when I was five years old, my mother and I were sitting on the couch together. As we sat there, she shoved her freezing cold feet under my legs.

"What're you doing?" I asked her.

"I'm warming up my feet," she muttered petulantly.

Huh? I thought to myself as I shook my head. I got the very clear impression that somehow, despite our ages, I was the adult and she was the child. She burrowed into me, totally unaware of the fact that she was causing me discomfort. She took what she needed, without any thought for those she was taking from. Just like a child.

"How *old* are you?" I asked her.

She just rolled her eyes at me.

As I grew older, with no guidance or understanding from the adults around me, I could only raise my eyebrows at her antics and think, "Does she realize *I'm* the parent here?" A silly thought for a child, perhaps, but it kept popping up in my mind.

This isn't to say that I didn't look up to my mother. The things that came out of her mouth were shocking—especially when she was talking about me or to me—but I think that all children look up to their parents in some way, and the efforts I made to understand her only left me more confused. I doubt if she remembers saying half of the things she did. In fact, she'll probably be shocked when she reads this chapter. Every mom wants to think she's a great mother, right?

A few years ago, Carla confirmed my theory for me. She said, "You know, they don't just hand you an instruction manual when you get pregnant. But every one of my kids is successful, so I guess I did a pretty damn good job with you, even though I had no idea what I was doing."

This is good stuff, I have to tell you. I did a lot of things in my life and made certain choices because they were the polar opposite of what she would do. I wanted to be as little like her as possible. But, in one aspect, I agree with her. There is a certain element of courageousness in how some of our parents brought us into the world. They may have messed some things up royally, but they did their best with the tools they had to work with.

So where is Bob in all of this? I have far more memories of my mother during my younger years. He didn't come into my room at night, when he got home, the way Carla did. He didn't cut me down, or compare me to my brothers—but he didn't stand up for me, either. Sometimes, if I was crying or talking too much, he'd grin and tell me to "Stick a tampon in it, Cindy." It wasn't until I was older that he really started butting in on my life. Still, he was just never tuned in to get it.

He may not have been around much at night, but my dad was definitely there in the mornings. Every day, bright and early, he would stomp into the hallway between my room and Timmy's and start singing, "Good morning to you! Good morning to you! Good morning, good morning, good morning to you!"

If I'd had the words back then, I would have said, "Dad, you're an ass." Instead, I pulled the pillow over my ears and muttered under my breath, "Ugh!" When I was feeling particularly brave (or irritated), I'd grumble "Dad, stop it! Leave me alone!" These were performances of love—the same kind of performance he'd given in that street before he proposed to my mom. At the time, though, I thought he was seriously messed up for waking us up like that. Why bother with alarm clocks when we had Bob Glickman?

The house on the hill was much nicer than the one we'd lived in for the first year in Valencia. This house was unique, one of nine on a cul-de-sac, and out front it had a big blackish rock with our address set onto it in iron and backlit so you could see it at night. You had to take a step up from the driveway to get onto the lawn, which spread across the entire front yard, broken only by one big palm tree smack in the center. Our huge living room window looked out over the lawn to the street. This house was the closest we'd come yet to living like Uncle Al and Aunt Judy, and I liked the fact that it was so pretty and well-kept.

I didn't know what Brian was doing downstairs in his separate room most of the time; I was just glad I got to be upstairs with Timmy. He was my best buddy, and I wanted to be just like him. Timmy ate roast beef sandwiches, so I ate roast beef sandwiches. Timmy liked catching lizards, so I liked catching lizards. Timmy played baseball, so I wanted to play baseball. For a long time I thought of his friends as my friends, even when they teased me about being fat.

Except for Annie and Julie, who lived across town, I hung out with the boys most of the time. I didn't mind and, like I mentioned before, I was a total tomboy. I'm not sure if it was nature or nurture— the fact that my parents so blatantly favored my brothers, or that I had no positive female role models—but for a long time I couldn't be bothered doing anything remotely "girly."

Tim was a total comedian as a kid (and still can be, when he chooses). He could find the humor in anything. When people would ask him questions, he would answer in commercial slogans. He could have whole conversations this way. When my mom was upset, he'd sing, "Roto-Rooter, that's our name! Call Roto-Rooter and all your troubles will go down the drain!"

We got along so well because we made each other laugh. His hair was lighter than anyone else's in the family, and the fact that he didn't look like the rest of us made him the butt of most of the family jokes. I don't know how many times Brian and I asked him if he was the mailman's son.

While his grades weren't as good as mine, Tim excelled in other areas. He was a star athlete and was always at the top of whatever sport he played. He won enough trophies to decorate the whole house and was always on the All-Star teams at the end of the baseball season.

Because Tim played baseball, naturally I wanted to play, too. They didn't have girls' baseball or softball teams back then, so I got to play at the same facility as both of my brothers. The name, Wm. S. Hart Boys' Baseball, was posted on a sign at the head of the dirt road that lead to the sports facility.

Yes, it was still acceptable to call it "Boys' Baseball" back then. This was the Seventies, after all.

If anyone thought the name would be a deterrent for girls like me, they were wrong. I went straight ahead and signed up. There were four leagues divided by age, and each one had several teams. My league (the youngest) played on the farthest field at the southwest corner of the lot.

One other girl was on my team. I didn't really connect with her, however. Skinny and tomboyish, her mother was the Team Mom, so she got special treatment—but I respected her because, like me, she wasn't afraid to tough it out with the guys.

Tight white pants that looked like knickers, white sweat socks that came up to our knees, colored stirrups to match our team shirt, cleats, and a stiff-brimmed baseball cap rounded out our uniforms. We were called the Indians, and our hat was an exact replica of the one worn by the Cleveland Indians—a red Indian with a big white smile on his face and one red feather on his head. I thought my uniform was the coolest thing ever. When I wore it, being chubby didn't quite matter so much, even though we had to tuck in our shirts and I couldn't cover up my big belly where it stuck out under the waistband of my pants. I was part of a team, and I was *good*.

My glove was awesome. It was a Spalding and a perfect fit. You know how when you first get a new leather baseball glove, it's usually hard and shiny and not flexible enough? Tim showed me how to rub leather softener into it and then put it under the leg of a table so it would get pressed down. Thanks to that—and all the hours I spent practicing with it in the back yard—my glove was a perfect fit. I was pretty good at handling a bat, too, thanks to Tim.

When I connected with the ball, I could knock that puppy all the way into the outfield, sometimes even out of the park. My hand-eye coordination wasn't always the best, though, so sometimes I'd miss the ball completely and swing myself around in a circle. The bat would fly out of my hands, sailing end over end toward the score-keeper's box, where my mom was supposed to be sitting. At least I didn't hit like a girl.

My mom was *supposed* to be in that scorekeeper's box, but she wasn't—at least, not after the first few games. She helped out a couple of times, but then she defected to Timmy's team.

Apparently, they didn't have enough people to be coaches (because there was no way my mother was qualified to coach boys' baseball) but there she was, Coach Carla, smoking her cigarettes while she rooted for her team, screaming like a banshee every time Tim scored a hit.

I was silently jealous. I mean, I knew that Tim was unquestionably Carla's favorite child. She was always talking about him. Tim was the smartest of all of us. Tim was a genius. Tim was going to be a rock star one day. Tim knew how to love. Blah, blah, blah. But it still hurt to have it rubbed in my face like that.

Our team practiced every week in a field near the school and then we held our games on the weekends at the Boys' Baseball Park. On Saturdays, we got all dressed up in our uniforms and headed out to play. Along the sides of the field were two dugouts: one for the home team and another for the visitors. Bleachers for parents, family and friends lined each side. The manual scoreboard stood high just outside of the outfield fence, with little hooks to hang the numbers on. Before I was old enough to play, I would hang out on the scoreboard and change the numbers for Timmy's games. (I loved to do this because, when I volunteered, I would get free corn chips and chili at the snack bar.)

A strong throwing arm and a lot of weight behind me to get distance on the ball earned me the position of third base. I was one of the only team members who could actually throw the ball to first base from third.

One day an argument erupted in the dugout. Mark was a scrawny little boy who always got stuck in the outfield because he wasn't a very good player. He kept bugging the coach to put him on third base and wouldn't relent, and today I was starting to get really pissed off. I didn't know why he was so determined to play my position, but I wasn't going to let him have it. That was *my* spot; I'd earned it.

Instead of acting pretty selfish, I suppose I should have let the poor guy have a turn. But I was sick and tired of being ignored and shoved aside, and there was no way I was going to give up my hard-won third base spot to this whiny little brat.

BAM! — I punched him in the nose.

I hit him so hard that his head snapped back and slammed up against the brick wall of the dugout. I was totally shocked at myself. Gaping at my clenched fist, I thought, *What did I just do?*

Ohmigosh! I hadn't really meant to hurt him. But he'd made me so *mad*, and Timmy had just taught me how to throw punches using our big, life-size Teddy bear, and… Mark started wailing as he dragged himself out of the dugout. His parents came running up, exclaiming over his bleeding nose. I just stood there, paralyzed.

The coach and all the parents crowded around Mark, bombarding him with questions about what had happened. As he explained in a mushy voice what I'd done to him, I'm pretty sure I turned purple with embarrassment, especially when people started asked him, "Come on, really? *She* kicked your ass?"

For the first time, I was almost glad my mother was across the way at Timmy's game. Needless to say, Mark didn't play third base that day. I kept my spot, and we won the game, but the sweetness of victory was gone. When Carla came to pick me up later, I didn't know what to expect. I was afraid she was going to start shouting at me right there in front of everyone. I felt horribly guilty, maybe even like I deserved to get yelled at, so I braced myself for the storm.

An awkward moment for certain, but it was because Carla was trying so hard not to laugh in front of Mark's parents. When she told my dad about it, he let out a big chuckle. Sweet little crybaby Cindy, kickin' some boy's ass. They thought it was hysterical.

Second Best—Maybe Even Third

Everybody loved Mrs. Brown. Ecstatic that I, too, would have her as my third grade teacher, just like Timmy, I couldn't wait for school to start.

My mother worked full-time as a teacher's aide in Tim's class for the entire year before. Mrs. Brown made a deal with my mom: She would make sure that I got into her class the next year in exchange for my mom helping her again.

My mom marched me to class on the first day of school, where she dumped the news on Mrs. Brown. Standing outside that big blue classroom door, Carla explained, "I can't be your teacher's aide this year after all."

Mrs. Brown frowned with a look like a deer caught in the headlights, almost as if to say, "*What*!? So you are telling me this now, on the first day of school?" I could sense the disbelief and lack of respect she felt.

Carla did go on to explain, "Well, see, I got a job at a bank and won't be available during the day."

I was *so* let down and horribly embarrassed. I felt responsible for my mother's actions when I saw the disenchanted look on Mrs. Brown's face. I had no clue why my mom had decided to be a teacher's aide in the first place—it just didn't seem to fit her. But, my mom had made a promise, and she'd broken it without a second thought. Part of me had actually been looking forward to having her around and, for once, enjoying the same attention that Timmy got. But no such luck. I was mortified.

Carla didn't mean to burn me, but when it came to me, she never kept her promises. She would tell me she loved me sometimes but it always felt insincere. The same way it felt when my dad said it. Later, I realized my mom, just like so many souls out there, didn't have a full tank— she herself was empty inside so it wasn't possible for her to give out love that she didn't have inside for herself.

My mother may have played favorites, but my father broke my heart. Not because he favored Brian over me—although he did, Brian being his first son and all —but because of Dawny. My cute, petite little cousin was over at our house a lot, and my dad would give her so much attention that it made me miserable. Seeing her getting coddled and cuddled and exclaimed over made me really start to hate myself. I wasn't even cute enough for my own father to like me. I wasn't the special girl. Nobody even noticed that I was hurt. *Ugh.*

I wasn't the only one who felt my parents' disregard; I was just the only one who got it from both sides. My mother and Brian didn't get along at all. He really took the brunt of her wrath. She got so mad at him sometimes that she'd chase him around the house with a tennis racket. Now, I don't know what kind of a punch a tennis racket packs—probably not much; it would most likely have bounced right off Brian's bony ass—but Carla's incoherent screaming was definitely painful. Tim and I would be doubled over laughing with our hands over our ears. I think Brian was laughing, too, even while he was running away from her in terror, because he knew my dad would stand up for him when he got home. After all, he was the oldest son, and the oldest son is always Daddy's favorite.

On the other hand, Timmy, while obviously my mother's pet, caught a lot of flak from my dad. The two of them would have strained conversations about Timmy's grades, or whatever else he was doing wrong, and then Carla would jump in and come to his rescue. It was an interesting dynamic, with Brian and Tim like two dolls that my parents could fight over, tugging arms and legs until there was stuffing all over the living room. I, on the other hand, was like the doll no one wanted to play with. But when Bob and Carla were really going at each other, I was happy to fly under the radar.

The battle between my parents had very little to do with Brian and Timmy. In the end, it was all about them. If they could pit us kids against each other in support of their respective causes, they'd feel like they had won the day. I guess some grown-ups just play that way.

CHAPTER 1

What the Hell is Wrong with You?

The Nannies—"Come and Take Your Medicino!"

"Come and take your *medicino!*"

Tapping a silver teaspoon on the countertop, Concha shouted for us to come and take a dose of whatever she was handing out. When we didn't come on our own, she pulled us into the kitchen by the ears.

No, we weren't rich—but yes, we had live-in maids. When we moved to Valencia, my mother began to travel with my father more often, and it was helpful to have a nanny around to take some of the burden off Carla's shoulders.

Always frugal, my dad got us some assistance direct from Mexico. I remember sitting in a cramped, dingy waiting room with my mom, surrounded by a group of quiet, dark-haired Hispanic women waiting to be interviewed. Their eyes widened as they took in Carla's fluffy black hair and flashy clothes; I tried to smile at them, but most didn't smile back.

Concha was our first maid and nanny. A tall, thin woman, she wore her black hair cropped really short. Femininity wasn't one of her strong points. I don't remember ever seeing her wear makeup. Being a tomboy myself, I sort of admired this about her. But she was really hard, too—all jutting bones and jagged edges—as though life had worn her away.

When she came to live with our family, Concha didn't speak a word of English but her communication skills were excellent. When we didn't do what she wanted, she would grab us by the ears and shake us until we got the point. It was damn painful! We got the hang of deciphering her rapid-fire mix of Spanish and American slang pretty quickly. And it was a good thing, too, because, for a long while, she was more present at the house than my parents. It got easier after my parents sent her to night school to learn English.

When we moved into the big house on Plaza Gavilan, Concha came with us. She cleaned and did laundry, studied for her English classes late into the night, and still had plenty of time to chase us around. Being typically mischievous children, Tim and I were quite a handful.

One day, while swimming in our big blue kidney-shaped pool, it started to rain. It was eighty degrees outside and the water was even warmer. We didn't see the sense of getting out for one silly rain cloud. We were already wet, so what was the difference?

Concha shouted at us in broken English, "Get out the pool! Get out the pool!" Once she'd exhausted her limited English vocabulary, she started muttering in Spanish, "Dios Mios!" and other unrecognizable statements under her breath. Our parents were at the office, and so when we ignored her threats, she decided to come in after us.

We paddled out to the middle of the pool, laughing so hard that we choked on the water. Hanging off a Styrofoam float, kicking our legs idly, we giggled and giggled as Concha got madder and madder. She started to take off her shirt—like she was planning to jump into the pool, capture us, and haul us off by our ears. Tim and I looked at each other incredulously. Her shoes and socks came off next.

The more she threatened us, the funnier the whole situation became. You see, Concha didn't know how to swim. This whole performance was just a scare tactic. Standing there, flat-chested and skinny in nothing but a black bra, our nanny ranted in unintelligible Spanish, spitting mad and on the verge of tears—and we just kept laughing. As long as we stayed in the center of the pool, Tim and I knew we were safe.

Finally, she stormed into the house and picked up the phone. "I call your parents," she declared very clearly from the doorway. I don't know why she thought this would work on us. Since our parents wouldn't care if we were out in a lightning storm, they certainly wouldn't care if we wanted to stay in the pool while it drizzled. They let us do just about anything.

Concha made sure to stand in front of the sliding glass door so we could watch her pick up the phone. She kept glancing our way, punching each number with dramatic flair, then pretending to talk into the receiver.

"Look," Tim whispered. "She isn't even calling them. She's holding down the button."

By this point, I didn't know whether to laugh or feel bad for her. I decided it was too funny not to giggle. By the time Concha finished her little charade, the sun had returned. Humiliated, she came back outside to gather up her shirt and shoes. I don't think she spoke to us for three days after that. Ear-pinching and wrist slaps abounded.

That day, I learned that while adults like Concha may think they're always right, sometimes it's the kids who are the smart ones.

Such childhood memories, while amusing and seemingly trite, actually hold deeper meaning, with clues for greater self-empowerment in our lives. They teach us that sometimes we have to use our own heads instead of obeying a silly command, without question, in Pavlovian fashion.

Just because people like Concha represent authority figures, it doesn't mean they're always right. So, who was the Concha in your life and what did she teach you?

Nanny No. 2

Olivia, nanny No. 2, was only a teenager when she came to work for us. Like Concha, she came directly from Mexico. She had very light olive skin and shiny black hair that fell nearly to her waist. I thought she was lovely.

While Concha didn't really make an effort to hide her resentment of us, Olivia's approach was different. She sat out on the swing set with me for hours, teaching me words in Spanish, so we had a secret language that the boys couldn't understand. She liked to brush and braid my hair, and sometimes she told me stories about her life in Mexico. Even though she scared the bejesus out of me, I really dug her.

While Concha had her ear-pinching technique, Olivia's game was to scare the crap out of us until we had no choice but to behave. One night, when we were home alone, she sat me down on the couch in the family room and told me a story.

"The Devil," she said, "does not like it when you do things you are not supposed to. In Mexico, sometimes young women will sneak away to go dancing at night, when they are supposed to be home in bed. And the Devil will come out to dance with them. He will charm them, sing to them—*serenade* them. They fall in love with him, the Devil, like he is the best man in the world. But when they come to trust him, he knows it, and he comes to find them later. He slashes their backs and marks a red X on them in blood!"

"And then what?" I asked with some trepidation.

"Then, they belong to him. They are his. All because they did not do as they were told."

"But he could pop up anywhere and we would never know it!" I exclaimed. Olivia just smiled, and I shivered.

In my mind, the Devil looked like a cross between a wolf and a sleek Italian man. He had prickly spikes on his body that ruffled when he was mad, and slicked-back black hair that parted around his curving horns. His face was handsome but cruel, like the vampires in the movies. *Definitely* not someone you'd want to dance with.

After Olivia told me that story, the night was a different place for me. Once I was in bed, I didn't get out unless I really, *really* had to. I was terrified to go to the bathroom by myself. Tiptoeing down the hall from my room, I wrapped my arm around the door frame to turn the light on before I stepped inside, because the Devil might be hiding in the darkness. I wouldn't sit down to pee until I checked behind the shower curtain and in the cupboards. I got in and out of there as fast as I could, refusing to turn my back to the mirror in case he came after me.

Later, when my friends learned to play Red Rum, I thought about Olivia's story. It seemed almost like the same thing—calling in spirits to dance with you, or do something for you. I never tried that game. I wasn't sure what kinds of spirits my friends were calling in, but I was pretty sure they weren't spirits I wanted to spend any time with. What if one of them was the Devil, coming to mark a big red X on me?

The visions tormented me for years after Olivia told me that story. I don't know if she realized what an impact it had on me—but then, again, maybe she did. Certainly I was on my best behavior when we were home alone. Concha was fierce, but Olivia knew the bad guys.

While Olivia was well-meaning, her story gave me the creeps and even haunted me for years as a little girl. It instilled a sense of fear—the *last* thing an already insecure, fat little girl like me needed. After all, I was already haunted and intimidated by all the images on those video covers. Weren't women surrounded by enough predators to have to worry about the Devil coming to get them? Interestingly enough, that's exactly what would happen years later...

Babysat by Trolls

When people hear the name "Valencia," the first thing they say is, "That's near Magic Mountain, right?" It's true: Magic Mountain was only a few short minutes from our house on the hill.

In the summers, when the nannies weren't around, our parents dropped us off at Magic Mountain for the day. They would give us each twenty bucks and send us off with a slap on the butt. "Have a good time, kids," they'd say. Sure! We had passes that gave us unlimited access to everything for the whole year. Restaurants, candle shops, puppet shows, live music, games—and of course, the coolest rides, all at our finger tips.

Back in those days, before the Bugs Bunny Gang, Magic Mountain's mascots were a bunch of trolls and other goofy characters. I used to kid around with Tim about how the trolls were babysitting us, because theirs were really the only quasi-adult eyes on us for hours at a time.

I loved Magic Mountain, riding as many roller coasters as humanly possible. The Revolution was one of the best—a white joyride with a big loop. But, after a while, all the attractions got old and the thrill was lost. Sometimes Brian and Tim's friends showed up and they would all ditch me. On those days, I sat by myself in the theater and hid out in a dark corner in between performances, just trying to kill time. I had a lot of alone time.

When I got bored of the theater, I strolled to the candle shop. Standing over bubbling pools of hot colored wax, dipping strings over and over, I created my own candles. Next, I ventured to the glass shop, fascinated by the workers who blew flames with torches to produce vases and jars. When I tired of that, I filled the glass jars with colored sand. The staff taught me how to push the layers of sand down to create birds, build rainbows, generate stripes, and complete other designs. Needless to say, I had quite the collection of candles and jars in my bedroom. When my creations turned out really nice, I gave them away as presents.

Finally, after what seemed like forever, five o'clock rolled around, and the boys and I headed out to the big circular driveway where our parents picked us up. Sitting on the grass, exhausted and full of junk food, we waited… and waited… and waited. No matter how many times my mom told us, "You'd better be out there at five o'clock sharp," she never showed up until six, or sometimes even seven. I got to the point where I hated going to Magic Mountain, because it was so obvious that it was just a place to dump us while my parents went about their lives.

While Magic Mountain was our summer and weekend day care, we also had after-school day care. When we were in elementary school, instead of going home at two o'clock, we took the bus to the Town and Country Farm School, where they had an after-school program for kids whose parents worked all day. We studied and did arts and crafts. Some of my school friends went there too, so I didn't mind it so much.

The program only ran until five o'clock, when we all line up out-side to wait for our parents. Thinking everyone was gone; the teachers locked the school doors and gates—and then came out to find me and Timmy still waiting on the sidewalk. "Where are your parents?" they asked. We could only shrug.

The teachers made phone calls, but most of the time they didn't get an answer. As the evening wore on, their efforts to find us a way home became more and more feverish—until, finally, my mom would pull up in her Mercedes with a cigarette between her lips, so totally nonchalant that the teachers couldn't say a word.

"What's the big deal," she'd ask them. "I'm here now, aren't I?"

This, to me, was far worse than being forgotten at Magic Mountain. I had no words to explain to the teachers why my mom didn't care enough to come get us when she was supposed to. Somehow, when I caught their pitying looks, I'd feel like it was my entire fault, even though there really wasn't anything I could do.

There was a girl at Town and Country Farm named Carrletta. Her parents both worked and they didn't have a lot of money. But every day at five o'clock sharp (or even a little before), one or both of them were waiting for her to come outside with her backpack, and I would stare in admiration. *Her parents must really love her*, I thought to myself, as I watched Carrletta hug her mom before climbing into the car.

I wonder what that's like.

Magic Apples

One day my mother asked me, "What do we need for groceries?"

"We need apples," I told her. I loved green Granny Smith apples.

"Are you sure?"

"Yes, Mom." I hadn't looked, but I really wanted green apples. Usually, we finished them before the week was done.

But when I went to check, I found that there were actually several red apples in the refrigerator. Not wanting my mother to find them (and scream at me for lying), I grabbed the apples while she was still upstairs and ran out into the back yard. One by one, I threw them over the wall by the barbecue pit.

I thought I was safe until the next day, when the neighbor showed up at our house holding a bag of apples. "Are these yours?" she asked, evidently pretty put out. "I think they are. Unless apples are magically appearing in your yard too?"

God forbid someone in our household might have the audacity to throw apples into her yard.

I was stunned. It had never crossed my mind that she might bring them back! Wouldn't any normal person just throw them away? I sneaked up to my room while Carla talked to the neighbor.

I hid for a while, afraid that I was going to be in even bigger trouble. But when Carla called me back downstairs, she couldn't keep herself from cracking up. She kept trying to say something, but all that came out for a while was, "Hmm…Hmm!"

Finally, she caught her breath, and asked me, "Did you do this?"

My face was flaming red, which pretty much gave it away. "Yes."

Still chuckling, she said the words that always cut me deepest. "What the hell is *wrong* with you?"

To Carla, the whole incident was too funny to merit punishment, but I was mortified. I learned my lesson that day: Think things out carefully before presuming anything.

I think the neighbor's appearance was a far more solid lesson than any tantrum Carla could have thrown. I tried to avoid walking past her yard for weeks.

I also tried to avoid the question gnawing at me: "What the hell is wrong with you?" I was different, no doubt, and certainly didn't have a life like most other kids. But there was something else bothering me; I was just too young at this point to fathom what it was. All I could hear was that same upsetting question playing over and over in my head.

Not too long after the apple incident, I was standing on the gold velvet upholstered chair that sat right next to an enormous plate glass window overlooking the front lawn and our lone palm tree. I'm not sure precisely why I was standing on the chair—but as I stood up and leaned over, the chair lost its balance and the back of it went right through my window. My mother heard the commotion and stomped upstairs to find out what the heck was going on. I started shaking. This time, I wasn't going to get a pass.

When Carla asked me what had happened, I said, "Ummm... umm, I don't know." I showed her the window but—since I was in fear for my life, or at least my behind (this was one she might get my dad's belt out for)—I couldn't put together the words to describe the accident. I wasn't any good at making up stories, either, so I just stood there, trying to look innocent and keeping my mouth shut.

After a moment's consideration, Carla decided that it must have been a sonic boom, or an earthquake, because whatever it was had made the whole house shake.

Could a sonic boom actually shatter a five-foot-high window? I didn't know, but Carla was off and running and I didn't try to stop her. She even went to some of the neighbors and asked if they'd heard anything, or felt the "earthquake"—which, of course, they hadn't. Confounded, she went round and round with it, gnawing at it like a dog with a bone. But she just couldn't figure it out.

Finally, I was so ashamed that I let her in on the secret. I could practically see the light bulb go on in her head. Needless to say, I got quite the verbal beating for that one, even though the whole thing had been a silly accident. I could make a fool of myself all I wanted, but there was no way in heaven or hell I was going to get away with making a fool of my mother.

What the hell is wrong with me? I'm not sure but I know something just isn't right...

CHAPTER ▦

Sex and Other Rude Lessons

The Sex Talk

How does the daughter of L.A.'s porn king learn about sex? From her older brothers, of course.

"That's an outrageous lie!" I told them.

Despite all the images with which I was bombarded during my formative years, the mechanics of sex didn't really make much sense to me. The posters in my dad's warehouse were explicit and graphic, but the whole picture still wasn't really clicking. I didn't understand the connection—or the disconnection—between sex and love. I thought love was what the girls in the posters were after.

Love was what they had and I didn't. Attention and adoration is what they really had. Of course, I didn't have that either.

It went down at our beach house. My brothers were about seven and eight at the time, but they spilled all the juicy details about how a man puts his penis inside a girl's wee-wee. The level of detail was astounding, if had we been anyone else's kids. Still, naïve little Cindy, age six, didn't believe a word they said. After all, most little girls my age were still trying to figure out how the pull-string worked on their Thumbelina dolls.

"Are you kidding me?" I exclaimed. "That's so weird! Why would someone do that?" Not knowing where else to turn, I ran to my parents and asked why Brian and Tim told me such an extreme lie.

My mother and father looked at each other, awkward as any parents might be with this line of questioning from a six-year-old. "Hmmm…" my dad said, trying not to smile. "Do you want to tell her?"

My mother demonstrated by making an O with her left hand, and using the index finger of her right hand as the penis. Then she showed me the actual act of a penis entering a vagina. Turns out, my brothers had been right after all. Oh my, I felt so embarrassed for all of us.

This rendition was devoid of any lubrication, so to speak, and included no information about foreplay at all. Love didn't even come into the conversation. Carla launched right into the good stuff like a man who's just looking to get off.

Some background information for a pre-pubescent girl as to *why* people would choose to engage in such a strange act might also have been helpful—but really, where would that conversation have gone? How can you talk about sex as a loving exchange between partners when you sell porn for a living? How can you tell a daughter, who you never wanted, how beautiful it is to make a baby with someone you love?

But I have to give Carla some credit. At least she didn't try the fluffy stork story on me.

Praying to God

Around the same time that we moved to our house on the hill, my parents bought a vacation house in Ventura a block from the beach. We had a special arrangement with other families and divided up the weekends so everyone could stay at least once a month. We were there so often that we began to make friends with the neighborhood kids.

We had everything we wanted: the beach as our playground, tri-motos (the ancestors of today's ATVs) to go "wamping" along the sand moguls, and parents who set us loose. Tim and I captured unsuspecting lizards and horny toads in the open terrain and played with sand crabs on the beach. The friends he made became my friends. I enjoyed hanging with Tim.

When the kids in Ventura found out what my parents did for a living, they had a field day. The pictures Tim brought back from the conventions made it even more apparent to them that this was very cool stuff—and that I, in comparison, was not such cool stuff.

"Why is your butt so big?" Tim and his friends teased. One time, they went on and on for so long, calling me names and singing songs about how ugly and gross I was, that I couldn't keep a smile on my face any longer. I ran away to my room and cried.

Lying on my bed, I prayed aloud. "God," I sobbed. "When I grow up, I'm going to be skinny. I'm going to be slender and beautiful. I'm going to show all of them! Please, God, hear me! Hear me!" I was crying so desperately that I didn't see Tim's friend sneak into my room through the half-open door. Pulling my puffy face out of my pillow, I looked up to find him standing over me with a big smirk on his face. He was enjoying my pain.

Punching him like Mark in the dugout might have been an option, but I was too hurt and embarrassed to do anything. With tears streaming down my face, I stared at him until he left, still smirking, on his way back to report to my brother.

That was the beginning of the end of my days as Tim's sidekick. We were still close, but I didn't want to be around his friends so much after that. I learned that I would rather be alone than become the "butt" of their jokes.

Since I hadn't bothered to make any friends my own age, I started hanging out with the adults. Part of me was interested to see what grown-ups did when they were alone.

Turns out that my mother just flat out made up stories.

She would tell the neighbors and the other kids' parents all kinds of stuff that wasn't even remotely true. At first I would try to correct her. "No, Mommy," I'd say. "It didn't happen that way. Don't you remember?"

She'd brush me off, obviously unhappy to be corrected—then, after the company left, she'd really lay into me. "You are such a spoiled brat. Do NOT interrupt me when I'm talking! Next time, you'd better shut the hell up!" There were a few more choice words thrown in there, too.

I learned to bite my tongue when Carla told her stories. I didn't realize that I was embarrassing her. I was just trying to keep her honest.

My mistake.

I understood what she was doing—slanting every story to make herself either the heroine or the victim, depending on the outcome. Stretching the truth, I didn't want her telling lies about me, but generally I just stayed out of it.

After that, she learned not to say so much in front of me either.

The funny thing is that I don't remember a lot of what she said while in Carla land, except that she created pretty wild stuff. Sometimes her stories had a kernel of truth at their center, but other times she just plucked them out of thin air.

Tim and I have both tried to recall some of the funnier whoppers she concocted—but since we both learned pretty quickly not to believe a word that came out of her mouth, we stopped paying attention to the details. As for the tales she told about me...Well, they weren't true, so they weren't worth remembering.

From Carla's perspective, it didn't matter if what she said was true or not. I learned that she just wanted to be the center of attention at all times, and she couldn't do that without good stories.

I'm so Happy I Could Just Sh*t!

One day, I saw the *coolest* thing. My mom and I were walking down the street in Valencia when we passed a T-shirt shop. In the window, the merchant had displayed a bunch of shirts with different interchangeable sticker designs. Anyone could buy a customized shirt in any color, size and design.

There it was! A green sparkly frog sitting on a lily pad; I just *had* to have it. I loved to bounce and hop like a frog. Plus, my friend Rose loved and collected frogs, so I loved frogs too. Rose would be so excited if she saw me actually *wearing* a frog!

Jumping up and down in excitement, I pointed out the shirt to Carla. "Isn't that frog great!? It's so cute! Can I make a T-shirt? Can I? Please, please, please?"

My mom looked at the shirt and laughed. "Okay," she said. Let's go inside and see."

I pointed out the frog sticker to the clerk and asked her to check if they had it available. I was very professional about it. When she came back to the counter to confirm that they had the sticker I wanted, I made a show of selecting the perfect color shirt to add it to. While I'd originally wanted green, my mom helped me decide that yellow made a better backdrop for a green frog.

The clerk (with a few odd glances at my mom) unrolled the shirt and placed it on a huge ironing board. There was another plate that lifted up from the top of the board that had steam coming out of it. She carefully placed the sticker on top of my shirt, and then slowly pressed the top board down. Steam shot out on all sides.

I gleefully observed this process with a huge smile on my face. I felt like I'd just won the biggest prize on the planet. How cool. I was getting something that had been created just for me. It was one of a kind. No one else in school had a shirt like mine. Bursting with excitement, I even gave my mom a hug.

When we got home, my mom and I were so proud of our new creation that we had to show my father. He took one look and quietly chuckled under his breath.

"That's cute, honey," he said.

The next day, I woke up early, buzzing with excitement. I was going to wear my new shirt today and I was so proud. It was a little chilly, so I had to wear a jacket over it. I decided that recess was the best time for the unveiling anyway, so I kept my creation covered up all morning. As the bell rang and we all rushed out onto the playground, I whipped off my jacket and ran toward the swings with a big grin on my face. I couldn't wait to show the other kids!

Mrs. Stewart was sweet, young, vibrant and beautiful—my favorite teacher in the whole world. When she saw my shirt, a strange look came over her face, and she motioned for me to come over. I could hear the other kids yelling and having fun on the playground, and I wanted to join them, but Mrs. Stewart kept waving me over.

"You are going to have to go to the principal's office," she said sternly.

"But why? What did I do wrong?" She'd never talked to me this way before. It felt like she'd slapped me.

"It's not something you did. It's your shirt," she explained.

"Huh? I don't get it; I like my shirt!" I protested. "I love frogs, and I didn't do anything wrong."

"Oh, boy," she sighed, looking a little sad. "I'm sorry, Cindy. But it is what it says."

"What's wrong with what it says? My mom and I picked it out together!" I said in my defense.

"Your shirt says, *'I'm so happy I could just sh*t!'* That is not acceptable language, and I can't allow it at school. You are going to have to go to the principal's office," she replied. "Off you go."

"Ugh, that's not fair!" I exclaimed. With my head hanging down, I went anyway. Who would have thought Mrs. Stewart was such a prude?

I guess when your parents sell pornography for a living, a little profanity isn't such a big deal. Compared to some of the stuff I'd seen and heard, this was nothing. It was just an innocent little frog, sitting on a lily pad.

As I walked to the principal's office, with my tail between my legs, I felt so humiliated. I couldn't believe that my mom let me go to school wearing a shirt that got me in trouble.

Even back then, my first response to humiliation was either total silence or outright laughter. I couldn't help but smirk when I showed the office staff my shirt. When the principal asked me what I thought was so funny, I just laughed harder.

The truth is that it *was* kind of funny. Who else but Carla would send her kid to first grade wearing a shirt like that?

I was still giggling when they called my mother to come get me. And, I was still giggling when they ushered me out of the double doors and onto the sidewalk. And there I was, sitting on the curb in my yellow shirt, kicked out of school—so happy I could just sh*t!

The Big Bully

By the time I was in fourth grade, I was so sick of getting picked on that I decided to get my revenge. I chose as my target a sweet boy named Johnny Larsen. I don't know why but, for some reason, he just bugged me off.

When we got to school every morning and lined up outside our classroom, I torment him. I'd push him between the shoulders so he'd fall into the kids in front of him and say all kinds of mean things, making him cry more than once.

When he finally told me to shut up, the teacher pulled him out of line and made him stand all by himself on the other side of the doorway. He looked so small, cringing over there like a little lamb separated from his flock. I felt bad for him, a little—but that didn't stop me from bullying him every time the teacher wasn't around. And when he'd try, in his scared little way, to fight back, the teacher yanked him out of line again.

I don't know how I never got in trouble for what I did. I don't think the school staff could credit a female bully back then—even one who wore obscene shirts to school. But every time I think of Johnny Larsen, I feel horribly guilty. I hope his life wasn't ruined because of what I did back then.

What would make me, a girl who was taunted herself, behave this way? I was obviously just mimicking the bullying inflicted on me by other kids and none of it was conscious. So Johnny became my punching bag, no different than I was to others. Still, while I was too young to really figure out everything that was going on, some part deep inside of me sensed that it wasn't right. When we treat people this way, we're just punching ourselves in the long run. So I learned to think twice before behaving that way ever again.

If you're out there, Johnny, please forgive me.

CHAPTER 4

No Boundaries

Lessons in driving, death and living on the edge

I n their book *The Vortex* (Hay House, 2009), Jerry and Esther Hicks write about allowing children to find their own emotional guidance system. My parents, apparently, were early proponents of this strategy.

Rules? What rules?

Case in point: Who else but Bob and Carla let their ten- and twelve-year-old children drive their cars? The same parents who taught their kids about sex in first grade and let them go to school with shirts that implied profanity.

Brian used to move the cars for my parents. I don't know why the cars needed to be moved all the time, or why this couldn't just be done when one or the other of them were leaving for the day…

Anyway, on this particular day, Brian asked me to help him. The plan was for him to back the funky, tie-dyed van out of the driveway and then back the equally funky station wagon out to make space for the van to pull in. (Yes, we had a station wagon. I guess Bob and Carla had a momentary desire to own a family-friendly vehicle.)

After he'd backed it up onto the street, Brian put me in the station wagon and told me to drive forward when he was done moving the van.

I couldn't really reach the pedals, but I nodded anyway, not wanting to admit that I had no idea how to drive. Hello? I was only ten!

I still don't know what I did, exactly. But, as Brian pulled back, I started moving forward.

Omigosh! What do I do now? I saw the front end of the station wagon edging closer and closer to the back of the van, but I had no idea what to do! I stepped on one of the pedals…

Crrrrunch!

Brian dashed up and started yelling at me. I threw up my hands and said, "What was I supposed to do? You never told me how to stop it!"

Only then did he explain to me the intricate system of brake pedal versus gas pedal—all the while looking sideways at me like I was mildly retarded. Unlike him, I didn't know from birth how to operate a motor vehicle.

I don't know how we got away with that one. We just didn't tell my parents. When my mother noticed the gash in the van's rear bumper, we just shrugged and tried to look blameless. I might have suggested that she ran into a shopping cart at the market.

Certainly I didn't have enough awareness at this age to say, "No, I can't and won't drive a car!" But the important thing to consider here is how, as adults, we often fail to say no or take responsibility or question what we're being asked to do when we know it's not right.

NA-NA-NA…Wonder Woman!!

Brian's unorthodox teaching methods also extended to riding motorcycles. Settling me on the seat of a little blue motorbike, he put my hands on the handlebars and said, "Okay, go!"

What he *didn't* say was that the accelerator was on the right handlebar and, when you pulled it back, it made the bike go faster. A little twist in my death grip and the bike shot away so fast it flung my legs up in the air. As my body flew out like a flag, my hands pulled tighter and the bike went even faster.

For a split second, it was like flying. If I'd had a cape, I would have been Wonder Woman. Then, reality set in—and I wiped out in the middle of the street.

Brian laughed so hard that I thought he was going to throw up. Only then, after he'd had his fun, did he decide to tell me how the whole handlebar thing worked.

I wonder now if this was his way of making things the same for me as they were for him. Certainly, no one showed him how to ride a motorcycle. Probably, no one showed him how to drive a car, either. Out of all of us, he probably got the least guidance. My dad expected him to behave like a man from the get-go. My mother…Well, she had her tennis racket and her loud mouth, but if she shared much else with Brian, I didn't see it. He learned by trial and error—and therefore, so did I.

What fun for him.

I was a little gun-shy around motorcycles after that, so I settled for the next best thing: my awesome powder-blue bike. It had a long, wide seat with stripes that ran across from side to side, white training wheels and little white streamers flowing off the handlebars. I took my feet off the pedals and coasted down the hill near our house.

The first time I rode without my training wheels wasn't quite as exhilarating as flying off the back of a motorcycle—but (after a little zigging and zagging) I still flew down that hill like a superhero.

Sometimes learning by trial and error is simply the best teacher, especially since there are no mistakes in life!

Three-Wheeling

Sex, drugs and rock'n'roll, baby!

My dad might have met my mom over a Diet Coke, but he coaxed her back to his apartment with a Harley.

"I have a Harley hanging over my fridge," he told her.

"You're kidding!"

"Nope. Want to come over and see it?"

Well, who could resist the sight of a Harley hanging over a fridge?

When Carla got to Bob's apartment, she found that there was, in fact, a Harley—or at least, there was a Harley *motor*, sitting right on top of the refrigerator in all its greasy glory.

A big part of my dad's charm was his ability to draw people in with only half the story. When he started making money in the business, my dad bought motorcycles for himself and Carla. After all, porn and Harley-Davidsons go hand-in-hand. My father rode an orange touring bike, and Carla had a three-wheeler.

My mom's gleaming white trike had an enormous front wheel with chrome spokes and foot pegs set so high that they looked like the stirrups at the gynecologist's office. Once she got going, she pulled her legs up in the air and placed them on the pegs, while her arms reached comically for handlebars that were almost over her head. Her cheeks would flap in the wind and the tendrils of her black hair spiraled out of her bandana. With her ripped jeans, leather jacket and big brown-fringed motorcycle boots (not to mention the studded belt!) she thought she was quite the motorcycle mama.

She was hilarious—and at the same time, kind of awesome. Her trike had a U-shaped leather backseat that wrapped over the top of the two rear tires. Each leg of the U was a seat. When we went riding, my brothers got the seats on the sides, while I had to cram myself into the narrow, center part of the U, straddling the white fiberglass casing that covered the motor. I tucked my feet up under me, Indian-style, and tried to balance as we flew down Lyons Avenue. My brothers held onto the handrail in back of the seat and I held onto them.

Each of us had our own little open-faced helmet with glittery decals—but that was the extent of our protection. Forget seatbelts. Forget face guards or goggles. (Of course, back then, helmets weren't even required in most states. My parents probably thought they were being extra-specially careful.)

Lyons Avenue was the main drag in Valencia at that time and sometimes, when Carla shifted gears, she did it so abruptly that the trike popped a wheelie. Or, we'd be at a stoplight and, when the light turned green, she hit it. Our heads slammed back, sometimes stopping mere inches from the ground. We all thought it was the coolest thing ever. Carla probably did, too—which explains why she kept doing it even after she got better at driving the bike.

My father, on the other hand, was a total badass on his Harley. Sometimes he used to take me for a ride on the back, which was awesome—but, more often than not, I ended up crunched on the back of my mom's trike. They said it was safer. Maybe if Carla hadn't been driving…

A lot of my parents' friends had bikes and they cruised together. My favorites in the biker crew were Gary and his wife, Rose, whose love of frogs had inspired my unfortunate choice in T-shirts.

One year a big group of them decided to take a three-week motorcycle tour through Mexico. They were having a grand old time until one day, when Ray was approaching a big truck on the road. Something happened—no one was ever sure what—and his bike slid out. Rose, riding on the back, flew ten feet in the air and landed on the side of the road. The paramedics, when they finally got there, were able to save Gary. Rose was already gone.

When they got home, my dad didn't say a word, but my mom very gently sat me down and said she needed to talk to me. Since she was never this soft with me, I figured it had to be something extraordinarily strange or serious. Or, she was setting me up.

She said a couple of things I didn't understand, about heaven and angels, probably trying to soften the blow. When she finally told me that Rose was dead, I didn't believe her. This didn't seem like the kind of story she normally made up—but then, you never could tell with Carla.

This was my first exposure to death; there was no precedent in my world for this kind of thing. My first thought was, "Why didn't she just come out and tell me?" The next was, "How could Rose be here one minute and gone the next?" I was stunned.

I really loved Rose. She paid attention to me, which meant a lot, and I felt really comfortable with her. She didn't care that I was chubby or that my dad sold porn. I felt like I should miss her, like I should be crying—because that's what you did when people died, right?—but the tears didn't come. I just marched off to my room in a sort of somber daze and lay down on my bed.

After a while, I started to talk to Rose. I had no idea if she could hear me, but I felt like she could. I told her how much I loved her collection of frogs. I asked if it was painful to die, or if it had been quick. I said I hoped she didn't suffer. Finally, I told her that I would miss her.

After that, my parents didn't take any more motorcycle trips. A few months later, the Harley and the trike disappeared from our garage. I guess when you see something like that first-hand, freewheelin' down Lyons Avenue doesn't seem like so much fun anymore.

CHAPTER **10**

Now We're In Business

Adults Only! [Rated X]

My dad got his start in sex stores. Before video stores even existed, films were only available on eight-millimeter reels. He started out, when he worked for Steve, pounding the pavement and selling reels to boutique stores. With the advent of video, mom-and-pop video stores started to crop up. Some confusion arose at first as to whether video would go the way of VHS or Beta, but that soon smoothed itself out.

Pornographic videos rapidly caught on. Connoisseurs snuck into those dark and secret rooms in the back of the video shops—the ones always half-concealed behind dirty black drapes and "Adults Only" signs. Now adult videos were mainstream, making Bob's job a lot easier.

After he bought Norm and their third partner out of their shares of J&I, my dad's business evolved with the times. With the advent of VHS, he was able to cover ground a lot more quickly, selling over the phone to regular video stores. Despite all the trouble that phone calls had gotten him into with Steve and the feds, Bob was quite the little telemarketer. He had accounts all over the country. All he needed to sell his product was a desk, a phone and a few choice adjectives.

"You can't afford *not* to buy this one," he'd tell the store owners. And they'd bite.

Soon, he had an office space in the San Fernando Valley, which was apparently the porn capital of the world in the late Seventies. He and my mother created a new company called BTC Enterprises, which was short for Brian, Tim and Cindy—a true family business (see, no one could say they didn't love us!) and from there, they proceeded to rake in the dough.

Carla never stuck with a job, so working with my dad offered the perfect solution for her. Obviously, there was no way she could get fired—not if Bob wanted to remain a married man. But she wasn't exactly invested in keeping the peace.

In my mother's humble opinion, she was the mastermind behind the entire operation. BTC and Cinnabar Video were *her* businesses— and who the hell was Bob Glickman to tell her how to run them? If it wasn't for her, she postulated, he'd still be slaving away in construction.

Carla talked to my father the same way she talked to me: like he was stupid. She was right; he was wrong. And clearly she was going to have to educate him even on this most obvious of facts.

The two of them used to get into screaming fights in the middle of the office. It didn't matter if the employees were there—in fact, it was even hotter when they were. (I think my mom was hoping the sales guys dug her, or at least would take her side against my dad, since Brian and Tim weren't there to use as bait.) It was relentless and endless: Each accused the other of being wrong about some minor point and then stormed around trying to prove that he or she was right. Sometimes, they took the fights home, where we kids had the pleasure of witnessing them. I think, by the end of the day, they were fighting just to fight, because it was the best way they knew how to communicate.

The truth is that they might have made an excellent team, if they'd been able to stop bickering about who was in charge. No matter what stories my mom told, it was clear that my father was really the driving force behind the business. His strengths were in marketing and cold-calling, and he could get down to the grindstone like no one else. He believed in working hard to make a buck, so that's what he did. He could hire sales agents, and he did: a bunch of wide-eyed twenty-year-olds who couldn't think past the fact that they got to sample the "product" in their spare time. Not one of those boys could work the phones like my dad. (Maybe they were too distracted by the posters hanging on all the walls, taped to the fronts of the bins and pinned to the cubicles... It was, I imagine, a lot like working in a donut shop for me: days full of guilty pleasures, unable to resist taking a bite here, a bite there.)

My mom, on the other hand, ran the administrative side of things. She took care of everything from decorating to bookkeeping. She had a great imagination and a flare for design, but I don't understand why she thought she'd be good at the rest of it. She started bringing me in to help with the accounting by the time I was ten. I loathed it and told her so. (Bookkeeping, by the way, is the most boring thing in the world, when you are an extrovert.)

But she couldn't ask anyone else for help, because that would have been admitting defeat. She was determined to prove that she was the boss and that Bob was every bit the inferior piece of crap she told everyone he was. I think part of her was still trying to prove to her own father that she was smart enough to be successful.

I hated being at the office. I hated the way the files were never quite in alphabetical order and the way my mom asked for my help only to tell me I was doing it wrong. I hated the huge posters of women with their legs spread open and men holding their own erect penises—although, at this point, I was completely desensitized by the images. But mostly I hated to watch my parents fight.

I don't know why my dad let Carla tear him down to a bite-size of a man, over and over, but he did. He'd battle it out for a while, but then you could just *see* him giving up. With his tail between his legs, he'd concede to whatever irrational argument she was making and try to get back to work.

I promised myself I'd never have a relationship like that, no matter what my mother said was impossible—but I didn't have any idea what a good relationship looked like. I started thinking that maybe marriage was out; it appeared so complicated. I wanted to stay free as a bird forever. No kids, either. There was no way I was going to subject someone else to this torment.

"Let's Go On Vacation, Kids!"

When I was about fifteen, Timmy and I got to talking about the family business. As you can imagine, it was a frequent topic of conversation.

"You know they used to film at our house on the hill," he said.

"Shut up!" There was no way that could have happened. I mean, that's just creepy. And my parents had *some* boundaries, didn't they?

We argued about this for a while. Finally, Tim threw up his hands and said, "Fine. I guess I have to prove it to you." He turned and walked out of the room.

A few minutes later, he came back. Smirking in his most endearing way, he handed me a shiny, full-color VHS case. The front was decorated with open-mouthed naked women and close-ups of big schlongs. But that wasn't what was shocking about it—although I'm sure, for anyone else, the cock-and-balls would have been enough.

No, what shocked me was that the pictures appeared to have been taken at our childhood home on Plaza Gavilan, at the end of the cul-de-sac.

I felt my hands start to shake a little. Tim stepped back and stuffed his hands in his pockets. I studied that box top to bottom, side to side—but there was no mistaking it. There was our dark brown shag carpet and our stairway finished in dark brown wood trim. There were our brown-and-orange striped couches—only there were naked girls sprawled all over them.

Eeeewwww.

This was no joke. Even though he was laughing his ass off at my naiveté, Tim wasn't playing a prank on me.

Tim turned the box over. "Recognize the pool?" he asked.

Of course I did. I'd know that kidney-shaped pool anywhere. I'd slid down that blue fiberglass slide hundreds of times and climbed up that white ladder with the metal handrails. We'd had birthday parties around this pool. We'd tormented Concha from its deep center.

And there was the barbecue pit, and the tree where I sat and talked to God when I was lonely, and even a corner of the swing set where Olivia used to teach me Spanish.

"Are you friggin' kidding me?!" I exclaimed.

"Yeah, that's our house," Brian chimed in from the doorway.

I had no idea how to feel. I mean, I knew what my parents did for a living, but I had no idea that they'd ever brought it *home.* Or had I?

I'd often had the pleasure of encountering scantily clad actresses on our front walkway, stumbling toward the house with their eyes glazed over and their sky-high heels catching on the red clay tiles— but I hadn't put it together that they were at our house to *act.* I couldn't believe I'd been so blind and stupid about the whole thing. Silly little Cindy, blind as a bat in a box.

Standing there with that video box in hand, I flashed back to one day in particular. I must have been seven or eight years old. That morning my parents announced that we were going on vacation. No big deal—we were just going somewhere to have fun for a couple of days. We each packed a small bag with clothes and bathing suits.

Then, they told us where we were going.

I asked my mother, "Why are we going on vacation at a hotel that's only five minutes from our house?"

"Oh, it will be fun," Carla said, waving a long-nailed hand. "You guys can play in the pool."

I was totally perplexed. Didn't we have a perfectly good pool right here at home? Most hotel pools didn't even have diving boards!

As we were getting ready to leave, people started bringing things into our house. Big lights, tripods, big black sheets, bags of equipment.

"Mom," I asked. "Why are those men hanging lights on our stairway?"

Carla was quiet for a while, then said, "They are going to film a movie here, sweetheart."

I gasped in delight. "Oh! Our house in a movie? Cool!"

"Umm-hmm…"

"What movie? Will we be able to see it? Is our house going to be famous?"

She didn't answer, only shuffled me out the door. I bounced along in front of her, dreaming about our house on the silver screen, with no understanding of what was happening right under my nose. Duh!

As I came out the front door, two skanky chicks stumbled up the long front steps. They had ratty, teased-up hair—all the rage in the Eighties—and loads of black eyeliner circling their eyes. Their boobies bounced around under their thin T-shirts. They were leaning on one another, as if they couldn't stand up on their own. I don't think either of them saw me as they fell through the front door.

My face crinkled up. "Huh?" Those didn't look like Hollywood actresses to me. Those girls oozed "slut" from their very pores. They looked like... the girls on my dad's video boxes.

Curious now and a little creeped out, I told my mom I had to pee and then followed them back into the house. I wanted to make sure these girls weren't doing anything to my room. I sprinted to the upstairs bathroom. The girls themselves were nowhere to be found, but in my bathroom I found a bloody Kotex in the trash bin. They didn't even wrap it up and just left it out there for the world to see.

And apparently, while we were "on vacation" three miles from our house, these Kotex-chucking superstars were doing all kinds of things I never could have imagined—in my waterbed.

Until that point, I'd had it in my head that my dad was just selling smut—not actually *making* it. It took the shock of seeing my own house on a video cover to bring it home to me. Yes, my dad was the Porn King of L.A.—but so much about my family seemed normal. We ate dinner together sometimes and my brothers and I played ball in the street when we were little, just like the other kids.

This shifted things in a way I couldn't describe, but I felt the tremor all the way to my core.

My brothers seemed to have a much better scope of what was going on in our parents' world than I did. They not only knew about the filming in our house but had actually watched the videos when they were eleven and twelve years old. They even went so far as to show the videos to their friends, proud of the fact that their dad was a "filmmaker."

To me, the fact that my dad sold porn for a living was a BIG secret. Or at least I wanted it to be. The less the world knew about it, the better.

When the kids in the neighborhood introduced me to their friends, they'd say, "Cindy's dad is the porn king of L.A." Mortified, I would turn red and stammer, "Well, that's not *really* what he does…"

I downplayed it whenever I could, even though everyone already knew. It's not exactly something a girl wants on her record, you know?

CHAPTER 11

No Religion

G uzzling down a huge bowl of Cap'n Crunch—or, in my case, two or three bowls—was a great start to a weekday. If we were really on the go, my brothers and I ate Pop Tarts while we waited for the bus. Bob and Carla were already off to work by the time we were getting ready for school.

On the weekends, however, my dad played chef. We celebrated our Jewish heritage with bagels, lox and cream cheese. We delighted in them the traditional Jewish way—or, at least, *his* traditional way— with tomatoes, purple onions and capers. Delicious! Yes, I was a bit of an oinker, downing at least three of these yummy bagels in a morning—one of my FAVORITE things and the only meal we sort of ate together. Sometimes we even had guests.

My dad also cooked his famous scrambled eggs infused with lox and onions. Much later, when I finally dated a Jewish boy, I learned that this concoction was called a "LEO" for lox, eggs and onions. What a big event! This was our version of being "Jewish."

We weren't really raised Jewish, so to speak, since my father did not encourage us to study that path because he had been discriminated against. He just didn't want us to have to incur what he did as a child. The interesting thing was that the two girls who went to school with me and lived on our street were both Jewish, but the only thing we really learned about while growing up was celebrating

97

Hanukkah. My mother encouraged it because she didn't understand that Rosh Hashanah was a high holy day for the Jews and much more significant than Hanukkah.

As a kid, I never knew any difference between Hanukkah and Christmas; it was all the same to me. I thought it was totally freaking awesome! Why would a kid complain when they were getting gifts for eight days and then more on Christmas too? I was thinking that I really liked this being Jewish thing until I discovered I actually knew absolutely nothing about it.

The most exposure we got to a more traditional American version of Judaism was through my Uncle Al and Aunt Judy when we went to their house and celebrated Hanukkah. I don't remember celebrating any other holidays with them, but I did get to see my cousins have their Bar Mitzvahs and the whole temple thing was so fascinating to me; I just loved it. I loved the Hebrew singing and the little hats called yarmulkes and the scarves the men wore. Dang, I thought that sure was a cool gig.

I enjoyed the experience but had no clue about it. My brothers and I did attend some Sunday school where we learned a few Bible/Torah stories or something like that, but I still don't think we learned much about the religion or the Hebrew and Yiddish languages—probably due to the fact that what we learned wasn't reinforced at home. We did learn the Hebrew alphabet and something about the Jewish calendar, but that was the only exposure we had.

Religions began to fascinate me. I elected to go to church with my Aunt Diane to grasp what occurred under that steeple and even more over requested to go to Catholic school searching for answers. But, when they filled out the application and had to say, "Well, we sell pornography," I am guessing the Catholic Church was probably not *so* cool with that. Extramarital sex was frowned upon, in general, never mind extramarital sex on video with props and a soundtrack.

Needless to say, I didn't get to go to Catholic school or wear those cool, long white sox with those plaid skirts and white blouses. Blasphemy! In my mind, the schoolteachers wearing those nun outfits would have been the bomb! So, when my mom told me they couldn't let me in, I was bummed.

As I got older, I started to check out what my friends were doing in terms of religion because it all seemed so totally fascinating to me. Growing up in California, we had all kinds of people in our schools and all kinds of ethnicities, races and religions. However, it was, with no question, highly white-dominated. We still had a mix and I think that I learned not to see the differences in people but the oneness in everybody. One of the great lessons learned from the scrutiny I faced by some about my background or what my parents did for a living helped me to actually understand things better and be less judgmental of others.

We may have chosen to live this life before we got here, as many people believe. But, once here, we have a choice. In every moment, we have the opportunity to decide who we want to be and who we want to become. If you do not like something in your life, change it.

Just because there was some silly stigma around what my parents did for a living, the truth was that they were doing this, plain and simple, for a living because there was money to be made in this industry, and there still is. Countless millions of people every day in this technological era access pornography on the Web and spend nearly fifteen billion dollars a year in the U.S. on pornography in some form, from DVDs and Web sites to live lap dances or even the unthinkable—prostitutes.

Keep in mind that I am not condoning the industry, but merely dismantling the façade of all the taboos and hang-ups and hypocrisy surrounding it.

So, if we all stop hiding behind ridiculous rules we have created around things in our lives and what is right and wrong based on a rule, rather than what you know in your heart to be good for you, then people could step out of their judgment and recognize that there is a reason people continue to reach out for this external pleasure.

Ever thought about having compassion for people who are prostitutes or johns? How about examining the deeper issue within driving them to engage in such activity, with no internal happiness in their hearts? Now that could also be looked at as a judgment. However, if you really dig deeper and ask someone like Dr. Phil, you most likely will find that this is just one addiction, or form of searching for something outside of yourself, to achieve a moment of happiness that truly can only be satisfied by going within and learning about who you are—living your life on purpose, following your divine purpose and tapping into your true potential and self-love.

Judgment on either side of the coin, in this situation or any other, doesn't need to exist. There is a desire, and there is something fulfilling that desire.

My parents made choices to live a better life and to keep up with the Joneses, or whatever their ideal was. It didn't matter to them what type of industry they were involved in; it was just a business. And, I decided at a young age that I was not going to be anything like these women oozing smuttiness who were stumbling up the sidewalk to our home. I saw these women on the box covers doing unmentionable acts with themselves and on men and I decided that was not what I wanted in my life.

I did not depend on my parents to give me those rules or boundaries; we never discussed them. But I listened to my internal guidance, which told me that it was not for me. That lifestyle was not who I was.

I was on a mission to prove that women had something more to contribute and offer the world than a sexual act in a video.

For me, that mission would begin with higher education.

An Education and a Mission

My grandmother, Mildred, said to me once that *valuing* education was a tradition passed on among the Jews. Education wasn't a privilege; it was actually sacred. The one thing that no persecutor could take away from the Jewish people was their knowledge. No matter what torture and torment they endured at the hands of the Nazis or anyone else, our people carried our knowledge, language, and history within themselves—a treasure greater than any other.

As the Nazis began to take over Europe, the Jews hid in fear for their lives, and one of the first things they did was to create secret underground hiding places for their books. Not even the Nazis were going to stop them from learning. The challenge these men and women faced in maintaining and continuing their tradition of education was greater than any obstacle seen by subsequent generations. To wake up every day in fear that someone might, at any moment, kill your family and strip you of everything you owned had to be devastating. But, as long as they were alive, the Jews were going to keep amassing knowledge and wisdom, because these things could never be taken from them.

Mildred told this story so powerfully that I felt it to the core of my being. I could see, in my mind, images of Jews like my grandfather, Joseph, sneaking through underground tunnels to their hidden libraries, where groups gathered to read by candlelight. I couldn't have been more than six years old at the time, but I knew that education was going to be just as important to me as it had been to my father's parents.

In fact, I was going to be a doctor.

I never saw myself as a medical doctor; I knew that wasn't my path. For me, it was about obtaining a doctorate and reaching the highest pinnacle of education in whatever subject I chose. There was nothing greater I could achieve.

I informed my parents of this decision while we were in the car one day.

"Okay, honey." At least my mom managed not to roll her eyes. My dad said nothing.

My parents didn't hold much stock in my ambitions. Bob had never finished college and, while Carla had gone to beauty school for aesthetics, she'd never done anything with it. Higher education wasn't a priority for either of them. Education was only valuable in proportion to the amount of money it allowed you to make.

My desire to learn was reinforced by my Uncle Al and Aunt Judy. Simply being in my uncle's presence was enough to inspire me. His children were going to be educated, and that was that. Mildred, for her part, didn't have much to say on the subject beyond her World War II stories. I think her interest in our family was superficial at best. She'd tell her stories and get her digs into my dad when she could, but when it came to our futures, she couldn't have cared less.

It was going to be up to me to rise above my circumstances and get the education I craved. I didn't know how, but I knew I would do it.

CHAPTER 12

Fairytales with a Twist

The Cops are Coming! The Cops are Coming!

D oesn't everyone get their house turned up by the feds at least once in their life? My dad actually had more than one run-in with The Man. I guess that's what happens when you're in the porn industry.

First, there was that mess with Steve, when my dad's phone conversations were taped. Then, my parents' office in the San Fernando Valley got turned upside down over some issue regarding porn sales in states where smut was illegal. The detectives rifled their records to see where the videos were being sold, looking for evidence of sales to prohibited areas. After that, my dad hung a huge map in the sales office with the "legal" states highlighted in bright yellow.

There was also the issue of underage actresses in the films my dad was selling. Thankfully (for us, anyway), he wasn't involved in filming at that point —only distribution. But I saw his friends on the evening news, flinching from the cameras as they were carted off to jail. Later they were shown in courtrooms across Southern California, wearing orange jumpsuits and looking skittish. Many of them ended up serving hard time or paying hefty fines.

Too young to know any better, I asked, "Why are they taking your friends to jail, Daddy?" He did his best to explain, but I didn't really understand the severity of it. The girls had lied about their ages—no one ever thought to check IDs or birth records back then—and the men had filmed them. I didn't realize how (depending on your viewpoint) these girls had abused the system, or been abused by it.

Many girls got sucked into it as teens and some did it to support substance addictions, creating a double-edged sword. For some, it's a better alternative to living on the streets in the face of poverty and few options. My parents faced a similar situation in a way when deciding to go into the business because it was better than facing welfare to support a family. How many people today, faced with foreclosure or losing everything, haven't considered doing something outside of their morals to pay the mortgage? What would *you* do?

It wasn't my dad's responsibility to check up on this stuff—otherwise, it might have been him in one of those ugly orange jumpers. I'm sure he was relieved, although my dad always had a poker face that made it hard to tell what he was thinking.

After the office was tossed, my parents decided it was time to do something else. Not only was it a pain in the neck to deal with the FBI's suspicion, but it was costing them an arm and a leg in legal fees. So they decided to sell off their video distribution rights and use the money they'd been saving for retirement to buy a restaurant in Grass Valley.

Yep, you heard right. The hard-partying, porn-pushing Glickmans were going to settle down in a small Northern California town and scramble up some eggs.

It had always been a dream of my dad's to own his own restaurant. After a few months of searching, he and Carla found a famous mom-and-pop restaurant down a back street in the commercial part of town—a real local treasure called The Omelet Pan. It already had a high volume of business and offered my dad's favorite kind of food: home-style breakfast. We went there a few times before my parents took it over. There were thirty-one omelets on the menu, just like the ice cream store, with flavors like I'd never imagined. I don't know what they did to those eggs but when the omelets came out, they were—no joke—five inches high, stuffed to the hilt with veggies and meat and cheese. They had a big white barrel in the back to hold all the eggshells they cracked every morning.

The owners were in their seventies—a bit country, but nice enough. The gal wore her hair in a beehive hairdo, just like Carla did in the Seventies. The man was grandfatherly and white-bearded, totally at home in overalls and a flannel shirt. My parents liked them a lot, and they all became good friends while negotiating the sale of the business.

Once the transfer of ownership was completed, my parents went to work. My dad cooked and my mom did the bookkeeping and the ordering. Their employees included Tony and Jeff, twins who had worked for the previous owners, and Barbara, the waitress. Then, there was Brian B., a 17-year-old prep cook with kinky black hair cut in a strange, fluffy mullet. Brian was still in high school but came in for the early morning prep shifts, showing up promptly at 4 a.m. on the weekends.

Oh, I loved that restaurant. Of course, our parents enlisted our help when they needed it—but I didn't mind, unlike the way I minded helping out at Porn Central in Valencia.

The Pan was an old-fashioned, quaint little dream of a restaurant, filled with wooden tables and chairs with padded seat-cushions in paisley and plaid. The top few feet of the wall that separated the kitchen from the dining room was made of glass, so you could see the chefs at work. In the back, there was a huge stainless steel stove where they fried up mountains of hash and flipped those huge fluffy omelets. All morning long, the old-fashioned stainless circular hanger for the food order slips filled up and kept spinning. In the front of the house, Barbara bustled around, filling the white coffee cups and smiling at everyone.

When I worked, I served as the busgirl. I cleaned the tables when people were done eating and reset them for the next customers. Timmy washed dishes in the back, where we had an enormous dishwashing machine with a conveyer and hanging plastic fringes and a deep metal sink. He sprayed the dishes with the hanging hose, sending steam billowing everywhere, and then pushed the dishes through the machine on plastic trays. I thought it was the coolest thing—like a car wash for dishes.

Who would have thought a normal life could be so much fun?

***

Grass Valley is near Nevada City, where the nineteenth-century gold miners came to make their millions. The story goes that the people who really made the money were the ones who sold the sifting pans. Nevada City even has a commemorative stamp that shows a miner squatting on his haunches with a pan in his hands. The symbolic gold-digger.

The main reason my parents chose Grass Valley was that they had gotten a heads-up from my Aunt Bobbi, who had moved up there from Oxnard a couple of years earlier.

Aunt Bobbi, who was dark-haired like my mother, had a wide rear end. It looked odd because she had a teensy waist and a skinny upper body. I don't know where she got it from because my mom was exactly the opposite: as broad-shouldered as a man, but with tiny little chicken legs. The third sister, Diane, was a twig who freaked out if she gained five pounds.

Where my mother was a bruiser—outgoing and brash—Bobbi was mousy. Like me, she was much more likely to eat her pain away than raise a fuss about it. She always seemed apprehensive, and wasn't intimidating at all (which might have explained why she used to spank us with a wooden spoon when we were little: that was the only way she could keep us in line).

Her husband, my uncle Carl, rolled a pack of cigarettes up his white T-shirt sleeve, Marlboro Reds. He drank a lot and had a tear tattoo next to one eye—a cool "cholo" or gang member thing to do. (Apparently, he'd forgotten somewhere along the line that he was a middle-class white boy.) She had one son named Michael, but she always looked bitter when she called him. I think he was always in trouble.

Anyway, Bobbi told my parents that they should come to Grass Valley, and they listened to her. I thought that since we were neighbors now—our houses were only about half a mile from one another—we'd see one another more often, but this wasn't the case. Sometimes she babysat for us, but other than that, she didn't come around much.

Before we moved to Grass Valley, my parents sold their distribution rights to a number of popular videos to a guy named Teddy. He wrote them a bunch of post-dated checks and promised that he was good for the money.

They also put the house in Valencia up for sale. At the time, property sales were low, even in nice neighborhoods, so they got into an owner-financing deal. This allowed them to sell the house even though the buyers didn't have very good credit. If the buyers default-ed on the loan, ownership of the house reverted back to my parents.

With the Valencia house sold, we were able to buy a cool three-story wood house in Grass Valley, which at that time was really in the boonies. All around our new house were beautiful old pine trees on an acre of land. It was amazing to look out the window and not see the neighbor's yard. We had parties with our friends under the stars on the back deck where we could grill or soak in the spa.

I liked Grass Valley a lot. *People up north were different*, I thought. *Not better, really, but a little more real.* I couldn't wait to go to school and make new friends. Timmy and Brian, on the other hand, really missed their friends and so were sort of ambivalent about the whole thing.

Of course, they would be. They didn't get teased and called a blimp all the time. *I* certainly wouldn't miss their friends.

At first, life was simpler in Grass Valley for all of us. There were fewer parties and social engagements, since there wasn't really much to do out there in the country, and far fewer people to do it with. Plus, now that my dad was (supposedly) on the straight and narrow, his old crew didn't come around as much. The only one we saw a lot of was Ray. He, like my dad, had extricated himself from the business and moved up to Grass Valley to enjoy an early retirement among the pines—which basically meant that he hung around and smoked a lot of pot.

Our house was so far from the school that we had to take the bus—or else ride ten miles on our bikes to get to class. Our bus driver was an older woman—a bit rough, with blonde hair that was short and feathered back on the sides. She was a cool lady, though, and I liked her. She talked to me like I mattered.

After school, Tim and I rode our tri-motos behind the house. We drove around and around in a big oval so many times that it created a perfect dirt track. When we got bored of that, we'd ride to the end of the road, where there was a private neighborhood with a lot of dirt and big rocks, and really do some "wamping."

At first, the Grass Valley adventure was great fun for everyone. It was all very innocent, with our suddenly "normal" parents working hard at their restaurant, the country atmosphere of space and safety, the lumbering yellow school buses and the days spent roaming in the woods behind our house. I felt free and happy for the first time in a long time. Up here, it didn't matter quite so much that I was fat. I didn't have to hide what my dad did for a living. I still got teased at school, but even that felt a little less cruel somehow. I thought we'd finally found *home*. And a normal life, far from the sordid world of porn and its boob-filled posters.

But after a while, the daily grind started to get to my parents. The hours were long; the work was hard; and getting up at 4 a.m. every day was something neither of them had ever attempted. Then, Teddy's post-dated checks stopped clearing, and the playful feeling of "working for fun" evaporated.

And so, always the entrepreneur, my dad, the former Porn King, started making other plans.

Prince Charming

Driving in the car with my mom, brothers and Aunt Bobbi on a trip to Yosemite, I told my mom, "Someday, I'm going to meet Prince Charming. He's going to be smart and nice and really love me for who I am."

Everyone else was sleeping, so Carla kept her snort at a reasonable volume. "Yeah, good luck with that," she conveyed with cutting sarcasm. "That's *ridiculous*! There's no such thing as a man like that.

That stuff only happens in fairy tales." The more she talked about it, the more I could feel the bitterness rolling off her in waves.

Despite their early romance, I think my mom felt like she ended up with my dad by default. No one better had come along, so Bob it was. White horses and sweeping romance were not part of her experience—and, therefore, they didn't exist.

I knew in my heart that it could exist, but there was no use trying to tell my mother anything she didn't want to hear, so I shut up. But I couldn't help thinking at the time, *It just didn't happen for you.*

As time went on, I got more and more jaded about relationships, in general, and about marriage in particular. But I never gave up on the idea that I might someday find my Prince Charming. (If you must know, I'm still looking…)

It was beyond my mom's reality, at that time, that a healthy loving relationship was possible. Carla came from an abusive upbringing with her father, an aborted pregnancy and a court battle with her first drug-addicted husband. Tainted by the porn industry and a dysfunctional relationship with my father, she unconsciously perpetuated these patterns that she was creating in her life— the beliefs that manifested her reality. Either way, she believed that misery in relationship was all there was— so, she was exactly right.

As Henry Ford said, "Whether you think you can, or you think you can't— you are right." In other words, our unconscious beliefs create our reality.

Eddie and Linda

Eddie D. was a friend of my dad's. He owned a company called 4Play Video that he ran with his significant other, Linda. He wore thick glasses and had this funny big belly that looked even bigger next to his skinny arms and legs. He also had an under bite that made his chin protrude, so he wore a mustache and a beard probably to disguise it. Eddie didn't talk a lot, but he smiled all the time and was convinced that he could lose weight by chewing but not swallowing his food.

I think Linda was in charge in that family. She was older and more outgoing than Eddie and a pretty neat lady. The two of them were more directly involved in the porn business than my father. Eddie had rooms in his facility that they used for filming, with projectors and movie cameras ready to go at all times. They even did editing in these rooms and often pieces of film were lying on the floor.

Quiet though he was, Eddie could be pretty decisive when the mood struck him. So when he decided to get married, there were no if's, and's, or but's about it. In fact, it was going to be a surprise. Originally, the event was supposed to be a surprise 50th birthday party for Linda. Poor Linda!

There she was, walking around the party, saying hello and talking to everyone, totally unaware that we were all holding our breath, waiting to see what would happen next. None of us knew what to expect or how she was going to react. I mean, a surprise birthday party is one thing, but a surprise wedding? It still ranks up there as one of the silliest things I've ever seen—but, then, Eddie and Linda's relationship was far from typical. Eddie was a pretty creative guy, and since he'd been with Linda for about eight years, he thought it was about time for them to tie the knot. So he invited all of their friends and family to his favorite restaurant in the valley and set about planning his wedding.

As Linda made her way around the room, things kept getting stranger and stranger. Eddie started pulling things out from behind a curtain, and a judge in a black suit appeared out of thin air. Someone handed Linda a bouquet, which she held dazedly, still not understanding. When she turned around to ask what was going on, Eddie got down on one knee. "Surprise! You're going to marry me now!"

Confused and caught off-guard, Linda just laughed and started shaking her head. Obviously, she thought this was a great joke. Eddie had to get up, take her hand, and ask her again. It wasn't until he pulled out the ring that she finally realized he was serious.

Eddie led his shell-shocked bride to the pastoral arch he'd set up in the front of the room, and the judge started the ceremony. After they both said "I do," everyone applauded, and we all sat down to start the reception.

Eddie was typical of the kind of guy who was friends with my dad. They were a real bunch of characters. But I have to give Eddie credit: It took a lot of guts and a pretty creative mind to come up with that wedding. I hate to think what would have happened if Linda had said no.

More than anything else, that wedding taught me that Princes Charming does exist. He may come in all shapes and sizes, even quirky ones. Whatever he did for a living, the love Eddie showed Linda that day was genuine and beautiful—and, young and disillusioned though I was, it gave me hope.

Based on my experiences, my thoughts of love and relationships were entrenched in many myths but, most importantly, based on the premise that I could somehow fill the void within myself by finding my prince. But I did not yet realize that the love had to be an inside job and the man who showed up would merely be a reflection of old patterns and how I felt about myself.

My First Sexual Experience

One of my cousins was about the same age as my brother, Brian. When we were kids, the two of them were good buddies. But when we moved to Grass Valley, Brian didn't seem to want much to do with him. I think my cousin was a bit gun-shy from living with my uncle. And Brian, at that age, didn't like anyone who couldn't (or wouldn't) stand up for themselves.

This cousin said to me once, "You and your brothers just had better opportunities than me growing up." I think he was referring to the fact that my parents had more money than his. Although he had his own traumas to deal with, he didn't have to live with the pornography, the screaming matches and Carla's unpredictable personality. I think he wanted to believe that we had a better upbringing than him so he could justify his own issues and lack of motivation.

I told him, "It doesn't matter where you come from but where you're going." He looked at me like maybe I was drunk.

Not long before we moved to Grass Valley, this cousin came for a visit. While the adults were busy, he took me into the upstairs bathroom and told me to take my clothes off. He got naked, too, and laid me down on the shaggy carpet in front of the sink. His little penis was funny-looking, hairless and white.

Then, he started to do to me what my mother had so graphically illustrated with her hands at the beach house in Ventura a few years before. We were both very young—I was nine, and he was only eleven—so I don't think it could be constituted as rape. I didn't fight him since I didn't have a clue what was going on. It was as if I was there in the bathroom but, at the same time completely disengaged from my body. I did what he told me to do, but I wasn't in control of any of it. It was surreal.

I don't remember feeling upset or fearful. I was more concerned that I would get in trouble if we got caught. When he was done, I simply got up, got dressed, and went on my way. It was all over so fast that the adults downstairs hadn't even missed us (not that they would have, anyway). Pretty soon, I'd managed to make myself forget about the whole thing. I was good at that, especially when I was armed with a box of cookies and a gallon of milk.

I suppose this explains why my hymen was broken when I went to the gynecologist at the age of twelve. My mother made the appointment for me because she wanted to be sure that I could get on birth control right away, even though I didn't have a boyfriend at the time and didn't plan on having one in the foreseeable future. When the gynecologist mentioned my "broken" condition to her, they both raised their eyebrows and turned to look at me. After all, a girl whose hymen was broken must have had sex already.

I could only say that I didn't know anything about it. I didn't want to get in trouble, and I didn't want to rat on my cousin. They asked a few more questions and then they let it go. Apparently the doctor had bigger mysteries to solve in the land of vaginas.

But they came to me again when it was discovered that my younger cousin, Dawny, also had a broken hymen. My Aunt Diane was in a panic. I'm not sure what happened or what she told Diane and my mom. But, from that point on, I was supposed to take her to the bathroom whenever she had to go because they were worried that someone was doing something to her.

I wonder if it was the same culprit.

Either way, the fairy tales with a twist continued to unfold in Grass Valley, full of wicked witches and big bad wolves...

CHAPTER 13

Reality Check

It's the Feds again!

"Timmy," I screamed. "Someone robbed us! Someone broke into our house!"

I dashed upstairs to my room to find my clothes strung out everywhere. Everything I owned had been pulled from the drawers and rifled. The suitcase of neglected Barbie dolls in my closet had been opened and tossed on the floor, with broken arms and heads and heels scattered all over the place. The trap door to the attic was open; whoever did this had been up there, too.

I don't know how long I stood frozen in utter disbelief. What a violation! I felt like everything was dirty now. Worthless. This was my stuff, and someone had been flinging it around like it was garbage.

I'd like to say that my parents' trouble with the authorities stopped once we moved north but it didn't. We'd been living in Grass Valley for about a year when the Feds caught up with my dad again. This time, it wasn't about lying sixteen-year-olds or questionable distribution practices. It was a lot worse.

It happened on a Saturday. The morning rush at the Omelet Pan was over, and the line didn't extend out the door anymore. Barbara was counting her tips, and I was busy bussing and resetting the tables, when two Cutlasses pulled up outside. I think I noticed the cars because they didn't pull into the normal parking spaces; instead, they were angled right up to the door. Both vehicles were painted black, with blackened windows and heavy black grills on their front bumpers. Not the type of vehicles you usually saw in peaceful Grass Valley.

A group of men in suits walked into The Omelet Pan. When Barbara tried to seat them, they shook their heads and started firing questions at her. "Do you know Bob and Carla Glickman? Are they here today? Can you point them out to us?"

My parents came out of the back. My dad was still wearing his grease-stained apron. They started whispering to the men in suits. My mother looked like she was about to combust. But there was no yelling or cursing. Only those awful whispers.

I snuck closer and closer, ducking behind the empty tables, trying to figure out what was going on.

"Will you come with us willingly?" one of the men asked. My dad glanced around the restaurant. There were still a few customers around. "Of course," he said, and then muttered, "Not that we have a choice."

Carla turned her back on the men. "Barbara," she barked. "Come here a minute." Then, in a softer voice, she said, "Look, I need you to take the kids home for me. This shouldn't take too long. Can you do that?"

Barbara, looking as scared as I felt, nodded.

"Tell Tony and Jeff to close up for the day," my dad said. "We'll be back in the morning."

They put my parents in separate cars. I couldn't see through the tinted windows, but I thought my dad waved at us as they pulled away.

We got home to find the house literally turned inside out. It looked like a tornado had touched down in my living room. Stuff was everywhere, tossed on the floor and over the chairs. Pictures had been pulled off the walls and propped in corners. The couch was missing its cushions. Every cupboard was open and every closet emptied of its contents.

Stunned, we picked our way through and into the kitchen. Pots and pans were everywhere. Even the food had been rifled.

And so my dad's friend, Ray, found me, in the midst of this chaos. Barbara must have called him the minute I went upstairs.

"Those guys at the restaurant were Federal agents," he said. "They think your dad is making counterfeit money."

As if the porn business hadn't been enough of a handful, now we were dealing with money laundering.

Apparently, my dad's friend, Eddie, purchased a special kind of copy machine that they could use to generate replicas of paper money. My mother later claimed that she heard them on the phone talking about a specific kind of paper they needed to "do it right," but that she had no idea what they were really up to. "I thought they were just playing around, being guys," she told me. "They were playing with all sorts of things, making monkeys and trying to see if they could get every hair in the perfect place."

Maybe that was true—but by the time our house got tossed, there were no paper monkeys to be found. Only money.

Eddie and my dad started with one-dollar bills and worked their way up to hundred-dollar bills. By the end, there were four guys in on the project. They stashed the evidence in the attic over my bedroom.

As Ray was telling me all this, I was thinking: *This is so ridiculous. He's lying.* But, sure enough, when I nudged a pile of clothes with my toe, there was a hundred-dollar bill lying there. When I picked it up, I could see that it was printed only on one side.

"It was really just a game," Ray said. "They never really intended to do anything with the money. This is all just a big mistake. Everything will be alright soon enough; you'll see."

Sure.

How the Feds caught on, I don't know. My mother mentioned that one of the women who cleaned our house might have found something. Ray thought one of the conspirators had passed some of the hundred-dollar bills in Sacramento. However it happened, the money-laundering scheme had been revealed at last, and I was missing two parents.

Ray stayed with us for the rest of the day and late into the night. My parents finally got home close to midnight. My mom launched in a tirade of the hell and torment her questioners had put her through, how they'd grilled her and yelled at her and disbelieved her, no matter what she said.

She'd gone with the agents willingly enough, thinking this was just some mix-up, or something to do with their old porn ties. No big deal, she thought. After all, they'd always gotten off easily enough before.

Sitting in a separate interrogation room, she waited for the inevitable questions. *"What is (or was) your business, exactly? Do you know it's illegal to sell pornographic materials in Utah?"* When they told her that Bob was passing counterfeit bills, she went ballistic.

"This is ludicrous! What the fuck are you talking about?" she demanded.

They showed her pictures of my bedroom, where they found the half-printed bills and the counterfeit plates taped to the bottom of my nightstand drawers. "Do you recognize this area?" they asked her. "Do you recognize this bed? This nightstand?"

Of course she did. That was her daughter's room.

If they didn't receive her full cooperation, the agents said, they were going to take her children away from her and make them wards of the state leaving her with nothing. They told her that Bob blamed her for everything. Well, that just rode right up her ass. Of course, this was just a tactic; as much as they bickered, my dad would never have thrown Carla to the wolves for something she hadn't done. But the assertion was enough to send Carla into a rage. If she'd actually known anything—which I'm pretty sure she hadn't—she would have dished it all, just to get back at Bob for being such a fucker.

My dad, on the other hand, looked more tired than angry. He didn't say much—only that he was not allowed to leave the state until this whole thing was cleared up. The agents had told him that Carla knew nothing and that she'd blamed him for everything. More than likely, it was true.

So that's how my father got busted for counterfeiting U.S. currency. The next morning he hired the best attorney money could buy and went back to cooking up bacon and eggs. Several months and $300,000 in legal fees later, he got off with a fine of $2,000 and three years' probation, during which he couldn't leave the country and had to get permission to cross state lines.

If Bob and Carla had been at each other's throats before, they really had it in for one another after the counterfeiting incident. Their arguments escalated to the point where I felt like I was living in a war zone.

One day, while my brothers were out, my dad stormed into the house like a thundercloud with blood on his knuckles. I was just about to ask him if he was hurt when my mother burst in the door behind him. She had blood on her, too, but I couldn't tell where she was bleeding from. I tried to make myself as small as possible as they set up a screaming contest in the front hall. Then they moved to the kitchen, and eventually to the family room, where I was hiding out.

Sobbing with fright, I finally stood up and said, "Dad, if you don't stop hurting Mom, I'm going to call the police."

He ignored me. I reached for the phone and started to dial—then, he rounded on me and ripped the phone out of my hand so hard he tore it out of the wall.

"Shut the fuck up and stay out of it, Cindy," he snarled.

I did.

I think that day was the beginning of the end of my parents' marriage.

Mom's Secret Lover

The end came after Brian B, the prep cook from the restaurant, moved in with us. My brother, Brian, got kicked out of his bedroom and had to sleep with Timmy. I'm not sure why Brian had to live with us—only that one day he was just there, with all his stuff.

Brian B had a few different girlfriends whom he juggled simultaneously. Tall and thin, with puffy black curls shaped into a mullet, he was quiet and a little smug, yet awkward at the same time. I guess he was a pretty typical kid. He worked hard, listened to music, drank beer, and smoked pot with my mom…

Wait, what?

Brian B. smoked a lot of pot. I think he may have influenced my brother, Brian, to do the same—although my brother was probably already experimenting with it by then, at least a little. Drugs were approached very casually in our house. "It's no big deal," my mom said, pursing her red lips around a joint.

I guess if you can justify dragging your kids to a porn convention, drugs look like small potatoes.

I found the pot-smoking so appalling. I was only in fifth grade at the time but knew this wasn't a cool thing to be doing. Plus it smelled awful and skunky, and the smoke permeated everything.

As you can probably guess, I didn't care much for Brian B., but I didn't have much say in the matter, either. He was one of my dad's best employees, and my mom…Well, let's just say he had other attributes that Carla admired. She started writing love notes to him right under my dad's nose. Soon, the situation escalated into a full-blown affair.

I don't know how they carried it on, right there in the house, without one of us catching them, but they managed for a while. Why Brian B. wanted to sleep with my mom, a woman almost twenty years his senior, I couldn't figure. She still smoked like a chimney, plus three pregnancies and years of yo-yo dieting had done a number on her body. I remember thinking, *Why on Earth would he want to do it with her?* Maybe he felt obligated, seeing as he was living in our house for free.

Steeped in the imagery of the porn world, I couldn't imagine that a woman like my mother might actually be attractive to someone so much younger.

Usually, when a man gives an eighteen-year-old boy permission to sleep at his house, it does not mean permission to sleep with his wife. But as furious as my dad must have been, he did a fairly good job of keeping his cool—at least when we were around. This time there were no bloody knuckles. There was only a terse family sit-down, during which my parents explained to us that they were getting divorced. No if's, and's, or but's. No why's or wherefore's. Only the stark reality of a marriage crashing and burning.

I wasn't exactly shocked. They fought so much that it was almost a relief that they wouldn't be living in the same house anymore.

My parents asked me which of them I wanted to live with, and I was afraid to say anything for a long time. If I had to choose, I'd pick my dad, because he seemed like the lesser of two evils—but if I didn't stay, what would my mom have left? I felt a little like a dog, standing there while my two owners slapped their thighs and whistled for me to "come here," like in those old family movies. Which one did I love more? Which way would I go?

In the end, they didn't give me a choice anyway. "Little girls should be with their mothers," Carla said, and that was that. So Brian and Tim packed up their room and headed back to Valencia with my dad, and my mom and I were left alone, stranded in Grass Valley in a big, empty house.

When I asked my mom about Brian B., she practically snarled at me. "That is totally insane," she spat. "Your father is crazy. Out of his mind. I had nothing to do with that kid."

Sure, I thought. *Except for the sex and the letters.* But she held her ground, and it wasn't until I was in my mid-thirties that she finally 'fessed up to me about the whole thing.

When I asked her why she had done it, she said, "I needed someone to pay attention to me." I guess despite all the screaming and passionate fights, she didn't feel that my dad gave her very much of his time. And Carla—always the victim—decided to look for what she needed elsewhere. After all, it was Bob's fault she felt that way. She didn't take responsibility, but at least she was being honest about it.

After my dad and the boys moved out, my mom stuck a couch in Tim's room and called it a den. It was really the only furniture we had left, except for her bedroom set and mine. We left Brian's room empty. I think that's where the affair had been carried out, and while Carla never expressed any real guilt or remorse, she never went out of her way to open that door, either.

Just in trying to fill her own void, she was running on auto-pilot. The desire to fill herself up eclipsed her familial obligations, and I, the beneficiary of this behavior, went on to do the same…

CHAPTER 14

Porn Stars for Breakfast

"Let's go to Glickman's house!" Tim's buddies cried out. "That's where the party's at!"

L iving it up in L.A., the three bachelors—my dad and two brothers—moved right back into our old house on the hill. The couple who'd bought it defaulted on the financing so it went back to my parents. After a few weeks, it was like the boys had never left.

With no restaurant to run, my dad needed a job. So he went back to doing what he did best: selling adult videos. In order to bring in more money, he decided to lease out the house for filming. He had to pay that alimony somehow, I guess.

When we were little, my parents took us on "vacations." But now that Tim and Brian were twelve and fourteen, there wasn't any need. The film crews came in while the boys were on their way to school, and they would leave late in the afternoon. Inevitably, however, there was some overlap.

Like the day when Tim came downstairs in his pajamas to get breakfast and found renowned porn star Traci Lords, sitting at the kitchen table in her see-through nightie and washing down her Cap'n Crunch with a bottle of Jack Daniels. It was 7 a.m.

"Whoa!" he said. Already snookered, she barely looked up at him.

On other days, Tim would come home from school to find the front door locked against him. He'd knock and knock until someone came to open up. More often than not, it was one of the actresses, swaying precariously on her six-inch heels, wearing nothing but a few scraps of lace.

"You're cute. Who are you?" the girl of the day asked.

"Uh, I live here. I just want to come in and get my baseball glove."

Sometimes they'd let him in. And most of the time he'd have to wait until whatever raunchy acts they were filming in the stairwell had been concluded.

As you may have guessed by now, my brothers received very little parental supervision. My dad bought a pallet of beer to keep in the garage and told the boys to help themselves whenever they wanted. There was pot in the house all the time, in addition to whatever drugs the film crews and actresses were doing, which could have been anything.

Tim reconnected with his old friends, Mike and John, pretty much the minute he got back to L.A. They did typical adolescent boy things: playing baseball, riding their bikes, and teasing girls. But when they got out of school, they'd both turn to Tim and say, "Come on, Glickman, let's go to your house!" Soon, everyone wanted to be Tim's friend, so they could hang out at the party house. The scene was usually in full swing, with the girls and the drugs and the cameras rolling all day long.

My father went back to wearing his open shirts and gold chains. On one of these chains, he hung a solid gold coke spoon and an angel. I guess that, without my mother around to keep him in line, he went a little wild.

Not long after, my dad invited Brian B.—yes, the same boy my mother had been secretly having an affair with in our house only a few months earlier—to work for him. Suddenly, the two of them were the best of friends. I don't know if Brian wiggled out of it by blaming the whole mess on Carla (which, knowing my mother, might even have been true), or if my dad just wanted to deprive his ex of her playmate. But, either way, Brian was now a fixture at the Glickman house again. Meanwhile, back at the ranch, my mom and I were roughing it in Grass Valley.

Mommy and Me

"Darling," Carla said, exhaling smoke in my face. "Darling, you want a younger man, because men die younger than women."

Ah. Wisdom from the Great Pontificator.

No sooner had Brian B. moved to L.A. to work for my dad than my mom picked up another young stud. His name was Tom and he wasn't a day over eighteen. I could only speculate as to why she'd want to date someone who was closer to my age than her own. Maybe it gave her a sense of control, like she could make him do what she wanted. She was a cougar before cougars were en vogue.

I didn't care about boys at the time, young or old. After watching my parents' relationship and then my mother's flings, I didn't see the point. I didn't know what I wanted, but it certainly wasn't that.

My mom kept The Omelet Pan, since my dad obviously couldn't take that with him to L.A., and she continued to get up at 4 a.m. to run the restaurant. She had me sleeping in her bed for a while so she'd feel less alone, and that meant I got up at 4 a.m. too—not that I slept very well between those cigarette-scented sheets. After a few weeks of this, I was pretty grouchy, but I knew better than to say anything. Better to lose a little sleep than suffer one of Carla's famous tantrums.

Speaking of someone sleeping in your bed…

One night Carla and Tom were making out on the couch—really going at it and groping one another like animals. Grossed out and totally uncomfortable, I headed up to bed—her bed, since that was the pattern she'd established.

I woke up an hour or so later to strange noises and my brass bed squeaking in the next room. What was going on in there? I got up and tiptoed down the hall to make sure everything was okay—only to see my mom and Tom, naked as the day they were born, getting it on in my bed. *In my bed!*

This was one of those moments that are so devastating you can't even summon up the strength to scream. I did the only thing I could do: I turned around and got back in bed, shaken to the core and hating her with every fiber of my being.

A few days later, Carla suggested that I should "Go ahead and start sleeping in your own bed again, darling."

"No way," I told her. "I am *not* sleeping in that bed after you had sex with that boy in it. That's so disgusting!"

She didn't apologize but at least she changed the sheets for me. And a few days later, she took fifty dollars out of The Omelet Pan's cash drawer so I could get my hair done at the strip mall salon near the restaurant. Maybe she really felt bad, or maybe she was just trying to buy me off again—but this time, I appreciated the gesture. My new blonde highlights made me feel *beautiful.*

Field Trip

It wasn't easy for Carla to run the restaurant on her own. She had Tony and Jeff, the twins, doing the cooking and prep work but, after my father and Brian B. left, there was too much work and not enough hands. Business slowed down, and things got pretty tight.

While she managed to find fifty bucks for me to get my hair done, my mom had to stop taking me to the man who'd been teaching me Hebrew at the Jewish center in town, and there was no way she could afford the five-hundred-dollar fee for my marine biology field trip to Monterey. But, oh, how I wanted to go! I was in fifth grade and I loved marine biology so much that I wanted to do it for the rest of my life.

I knew my mother simply didn't have the money, and I hadn't heard a word from my dad, so I was going to have to find another way to make this trip happen. Where was my dad, anyway?

I talked to my teacher—and, as it turned out, there was a work-study program that would pay for my trip. I just had to work really, really hard. Every day I took the early bus to school with my cousin, Michael, and the other high school kids. I had to get myself up and dressed on my own: my mom was already at the restaurant by then and, if I missed the bus, I was out of luck.

I worked in the library in the morning and at lunchtime. I re-shelved books and cleaned and did whatever else the librarians wanted me to do. Some mornings I forgot to set my alarm, or messed up the settings, and I woke up in a guilty panic, thinking they would take away my scholarship. On those days I'd work through my whole lunch and during recess too. The grown-ups at school were really nice about the whole thing and never yelled at me when I missed a morning.

Part of me felt resentful that I had to work so hard for what other kids just got handed to them. It wasn't fair that I had to deal with this. But, at the same time, there was this wonderful sense of accomplishment, like "Wow! I really earned this. This is *mine*."

That feeling has been a constant in my life since that school year. No matter how hard I've had to work for something, I've always persevered. It's as though a source greater than myself has been assisting me along the way.

So, against the odds, I got to go on my school trip to Monterey. On the morning we left, I woke up in a glow of excitement. I knew nothing could ever stop me. If I could make this happen, I could do anything.

After a long bus ride, my classmates and I went to Monterey's aquariums and then to the ocean to see the animals in their natural habitat. We learned about whale migration and fish spawning grounds. We even got to handle some of the starfish and sea urchins, which was *so* cool. All in all, it was the best trip ever. I think I enjoyed it more than anyone else, because I earned it.

Still, despite this accomplishment, little did I realize how scared my heart was— a little girl not hearing from her daddy for over a year. It was like I was nonexistent. Didn't he care enough to wonder how I was or even chat with me on occasion? I felt totally disregarded and left behind while he went about his life. Worst of all, I was so unloved.

Back Together Again

And just that quickly, my parents kissed and made up.

I don't know exactly when they started talking again, but one day Carla's latest boy toy disappeared like smoke on the wind. After that, we went down to L.A. for a visit. Tim was really happy to see my mom. I didn't know how to feel.

Since my dad was back in the porn industry, it was up to us to sell the restaurant and move back to Valencia. Tony and Jeff bought The Omelet Pan—not really a surprise, considering they were practically running it themselves anyway—and we sold the house in record time. Although I'd been in school in Grass Valley for two solid years at this point and had made some good friends, there was no discussion about my feelings. We were moving, and that was that. How I felt or how things would affect my life never seemed to matter.

The first thing my mother did when we got back to Valencia was to buy me a new bed. I guess she really did feel bad about her escapades with Tom. The second thing she did was start fighting with my dad again, just like old times.

Talk about a major downsize! After my mom and I moved back to L.A. from Grass Valley, my parents spent several months straightening out their finances. First, they had to recover from the losses around their business, now that Teddy (the guy who wrote the bad checks) was nowhere to be found. They sold the big house on the hill to get some start-up money for a new business and moved us into a three-bedroom-plus-den condo in Lake Shore. Shortly thereafter, they bought a three-bedroom single-level house and packed us all up again. At least they converted the garage into a bedroom for Brian, so he and Tim didn't have to share.

The extra money gave my parents the capital they needed to start their latest porn venture: Cinnabar Video. My mom chose the name "Cinnabar" from an Estee Lauder perfume. Cinnabar was a hard red rock, and their new company was going to be a solid as a rock in the industry. (On a side note, cinnabar is also a common ore for mercury and, therefore, poisonous. Who knows, maybe there's a metaphor there after all.)

It was good to be back in the same house with my brothers, but they'd changed a lot in the time I was gone, and we weren't so tight anymore. That summer I was left alone a lot since the boys were off playing with their friends. I had no way of connecting to anyone until school started up and didn't want to be a tagalong. And so I ate myself silly and continued to put the chubs on. It was a good enough pastime, better than watching TV. It certainly made me feel better. Food boxes didn't have pictures of naked skinny women on them, at least.

I did a lot of learning that summer, about who I was and what I wanted. I cemented my dream of going to college and earning a doctorate and made resolutions that mostly involved never, ever becoming like my parents. But I also spent a lot of time wishing that someone paid attention to me. Even day camp would have been a relief—but Bob and Carla figured I was old enough to take care of myself. After all, I would be entering junior high in the fall.

When I got really bored, I rode my moped in the paseos. I shouldn't have had a moped in the first place, being only twelve, but my parents had bought matching ones for Tim and me while we were still living in Grass Valley. And, thanks to Brian's "training" and a few months of practice, I had pretty good command of a motorcycle. My moped was red, with a white wire basket above the headlight, so I could go to the store and get what I needed when no one else was around. The fact that I didn't have a permit didn't matter to my parents at all. Why should it?

Because when the cops catch a twelve-year-old driving a moped without a license, they get mad, that's why.

But like everything else, Bob and Carla were totally nonchalant about legalities. Maybe such attitudes stem from getting away with posing underage girls for porn flicks and posing counterfeit bills for real ones…

When I caught sight of the police on my tail, I was on my way back from the store. I whipped into the paseos, screeched into my driveway, and stashed the bike in the garage. For a minute or two I thought I'd gotten away with it—but the cops must have gotten my plates because, just as I was starting to relax, two of them rang my doorbell.

"Are your parents home?" they asked.

"No." It was just me, like it had been all summer.

"Were you riding a moped ten minutes ago?"

I lied to them, because I really didn't know what else to do. "I've been home all afternoon," I said. But I could feel my lips tugging up at the corners. Why do I always have to laugh when I'm nervous?

"Open the garage."

Confused, I did as they asked. I didn't understand what the point was until I saw one of the officers put his hand on the engine.

Busted!

Really, I was a good kid—not at all a menace to society. I hated getting in trouble. Maybe the officer noticed that I was squirming in fear, or maybe he was just in a good mood, because he only said, "Don't do it again, okay?"

"Okay," I whispered shakily.

I was so freaked out that I didn't ride my moped for days. But, eventually, the thought of staying another minute alone in the house became too much to bear, and I was on the road again. But I was really careful when I saw a police car. And I no longer rode in the paseos.

Yet risking an encounter with the law was the lesser of two evils rather than staying alone in that house with just TV and food. That reality fell hard on the mind and heart of a young girl who took it out hard on her body by feeding herself silly and only making her situation even worse.

CHAPTER 15

What Makes You Think You're So Special?

Smart and Sassy!

After that lonely summer before seventh grade, it felt great to have friends. I wore crazy, colorful makeup, teased my bangs up as big as they would go, and sported clothes in bright colors adorned with huge shoulder pads. Everything about me was a bold statement, in true Eighties form, and I *liked* it that way.

At my junior high, they presented students with awards at the end of the year. The whole class voted for the winners in categories such as "Most Intelligent," "Most Popular," "Best Athlete" and "Best Musician." The school newspaper photographer captured the male and female winners in each category and then highlighted these students in the yearbook.

Thankfully, most of the kids in junior high had gotten over the fat thing, and my bubbly exterior made me easy to like. Plus, Timmy's stardom helped me get in with the cool kids, and then my friends started hanging out with his friends. Before you know it, we had a whole little club going on.

At the end of year, the votes were cast, and an unheard-of thing happened: I was voted not only "Most Intelligent," but also "Most Popular." *Omigosh! I was important! I was popular!* BUT, they also respected my intelligence. And everyone knew it! I felt such a rush of love and gratitude, I almost started crying.

One of the teachers took me aside. "We have never had such a thing happen in our school's entire history," she said. "And as much as we'd like to, we really can't give you two awards. It just wouldn't be fair."

I was a little disappointed but ultimately felt so honored and knew that things had to be fair. Since I was on the student body, I was allowed to pick which category I would keep for the yearbook. While I was surprised and humbled by both votes, I didn't want be remembered as a geek— oh, the thought process of a teenager. So I opted out of that and went for "Most Popular."

I practically floated home that day. Bursting in the door, I shouted, "Mom! Guess what happened today?" She was going to be so proud of me!

Well, not exactly.

"What now?" Carla snapped. I guess I'd interrupted her in the middle of… something.

But I kept right on gushing, too excited to see the telltale way her eyebrows bunched up, or how her jaw got that certain set to it.

"You're not going to believe this, but the kids at school voted me 'Most Popular' *and* 'Most Intelligent.' I won *two* awards! And it's never happened before in school history, and… "

"And what makes you think *YOU'RE* so special?" she interrupted coldly.

The sarcasm was so sharp that it could have cut my heart out. Those fatal words would stick with me forever.

Apparently, the fact that I'd won two awards made me a horrible child—a selfish, awful bully who didn't have any thought for other kids and their feelings. I was a brat, and there was no way I deserved to be honored with either of those awards. On and on she went, becoming more vehement by the minute.

Totally stunned, I couldn't even cry. I didn't know what I had done wrong. I only knew that, in my mother's eyes, it was a terrible thing to be me. Devastating—especially when it comes from the one person who's supposed to be your biggest fan.

The joy of the day evaporated in an instant. The miniscule sense of confidence in me got squashed yet again. Maybe she was right. Who did I think I was? What was so special about fat, stupid Cindy? I didn't even have the *right* to cry.

So, I did what I always did: I sucked it up. I didn't shed a single tear, not even when I was alone later. My mother condemned me for crying. Hell, she condemned me for laughing—after all, if I was laughing, I must be laughing at her. None of my emotions were good, valid or appropriate. But when I didn't show them, I was cold-hearted and incapable of love.

When the yearbooks came in, I didn't even open them to look at my "Most Popular" picture. I figured I was better off pretending the whole thing never happened.

An enormous gap existed between who my mother was and who I hoped she would be. This, of course, set *me* up for failure, expecting someone outside of myself to change. All I wanted to know was that she was, even in some small way, proud of me—but she could never give me that reassurance. At the time, she just didn't have it in her. She herself had done poorly in school and lacked of confidence, making it impossible to lift me up. Like taking a bite of a lemon, she never wanted to hear that I'd been recognized for anything.

I don't know why I was surprised by her reaction that day. As my father so kindly pointed out, I always seemed to set myself up for disappointment; after all, this wasn't the first time she'd shot me down. Maybe just *once* I wanted some validation from my own mother.

The last time I was ecstatic for being recognized was in Grass Valley, when it was discovered that the schools were a little behind those in Valencia. Since my grades were really good, the school wanted to let me skip a grade. Of course, I was beaming. I worked hard to get good grades, and this was proof that all my effort had been worth it—that I was special. And now, I would be in the same grade as Timmy!

My mother wasn't so thrilled about my accomplishments. Timmy was the smart one, after all. Timmy was brilliant. He was *amazing*. And I was not allowed to outshine him.

As a test, she asked me to spell something. Of course, she knew that spelling was my weakest skill—and of course, I got it wrong. Isn't that always the way it goes?

"Your spelling is atrocious," she said triumphantly. "I guess you're just not smart enough to skip a grade." (Funny, how I was smart enough to help her with the books for their business when she got frustrated, but not smart enough to be in the same grade as Tim. And, as for spelling, well… Let's just say that, thanks to spell-check, I was able to earn my Ph.D. without ever needing to know how to spell "insouciant.")

Later that year, the school wanted to put me in the gifted program. Again, I was thrilled—and again, my mother axed the idea. "She's too sensitive," she told my teacher. "She'll never be able to hack it."

Damn. I must have been a jacked-up kid. A bad speller, too emotional... Not knowing what else to do with that, I added these to the list of things that were wrong with me and tried to get on with my day.

It was getting harder and harder, carrying around this entire set of mental luggage. Sometimes I had to sit down and take an itinerary of my flaws just to remember them all.

Since I was still stuck in elementary school, I decided to run for class president. Now that was something Carla could get on board with—if only in a passive-aggressive sort of way. She helped me make posters advertising all kinds of impractical claims—things which probably weren't even realistic for a kid to do as class president—and even made lollipops that said, "Don't be a sucker! Vote for Cindy Glickman!"

A little inappropriate, maybe, but it was better than "I'm so happy I could just sh*t!"

As long as I gave her credit for having all the good ideas, she was happy to help me. But when I didn't win the election, she made it out to be my fault. It was a very bipolar situation.

The following year, when I moved over to Magnolia Intermediate School, my teacher gave us our report cards in the order of who had the best grades. When she called out my name first, ahead of everyone, I was beaming from ear to ear. It was so great to be recognized, even for such a small thing. She took the time to commend me for my efforts, right there in front of everyone, and called me a good girl.

Whatever my mom said about him, I knew that Timmy had never been called up first for his report card.

Where did THAT come from?

What makes you think YOU'RE so special?

Those words would hunt me silently, deep in my subconscious, all the way into my adult years. I operated under the assumption that I wasn't so special and that I was not here to shine my light too bright because it would be a poor reflection and perhaps make others feel bad about themselves. Until one day—long after that first incident—all of the coping mechanisms of eating and ignoring how I really felt could no longer cover this wound.

It suddenly surfaced on my way to work, on just another ordinary day, without any understanding as to why I was in such pain, nearly twenty-five years later. For some reason, I heard those haunting words resounding in my head yet again:

What makes you think YOU'RE so special?

Where did *that* come from? It had emerged so strongly that I couldn't ignore it any longer. I couldn't go to work before I got to the root of this problem. I needed to sit down and write out whatever was coming up for reckoning.

I headed for a coffee shop, but the one I'd intended to visit was closed. So I fished a notepad out of my bag and drove to another one of my favorite places: an overlook where I could see a small lake and all the beautiful houses on the water. Most of the time I would come here to daydream about owning one of those lovely homes, or to escape the constant buzz of my 5,000-square-foot office, my agents, and my staff.

Today, I could barely see the houses, or the water, or the grass. The minute I put my car into park, my eyes overflowed—and I wasn't even sure why. All I knew is that something was coming up out of the depths of my heart and it was time to face it dead-on.

For most of my life, I didn't listen to these internal messages. My parents were great at ignoring their "stuff"—their fears, love, jealousy and anger—and, in our house, emotion was often used as a weapon.

My own stuff manifested in various forms over the years, including an eating disorder, pitifully low self-worth and tolerance of abusive relationships. After a lot of pain and many trials, I'd finally learned to listen to the voice inside that had been with me all along.

But I still couldn't figure out why I was sad.

When we're feeling sad, we often think that the emotion applies to something that's happening in the here and now. But the truth is that we have coping mechanisms that don't allow us to deal fully with childhood pain. Some things are just too hard for a young mind and heart to process. The result is that this old, stuck pain bubbles up at odd times and for odd reasons and bursts into the mind when we're least prepared for it.

As I continued to ask myself what the heck was going on with me, I heard a sarcastic, all-too-familiar voice say: *"What makes you think YOU'RE so special?"*

Once I might have thought that the voice was my own. But I don't talk to myself that way anymore. This was coming from somewhere else. Yet it contained those awful, dreaded words.

I pulled out my phone and called my friend, Jason, a spiritual coach. When I told him what was going on, he asked the same question I had: "Was that your voice?"

"No. Of course not!" Part of me was trying to confirm this for myself. Had I failed in all my work? Had that negative, awful voice simply gone into hiding for a while, instead of moving out?

"Well," Jason said calmly, "if it isn't your voice, then whose voice is it?"

There was a dramatic silence. Part of me was screaming, "I don't know!"—as if I was determined to resist the truth, no matter what the cost.

"Just say the first name that comes to mind," Jason prompted.

So I did. "My mother."

I didn't want to believe it at first. But then, once I released it, I knew it was true.

"When was the first time she said that to you?" he asked.

And that was when the memory flashed before my eyes. I could see, vividly, the teal dress that I'd loved so much because it was, like, *totally* Eighties. I was grinning, nearly skipping, because I'd just found out that I'd won two of the superlative category titles for our eighth-grade class. Not only was I "Most Intelligent," but I was also "Most Popular." I felt like it was a real honor to be recognized not only for my intellect but for my likeability. After all, I'd put a lot of effort into being that kind of person.

When I waltzed in the door after school, I couldn't wait to tell my mother. I wanted her to be proud of me. I wanted her to recognize that I might, just maybe, be as smart and likeable as my brother Tim.

And that's when she said those devastating words: *"What makes you think YOU'RE so special?"*

As I was sobbing this story into the phone, I realized that I'd never really thought about that moment. I'd barely had a memory of it; in fact, I had totally suppressed it. It wasn't until today, twenty-four years later, that I felt the real blow. It was like I'd been punched in the stomach.

"If you were standing there with your thirteen-year-old self at that moment," Jason asked, "what would you say to her?"

I tried to envision my adult self there, in our old kitchen, standing next to a chubby pre-teen in a teal dress. I saw my mother, with her dyed-black hair and perpetual anger. Surprisingly, I felt compassion for my mom, even sadness. I know that she never felt that great about herself. What I had achieved that day was something she'd always wanted. My mother had never been popular, and she never believed she was intelligent because her father always told her she was a big dummy. So she did everything she could to prove that point on a subconscious level, and everything contrary to that point on a conscious level. She was constantly at war with herself. Lashing out at me was a way to avoid feeling other things—like pride, or jealousy, or vulnerability, or regret.

Jason was quiet for a minute. Then, he said, "The fact that you have compassion for your mom is wonderful."

I nodded against the phone, feeling good about my newfound understanding.

"But that is what you, the enlightened adult, would say. But what would that little girl in the teal dress say?"

Wow. That question changed everything! My little-girl self was angry, yes, but really more puzzled than anything else. So I planted my hands on my teal-covered, pudgy little hips, and blurted out the words I wished I'd been able to say to my mother back then: "What the hell were you thinking?! Why would you say something like that to a child? What is *wrong* with you?"

At the time, I felt like I had been sucker-punched. I was so stunned that I didn't even say a word. Besides, she was right. I asked myself, "Who DID I think I was to consider myself so special?"

And then, I laughed through my tears. Because really, it was kind of funny to think that I had held myself hostage to this belief for twenty-plus years. Who are we not to be special?

First Kiss: Dating the Daughter of a Porn King

The summer before eighth grade, I became a cheerleader.

Now, before you get too incredulous, realize that this was a paid gig. If your parents had the cash, you got to be a cheerleader. More money got you a burgundy skirt with white pleats, a white shirt a burgundy vest and a time slot to practice out on the field while the boys played football. Whoopi!

The fact that I didn't have to audition didn't make being a cheerleader any less exciting for me. I was a tomboy switching gears, and this was one of my first real steps into what the world views as girlhood. It was awkward; how do you bond with girls?

The dance routines were hard for me. I'd spent so long hating and hiding my body that I had no idea how to move it around on command. Also, I never practiced when I was at home, since it was pretty much guaranteed that my brothers would laugh at me. When we were out on the field, I tried to follow our coach's instructions, and when I lost my place, I'd try to follow the other girls and act like I knew what was up. I can't imagine it looked good from the field—but, hey, at least I was trying.

It wasn't easy being a cheerleader. I was so self-conscious about my thick legs that I wouldn't even wear shorts to school, so imagine how painful it was to wear a short skirt and matching undies in front of a crowd. It got to the point where I couldn't get dressed in front of the mirror.

Shanna—the *model* (and very Barbie-like) cheerleader, with long shiny blonde hair streaked by the Southern California sun—had a great body, a cute little nose and the Ken prototype boyfriend. I desired to be like her. When she stood next to me, I felt so inferior, as though I had suddenly shrunken four inches and turned into a troll.

I might as well have been a troll since I looked so heinous compared to her. Just like I felt at the porn conventions with all those hot gorgeous babes.

One day I actually looked down at my tree-trunk legs and said out loud, "I hate my big fat legs."

Shanna graciously smiled at me and shook her head. "You have perfect legs. They don't look fat to me at all. It's just that when you're looking down on them, they look bigger. That's all."

It sent chills through my heart that the prettiest girl on the team paid me this compliment. Even though I thought she was sugar-coating the truth, her kindness meant a lot. And I stopped looking down at my legs during practices.

Another good thing came out of that summer season: I met a boy who liked me. Mike was tall and thin, with brown eyes and short brown hair that stuck up at the crown of his head. I didn't know him from Adam.

Ah, summer love. It was so typically junior high. Mike told his friend that he liked me, and the friend passed the message to me because Mike was too shy to tell me himself. Since I had no idea who Mike was, I had to ask his friend to point him out. When he did, I got butterflies in my tummy. I couldn't believe that some boy actually wanted me—fat, ugly Cindy Glickman!

At that point, I don't think it mattered if Mike had webbed feet and warts on his nose. He was a boy, and he liked me, and that meant I was special. I was on top of the world.

"Are you sure he meant me?" I asked the messenger. "Really? Are you sure?" —thinking maybe it was a practical joke.

Mike's friend asked if he could have my phone number to pass along to Mike. I didn't have any words to say but "Yes! Sure! Here!" This was so completely new to me. I mean, he picked *me*! How could I not respond to that? (Thank God I have a little more self-respect than that today. But my little-girl self really needed that boost—that thrill of knowing that Mike could have picked any number of cuter, skinnier girls, but he wanted *me*.)

So, I gave the messenger friend my number, and Mike called me a day or so later. Wow, a boy calling me at home—how special! And then came the inevitable reaction: "Oh my God! What am I going to do now?"

The first time Mike called, my dad picked up the phone. "Who the hell is this?" he growled in his scariest voice. After a moment of silence, he said in his normal voice, "Oh. Okay. She's right here." I think he thought it would be great fun to make Cindy's new boyfriend poop his pants before he ever even met him. Of course, my dad wasn't actually going to stop me from dating—that would have been beyond hypocritical—but he loved freaking people out.

Ten minutes on the phone with Mike convinced me at last that this wasn't a joke. He really did like me. What exactly he liked about me, I have no idea. (I wonder now if he saw me on the field and simply thought, "That one, I can get.") And it didn't really matter anyway. Desperate for acceptance, I took his attention for the gift it was.

In our conversation, I sheepishly admitted that I didn't really know who he was, only that he was on the football team that our crew was cheering for—after all, we'd never actually met. To remedy this, we decided to meet on the night of a game behind the stands. (Behind the stands? How cliché can you get?)

He approached me slowly, like he thought I might bolt. The shadows hid his expression. He wasn't my idea of handsome, exactly, and he was very thin, which made me feel even fatter since I was so much wider than him. Shaking a little, I stepped closer, so I could get a better look at his eyes. We had barely said hello before he kissed me. I panicked for a moment, then surrendered to it.

I thought it was strange that I didn't fear him at all. But he seemed gentle and kind, and he was here, behind the stands, kissing me, just like they did in the movies. I don't know if this was his first kiss too, but it was a bit... sloppy. One might have thought that, due to my father's business, I might have been more experimental, but this was as far as I'd ever gone.

We kissed for about twenty minutes, then it was time to go. His parents would be looking for him, he said. I wiped my mouth with the back of my hand and nodded.

After that, we talked a few more times, but it was clear we had very little in common. I don't know who blew off whom, but it didn't bother me much when I realized that our summer romance was over.

I was pretty enough to be kissed, and that was all that mattered.

CHAPTER 16

Pot, Porn and Packing on the Pounds

Sliding into the stretch limo with a sense of dread in my belly, we were off to another porn convention. It was the summer before eighth grade, and I was really beginning to realize the power of being pretty—a power I did not in any way possess.

As usual, my parents had reserved one room for themselves and another for us. We all got passes to both the regular convention and the "Adults Only" area. Tim and I checked the whole place out, of course. It wasn't quite as shocking as it had been the first time around—but it wasn't exactly my dream vacation, either. Tim, less of a novelty now that he was nearing puberty, didn't get quite as much attention from the starlets, but he still got plenty of those trashy autographed photos, which he gleefully spread out all over our hotel bed.

I studied them surreptitiously, memorizing the curves of legs and hips, the flat planes of perfect bellies. Someday, I would look like that.

My dad had a booth, and he was really excited to market his latest video release, a film called "A Certain Sacrifice." It wasn't hardcore—but it *did* feature a luscious 19-year-old Madonna in the nude (hairy armpits and all) and that was big news. Bob could sell just about anything, but this one was really going to fly off the shelves. (On a side note, Madonna did *not* want that video released. Later, she actually sued my parents to try to keep them from selling it—but she lost.)

My dad put up his posters and set up all his materials on the convention floor—and then noticed that the guy next to him had the same posters. He was offering "pre-release" specials on "A Certain Sacrifice." Who did this schmuck think he was? My dad had cut a deal (on a napkin in a bar, but still a deal) with the producer, giving him exclusive rights to distribution. This was supposed to be his big day!

Then my dad recognized the guy as someone to whom he'd sold secondary release rights. Basically, the guy was supposed to be able to distribute the Madonna video—but only with my dad's permission and only *after* the convention.

Furious, my father picked a fight with the guy right there on the convention floor, yelling and waving his arms around. I guess they weren't resolving things fast enough, because my dad started to rip down the guy's posters.

"We had a contract!" my dad roared. "You can't sell it here. Are you an idiot? You'll be getting a call from my lawyer!"

"Looking forward to it!" the guy shouted back.

Clearly, this was not a good day for either of them.

After the disastrous convention, we rented a Volvo and drove up to New York City. I don't know if my dad needed time to cool down, or if he had accounts to see in the city, or what, but my parents gave Tim fifty bucks and set the two of us loose in Times Square. "Have fun," they said.

We grinned at each other. "Okay!"

New York was amazing to me then and it still is. We stared in awe at all the huge buildings. There were skyscrapers in L.A., but they were nothing like this. We drank in the stink of the summer air and diesel fumes. We stared curiously at the neon lights over our heads—dimmer during the day— and at the street people who held out their hands as we walked by, begging for money. There were no homeless people in Valencia. At twelve years old, I felt like I'd stepped into some sort of parallel universe, where everything was bigger and louder and closer.

After eating some real New York pizza from a street vendor, we wandered up to F.A.O. Schwartz, the biggest and best toy store in the world. We didn't spend any money in the toy store. Instead, Tim ducked into a head shop and came out with two small pipe-sized bongs. When we got back to the hotel, Carla asked him what he'd done with the money and he pulled them out to show her. "Oh," she said, raising one black eyebrow. "Is *that* what you bought?"

"Yeah." He wasn't defiant—just matter-of-fact.

And that was the end of that. Carla shrugged; my dad just shook his head. The bongs went into the suitcase and came home with us— precious souvenirs of our time in Manhattan.

King of the Castle

"Pass the bong, dude!" said one of Brian's friends in the smoke-filled room. His buddies crowded around in the garage on old dirty couches with cold concrete underfoot. Before the garage was transformed into a bedroom, it served as a low-end party station for my brother's friends. Mike, Vinny and Alan became regulars at this venue.

Alan muttered, "Wow, this stuff is stinky man."

"Yeah, dude, it's some sticky shit," another one of the guys mumbled.

Apparently, that meant it was good. Watching this scene was better than TV or any Cheech and Chong movies. While taking breaks from my math homework, I came in and just laughed my butt off while they passed the three-foot tall, see-through, blue bong.

They all laughed right back, rarely ever speaking directly to me. Mike said, "Check out Glickman's lil' sister, man! She's getting a contact high, dude. She's fucking funny!" I still remember the sound of the clicking lighter and the bubbling water as they took their next hit.

Brian, being king of *his* castle—or at least the garage—and having his own entrance to the house, creatively turned this into a profitable business venture. His friends were always in and out. Mike, his best friend, practically lived with us. The two of them smoked all the time, and we're not talking about cigarettes. You couldn't go into that garage without getting a contact high, and Brian himself thoroughly enjoyed making a killing at the same time. Like father, like son.

My parents were *so* proud—their son, an entrepreneur. And to think of Carla swinging a tennis racket at him years earlier, exclaiming, "You'll never amount to anything!" How wrong she was.

Brian always remained my dad's favorite, so he could do no wrong. It was assumed that Brian would follow my dad into the family business, so this peddling represented an entrepreneurial endeavor to develop his sales and marketing skills better than working for someone else. He was in business for himself—no menial labor for Brian!

While I *was* the white sheep of the family, I can't say I was an angel either. My friends, Steffy and Allison, and I smoked a little of the "wacky-tabacky" ourselves on occasion. It was easy to get the stuff; after all, my brother was the go-to guy in the neighborhood. We didn't do it often and it wasn't necessary to have a good time since my friends were already hilarious all on their own. Mostly, we got together and talked about boys, or studied, or did other normal "girl" things.

Sometimes we snuck vodka from the bottles my parents kept in the bar in our living room and then filled them up with water to hide our thievery. Of course, my parents figured it out pretty quickly. They laughed about the "weak" vodka with their friends and let it go.

Whatever Steffy, Allison and I did, it was nothing compared to what my brothers were doing. Brian smoked pot pretty much every day and used to get coke from one of my classmates. Between the porn, the pot, the booze and whatever else was going on, the Glickman residence was the neighborhood party spot and there was always some kind of debauchery going on.

One day, Allison came over for a visit. It was a non-pot-smoking day, so we were just sitting in my bedroom, talking about school stuff. All of a sudden, my mom barged in. Without any preamble, she started screaming at Allison.

"You are such a bad girl! You're a horrible influence on my daughter. How do you live with yourself, you little bitch?"

Are you kidding me?

I was stunned and absolutely mortified. We hadn't done anything wrong—in fact, we'd barely made a peep all afternoon. There was no reason at all for my mom to be acting like this. Allison's dad was a documentary director, not a porn king. She had a stay-at-home mom who cooked meals for their family and made sure that everyone got to their lessons and sports practices on time—not a crazy mother who made up stories about anything and everything just to get attention. Her brothers didn't sell drugs out of the garage, or smoke pot out of four-foot bongs, or do coke with her friends.

As suddenly as she'd appeared, my mom was gone. The door slammed shut behind her. I was so shocked that I hadn't even heard the last half of her tirade.

I turned to Allison, and whispered, "Oh, my God. What the hell was that about?" I hoped she'd figure out that my mom was crazy and unhinged, didn't mean it and was certain to lose memory of this conversation come morning.

But Allison didn't get any of it. She broke down in tears and refused to say another word to me. Perhaps, she thought it was my fault that my mom had gone off like that—that I had said something to make it sound like she—not I—was the troublemaker. And so I could only sit there, bent over in shame. She called her mom to come pick her up and repacked her bag—she had originally planned to spend the night at my house—and fled out the front door to wait at the curb.

Overwhelmed with guilt, I came out to stand with her. I kept apologizing over and over. When her mom got there, I apologized to her, too. At least her mom said she understood and that it wasn't my fault.

After Allison left, my mother continued the yelling. "You're a worthless piece of shit, Cindy," she told me. "It's a wonder you have any friends at all. You're a no-good bully. If you weren't such a know-it-all control freak, people might actually like you."

"But mom, I didn't do anything!"

"Of course you did. You're just such a bully that you can't even see it."

Deep down, I think I sensed that something wasn't right with my mom. But there was still that part of me that didn't know for certain. I mean, what's a mother supposed to act like? I thought she was just correcting me—that I really was too awful to see just how awful I was. *I have my problems, just like everybody else,* I reasoned, *and she's just telling me what they are.* Of course, I did not realize at that time that she was just projecting her own issues on me.

But, now, she'd graduated to correcting my friends, too. And she'd done it out of the blue, with no rhyme or reason. One minute she was fine, and the next she was raving. To me, this was normal behavior—but to Allison, it was devastating. From that point forward, I started to disconnect from my friends. I was still friendly with everyone at school but certainly not inviting any one over to the house anymore. Not if they have to go through an ordeal like that.

Hair Trauma

Squirming with excitement, I parked myself in the salon chair. My girlfriend Angie's older sister who was studying cosmetology needed a guinea pig and I was just the one. With my help, she could accrue more hours toward obtaining her license at the beauty school. I already donned blonde highlights and spiral curls, but my exposed brown roots screamed, "Trrrraashy!"

I thought, *Oh, fun! Let's try something new.* Plus, highlights broke the bank and going to a student in training required a lot less funds. Carla graciously funded the first round in Grass Valley as a peace offering, but the next ones were up to me.

Slopping hair color all over my head, Angie's sister clocked me and then stuck my skull in the bowl. She seated me back in the chair, took the towel off, and *voila*! My haired had turned orange! When they tried to fix it, it turned green! Holy crap! By that point, it was so fried that the only thing left to do was chop it. Hacked off to the nape of my neck, my hair was still green. The instructor advised, "The only thing we can do now is dye it red to neutralize the green."

With tears trickling down my cheeks, I cried uncle and whispered, "Just do it."

When I walked in the door with my new short, burgundy hair, my mother just about had a heart attack.

"It's horrible!" she said. "Absolutely hideous! What were you thinking?"

I shrugged my shoulders, already feeling miserable. Now Carla rubbed my face in it too—having no clue that she just added insult to injury. The trauma of this incident went way beyond my burgundy mop. How about being stopped and asked if you are a boy or a girl?

Once, while I was still in elementary school, I marveled at a woman with a really hip, super-short, spiky Eighties haircut. It stood up all over her head and had some longer hairs that ran down her neck. I thought, *Wow, that's the coolest rocker hairdo ever.* So I asked my mom, "Can I get my hair cut like that? I love it! I love it!"

Unfortunately for me, an angular-face sported that do nicely. But, with my round, chubby cheeks atop my plump little body, it did not exactly result in a feminine look. Stopped by a woman on my way home from school, she asked, "Are you a boy or a girl?" Devastated by the question, I paused and thought to myself, "Are you kidding me?" When I told her, she said, "Well, you don't *look* like a girl."

Any shreds of self-confidence I did have were totally obliterated. As if I didn't already hate myself enough. After that, I swore to never, ever cut my hair short again. I spent almost two years growing out that awful mullet. Even trims scare me now. (To this day, I freak out if a stylist cuts my hair more than I've asked.) So the last thing on my mind was an innocent highlight costing me all of my hair. Now, as my mom so eloquently reminded me, I was back to being an ugly, chubby, unlovable *boy* — right before we left for another porn convention no less.

Now, when I look at the picture from that summer, I realize that the haircut wasn't so bad. In fact, I was kind of cute—if still a little awkward. But I was so entrenched in the idea of my ugliness that I couldn't see the real reflection in the mirror.

Soon after, I started starving myself.

Dealing with the Enemy

Why couldn't I magically lose weight, like my dad?

Pops underwent gastric bypass surgery, before the days of LAP bands and laparoscopy. Back then, they opened you up, cut three-quarters of your stomach out, and sewed you back together. His scar ran from his left hip, up to his breast, and curved back down to his other hip—like a big frown.

When the surgery was first done, my dad ate very little. When he overate, he threw up. Great concept! After a while, he joked about it, sticking his finger down his throat and crossing his eyes. He swiftly lost more weight. By the time he and my mom separated, he'd lost about one hundred pounds.

"I'm gonna barf now," My father would say, after ordering whatever he wanted and getting his fill. At restaurants he'd do his funny act, then beeline it to the bathroom. When he came back, his eyes were red and watery, so we all knew what he'd been doing. He'd sit down, drink some water, and pick up eating right where he'd left off. When the entrees were finished, he'd suggest all sorts of yummy deserts, or talk about going for ice cream. My brothers and I rubbed our bellies, moaning that we were full, and he just laugh—like we were the suckers for missing out on the best part.

Fat and frumpy the summer before high school, I obsessed about my weight. My friends blossomed into thin and beautiful young women while my mind compulsively compared myself to them, producing a breeding ground of self-hate. The fastest way to get thin was to starve myself. That worked for only so long before I felt dizzy and foggy-minded, with that darn appetite rearing up. Modeling my dad's behavior offered the ideal solution. Devour whatever I wanted, so long as I threw it up after.

As they say: When in Rome, do as the Romans do.

In the Eighties, aerobics became the craze. I started taking classes at the racquetball club. Soon, I spent twice a day at the gym, racing to burn as many calories as possible. When I got hungry, I ate ice. If I really slipped up and consumed real food, I stuck my finger down my throat, like my dad, and the calories came right back up again. I didn't even need gastric bypass surgery! Yahoo!

Sadly, however, it developed into a battlefield, a win-lose game. Taunted by all kinds of delectable forbidden fruits, I fought my own inner demons. It was like having an angel on one shoulder and a devil on the other.

"No! Don't do it!" the angel said.

"But if it comes right back up again," the devil countered, "No harm, no foul, right? Just eat. Enjoy; you deserve it!"

"Be strong…" the angel said in a weakening whisper.

My head spun back and forth, until I couldn't see clearly. My body trembled until I couldn't fight it anymore and then recklessly I gave in to the "sin." Initially, I thought, *This is going to be great. All the pleasure without the damage.* But, then, once I was through filling my body with bliss, I passed the point of no return. My belly painfully distended and sheer panic set in. *Oh, God, I have to get rid of this! I have to throw it up. I have to get this poison out of my body! I can't give myself time to digest it. I have to get rid of it—now! Now!*

Hunched over the toilet, consumed by terror, I jammed my fingers down my throat until I choked. It was so disgusting, with vomit covering my fingers. I hated myself. Where was my self-control? How could food have this power over me?

Shaking, with my eyes watering as I looked at the masticated mess in the toilet, I swore to myself: *I just had to get rid of this, this one last time. Tomorrow is a new day, I'm going to stop. I'm never going to do this again. I'll be stronger—I won't eat, and I won't have to do this anymore.*

And all the while, that angel (now a little colder and sterner) shook her head.

My resolution lasted for a day, or two, or even a whole week. But then I'd smell pizza, or see a bag of donuts just lying there, waiting for me. Temporary amnesia set in, only remembering the pleasure of eating—and none of the consequences. Half an hour later, I'd be back in the bathroom with my throat on fire, sobbing over the mess in the toilet.

But, in a month, I dropped twenty pounds. I went from a misses' size nine to a size two. I thought I was brilliant (temporary amnesia again). Was this really all I'd needed to do? Why had I spent all those years as the fat girl?

That summer marked the beginning of my struggles with bulimia. More than twenty years later, maintaining a healthy relationship with food has had its challenges. It has been a crutch, a friend and a confidante. When I have no one to turn to, food has always been there. Sometimes, when stress is high, I feel anxiety and my first reaction is to eat. And since food is necessary for energy and so readily available, it is not a drug or addiction you can avoid or abstain from.

Rather than trying to conquer such an addiction, I learned to love it. It is my body's (and anyone else who suffers such challenges) way of telling me something is wrong and to pay attention. The many years of working with this disorder has been another gift from my upbringing. The gift in it was to learn how to really listen to—and love— myself and my body.

I don't blame my father for any of this; if I hadn't learned it from him, I would have picked it up somewhere else. My body image issues were already leading me in that direction. It just went way beyond body image; it became a way to temporarily feel a void in my heart. I am the one who turned it into my own coping mechanism, which became a terrible habit. And I hid my purging so well that it was years before anyone learned I'd been mimicking Bob's behavior. After that, my mom started following me to the bathroom whenever we'd go out to eat.

That first summer I undervalued the repercussions. And, the health risks of binging and purging were the least of my concerns. All that mattered at the time remained finally being thin, and beautiful and special—like the women at the conventions.

***

This life has been a journey, and many situations from childhood scarred me, like most everyone else. But, as an adult woman, I have worked through these scars, been honest with myself, changed my perspective and, ultimately, become a better person because of it. Rather than consume mounds of food to fill the void in my heart, I have discovered how to fill it with self-love, compassion and understanding for myself and all others involved. We make our own meaning out of these life experiences, so we can choose to be the victim or we can choose to be a victor, engaging in life and situations as catalysts for growth and evolution.

I have had some pretty big life challenges and some really huge blessings along the way. It doesn't matter who you are or where you come from; you, too, have been blessed. Look into your life and find the areas where you have been gifted. Find the silver lining to your clouds and use that to become the best person you can be today. They are the catalyst for your change and strength and the seed of what makes you special. Be grateful to your family and for whatever you have been given, whether it serves as a point of contrast for what you don't want or a signal of what you really do want. Some people have had role models and some of us have not. Find your own role models and become your own role model. Step into your power and be all you can be— right here, right now, today. That is all that matters. And that is what all this taught me.

CHAPTER 17

Sex-Capades

Suddenly Seducing Cindy

I think were alone now; there doesn't seem to be anyone around...

That hit, by Tiffany, was our song. Which is exactly what my first high school boyfriend demanded: for us to be alone, so he could get me into bed—or at least, into the bed of his truck.

Then, when he finally got some action, he dumped me. I was fourteen and traumatized. I don't recall it being enjoyable either—in fact, I barely remember it. At the time, it seemed like something I had to do rather than wanted to do— it felt like coercion. In order to be liked, I shamefully acquiesced having no understanding of sex as an emotional union or an expression of love. My parents didn't exactly educate me about that aspect, and who else was there for me to learn from—those convention queens or the starlets on our stoop? I don't think so...

A few days after the deed was done, he explained that he didn't feel right about it and had found a good Christian girl who teased him to his heart's content and never let him get past first base. Apparently, I was now dirty and he wanted nothing further to do with me. He had more in common with her than with me.

You can imagine my confusion. I tried to say no, but he just continued to pursue it. I hadn't realized that it was actually possible to say no and I thought I was doing the right thing to make sure he liked me. Apparently, when you're the daughter of a Porn King, you're expected to behave in a certain way. And I had done exactly that. Otherwise, I'd be labeled as a prude and a tease. (Just like the good Christian girls. Hmm…)

After harassing me, that boy took what he wanted and still it wasn't good enough. Unable to cope with his sucker-punch, I purged myself of the pain the only way I knew how.

Is That Your Penis?!

"It's a lot easier to roll up to your problems in a Rolls Royce, honey," my mother so kindly reminded me often. So— to get me back in the game, Bob and Carla became matchmakers!? What is the world coming to?

Marriage being a business deal and devoid of love, it was time for me to start dating again. My parents weren't wasting any time in pairing me off. My dad decided to set me up on a blind date with a thirty-one-year-old millionaire from Israel. "You're really going to like him," my dad gushed in his best salesman voice. "He's a good Jewish boy with good ethical values. He owns his own business. He wants a wife and a family, and he's ready to commit. He's perfect for you."

I had no idea what to think. But I knew better than to trust my parents' judgment of "good ethical values." And since when had marriage and kids become part of my foreseeable future?

Oh, and did I mention that I was *fifteen*?

"Marry that money and you'll be set for life," my mother said, sliding closer to me on the couch, lowering her voice to a confidential whisper. "You're going to need a lot more money than you'll be able to get on your own just out of college. Living on sixty grand a year is barely living, honey."

In the end, I didn't really have a choice in the matter. My dad coordinated the date with Rob, as in "Cradle Robber"—and I tried to feel good about it. By the time Saturday came, I was actually sort of excited and more than a little nervous.

I picked out a skirt I hadn't had much opportunity to wear. The material was soft but sort of shiny, with a stretchy waistband and feathery pieces that lay flat while I was standing still but flew out like wings when I twirled around. The blouse that went with it was plain, but made of the same material that faded from pink to deep purple, depending on the lighting. I took my time drying my hair, coaxing it into a leonine Eighties pouf with mousse and hairspray. Once I finished putting on my dark eye makeup, I could easily have passed for a young woman of eighteen. Maybe even twenty.

The doorbell rang, and I dashed to answer it. Rob wasn't a bad-looking guy—dark hair, dark eyes, conservative haircut, a little chunky, not too tall. Pretty much a typical Israeli businessman. He took my arm and walked me out to his car—a jet-black BMW M3 with immaculate leather seats, spotless black carpeting and all the bells and whistles.

Well, I thought. *At least he has a nice ride.*

The event we were going to was a family party—but first we had to go to his mother's apartment in the Valley. This was my first real, official, meet-the-parents kind of date, so I didn't know what to do except roll with it and try not to act like a little kid. We kept up the small talk all the way to his mother's front door. He seemed likable enough, if a little reserved.

Rob's mother was a short, round Jewish lady who spoke only Hebrew. My Jewish education had been kind of spotty, so I didn't understand most of what she said. I only sat there and nodded and smiled until my cheeks hurt. Rob translated between us, but I had no real idea what was going on. *Just get me out of here*, I thought.

Now, I understand the situation a little better. Rob was looking for a wife, and so it was appropriate for his mother to approve his choice of a potential mate. Rob was old for an Israeli to be without a wife and family. He'd taken a few extra years to get his business up and running, but now it was time to settle down. Given that my father had arranged this date, it was assumed that I was marriageable and willing—so everyone just got right down to business.

I don't know what his mother was looking for, or if she found it. For heaven's sake, I didn't know what *I* was looking for. Why was I even there? What was I thinking?

"Isn't the party starting soon?" I asked after a while. "Shouldn't we get going?"

Rob's mom said something unintelligible, and he laughed. He didn't bother to translate, so I assumed they were making fun of me.

Finally, Rob's friend showed up to collect all of us and bring us to the party. Once we were there, I was able to relax a little. It was a raucous family gathering, like the ones you see in old movies, with the whole family gathered in a big room to eat and dance and drink. Most of the parties I'd been to had consisted of a bunch of kids getting as drunk as possible and making out in closets—or my dad's friends, with their shirts open and gold chains dangling over their hairy chests, bent over mirrors or swirling glasses of scotch—and so this was a pleasant surprise.

I danced with Rob, and twirling in my dress was a blast. By the end of the night, I was back to being my giggly, outgoing self and Rob was obviously pleased at his choice of a companion.

When the party started to wind down, Rob's friend brought us back to Rob's mother's house. They talked about going to a club, but when the friend found out I wasn't twenty-one, he went his own way, leaving me alone with my date. Rob helped me back into his BMW and drove me up into the hills to a deserted overlook.

Entranced by the view, I got out of the car to get a better look at the sparkling lights that stretched on and on under the stars. Suddenly, I felt my back slam up against the car door as Rob stuck his tongue down my throat. I froze. He pressed himself up against the whole length of my body, and I could feel his penis harden as I clamped my mouth shut. Why was he so hard? I hadn't done anything! I hadn't encouraged him, or flirted, or anything! I felt like I wanted to crawl out of my skin.

And, this was flat-out creepy. I'd never had the sensation of a man rubbing himself up against me like that. Like I was a scratching post and he was a cat. Overwhelmed with disgust, I didn't care what kind of car he drove or how nice his mother was. I did not want this man's tongue down my throat or his repulsive penis rubbing against my thigh.

I ripped my mouth away from his, and he smiled. I think he thought I was shy. He moved in on me again, and I turned my head. "No," I whispered.

I don't think he heard me. I could barely hear myself. But I guess he got the message because we got back in the car. He rubbed my arm and took my hand and, although every hair on my body stood straight up in revulsion, I didn't fight. My tongue was tied and my stomach in knots the whole way home. The confidence I exuded at the party had vanished. I just sat there like a puppet, listening to him talk, allowing him to rub my hand and kiss my fingers as we drove for what seemed like hours.

Finally, we arrived at my house. I hugged him and said thanks, then turned and ran up the steps to the front door for fear that he might try to kiss me again.

Whatever he was, Rob was most certainly *not* my Prince Charming.

Later, while I was washing the makeup off my face and combing out my teased-up hair, I decided never to marry a man like Rob just to feel financially secure. Maybe I'd never marry at all, but if I did get married, it would be for love. I'd rather be poor than sleep with a man who made my skin crawl. Better yet, I'd make my own money and have all the things I wanted without compromise.

More than anything, I was furious with my father for putting me in this situation. He pimped me out! I know that wasn't his intention—he, like my mother, wanted me to marry for money so I'd be "taken care of"—but the whole thing made me feel so dirty. Like I was no better or different than one of those girls in the videos, trading sex for cash. And in the end, if I married Rob, wouldn't it have been exactly that?

My Best Friend's Brother

What better place for a bulimic than a donut shop, right?

During high school, I worked with my friend Carrie, who had been my friend since the move back from Grass Valley, at the same donut shop I used to frequent on the way home from elementary school. Insanely, we got there at 4:30 in the morning on the weekends, but clearly it offered a better alternative to my brother Brian's career choice.

Daughter of a Porn King

Other than working at the donut shop and attending school, I spent a lot of time at Carrie's house and felt really at home there. Her mother was wonderful to me. She sat down at the kitchen table and talked to me like I was a real person, not the brat who was always underfoot. It got to the point where I spent more time at Carrie's house than I did at my own—especially after the incident with my mother and Allison. I even went to their family's ski cabin in Arizona for Christmas.

I had a big crush on Carrie's older brother, Tom. He was in junior college while I was a sophomore in high school, and I thought he was *dreamy*. He never really paid attention to me; I was just Carrie's little friend. Until the day I got my braces off.

Finally, I got to lose the metal! So proud of my new teeth, I kept checking them out in every mirror. My face was finally starting to look like a woman, with defined cheekbones (thanks to my "dieting") and a narrow chin. My eyes looked bigger now that my cheeks weren't so chubby, and my hair was finally grown out from that disaster at the beauty school. I felt… comfortable. Maybe even the teensiest bit cute.

When I got to Carrie's house that afternoon, Tom was napping on the couch. I tiptoed in, running my tongue across my smooth, straight teeth. Trembling with excitement, I knelt down and shook him awake.

"Hey," I said, "Check it out!"

He opened his eyes, just inches from mine, and I flashed him my best metal-free smile.

"Wow," he said, staring at me like he'd never seen me before. "You look…You look great, Cyn."

My heart leapt.

From that day on, Tom and I were an item. Not surprisingly, Carrie resented this new turn of events. She barely talked to me at the donut shop anymore. It hurt a little, but I didn't mind: Tom loved me, and that was enough.

My parents took another trip to the East Coast when I was fifteen and they invited Tom to come with us. We went to Epcot and Disney World. Bob and Carla saw nothing wrong with getting the two of us our own hotel room. After all, they knew we were already having sex, so what was the big deal?

Tom didn't know quite what to make of all this. He was raised very differently than me. His father was much more of a disciplinarian, whereas my dad let most things fly by. Bob's jokes always had an underlying stab to them, though; it was how he got people to do what he wanted. This was how the "miscommunication" happened.

When Tom and Carrie's parents brought me along on vacation, they never expected me to pay for anything. But apparently, my dad wasn't expecting to cover Tom's share of the trip, even though it had been his idea to extend the invitation.

"I guess he can just pay for his own plane ticket," my dad said—and that's what I conveyed to Tom. But, when we got back, he started making jokes about how my boyfriend was a cheap bastard. Basically, he wanted more money. I never said anything to Tom about this, since I felt he'd paid more than enough—but from that point on, my dad considered him a cheapskate.

I don't know where my dad came up with this but he really hated Tom and sometimes I wondered if my dad was jealous because I had a boyfriend and was no longer his little girl. But it was probably because he was just looking out for me. It was important for him to know a guy could provide for his daughter, so maybe he was just acting out of love. Often we don't understand our parents' behavior but it usually boils down to love—even if we can't see it at the time.

Looking Back

Now, after all my "sex-capades" things have changed. I wait until I am ready, and I may never be ready. But I don't allow a man's desire to become my responsibility, nor do I take responsibility for his erection. If it is unwanted, he will have to deal it with himself.

When two people join their bodies, it is a union of their souls—an expression of love and their own private party. Wouldn't it have been nice if my parents had taught me about love and sex that way? Well, they did. It just wasn't a direct route. I had to take the completely opposite road to arrive in this place.

Now I am at a point in my life where I can truly value and appreciate all that a truly loving relationship offers as a point of comparison. As they say, without the darkness there is no light and without the light there is no dark. Hence, the greatest blessing and gift I have had to wait my share of Christmases for was the greatest gift of all—and that is love. Self-love and now unconditional love with my divinely intended soul mate—wherever he may be.

Just as I had to earn that trip to the Monterey and just as I had to work my way through school, through all of the challenges I have been able to gain a deeper appreciation for the glorious moments, the glorious gifts, the special people and the beautiful relationships. Guess I will have to earn this one too.

CHAPTER 18

Getting Out of Dodge!

By my second year of high school, I discovered that I could graduate early if I took some classes at the local junior college. That meant expediting my way out of the house! I didn't need any more incentive than that, so I went to see my school guidance counselor to discuss my options. Brian helped me go over the list of credits I'd need to graduate at the end of my third year, and I had everything mapped out.

My snippy little guidance counselor, Mrs. Flaherty, had it out for me. I don't know what I ever did to her, but she predetermined she didn't like me because she judged Timmy as a troublemaker. Anytime I came into the office, she just glared at me until I left. Maybe she was like that with everyone, but it sure seemed personal.

Despite her general bad attitude, I expected support from Mrs. Flaherty. After all, it looks good for the school when its students excel—but the first response out of her mouth was, "No way. You can't do that. High school requires four years, so you'll have to stay."

"Really? Are you kidding me?" This was unbelievable to me. My grades were perfect at that point, and I'd had nothing but commendations from my teachers. By any academic standard, I was ready for college. But the rules said no.

I picked up my bag and swept out of the office, thinking to myself, *Don't you know who I am? Do you have any idea who you're*

169

dealing with? Nothing can stop me! I grew up with no rules. I'm not going to start living by them now!

That day, a light bulb came on for me. It was the first time I'd ever seen my parents' lack of structure as a gift. But, in a way, it was. I didn't need to follow the school's rules when they didn't make sense. I could make my own.

If the guidance counselor wasn't going to see the sense in this, then I'd just have to go over her head. (There was another gift from my dad, who always used to say that a good salesman never takes no for an answer!) So I made an appointment to talk to the principal. By then, I had done even more research and mapped out exactly which classes I needed, where and when I could take them, and how my schedule operated for the next school year.

I presented my case confidently, thinking this would be a slam dunk—but, again, it was a no-go. School and district policies just didn't allow for early graduation.

"But if I earn the credits, I should technically be allowed to graduate," I protested. "Some kids take five years to earn their credits, and you let them graduate. What is so different about me doing it faster?"

"I'm sorry, Miss Glickman," the principal said. "But it's just not allowed. There will be no further discussion."

What a bunch of imbeciles. Obviously, this was a serious example of what happened when people didn't think outside the box. At a time when everyone was complaining about the laziness of Generation X, why the system wanted to squash a kid like me, who actually showed some ambition, was beyond me. The stupidity was astounding.

It occurred to me that had my mother allowed me to skip that grade in Grass Valley, I would have been graduating early anyway—no discussion required.

Just to cover all my bases, I spoke to another school guidance counselor. He was a little friendlier about it, but his answer remained the same. "It seems like you have it all mapped out," he said, with a little shake of his head. "I wish I could help, because this is really a great idea for you, but school policy…" Blah, blah, blah.

Well, I thought. *It's time to bust out of this joint and bring in the big guns.* What better way to get around school policy than to go to the person who made it? Using my most professional phone voice, I set up a meeting with the superintendent of the school district. I had a future in front of me, and I was tired of messing with small-minded people.

I had a few weeks to prepare for this meeting so, by the time I rolled up in my hot pink 1972 Volkswagen Bug, I was ready to argue my case to the superintendent in a clear, concise manner. (Yes, I was driving at fifteen after buying the car with my earnings from the donut shop. My parents didn't care that I drove without a license or registration. Having wheels made it easier, and I didn't have to pester them to take me where I needed to go. I learned to drive the same way I learned to ride a motorcycle: Brian provided some very basic instruction; then I just did it. Thankfully, there was no way I could fly off the back of the car.)

Once shown into the superintendent's office, I explained calmly that remaining in high school actually hindered my academic progress and diminished my passion for education. I told him that I planned to study astrophysics in college because this field combined my two loves—math and astronomy. I might even become an astronaut. I presented a timeline detailing exactly how I planned to pursue this goal and how I could fulfill all of the district's policy requirements for graduation by the end of my junior year.

Dr. Wexler, the superintendent, leaned back quietly in his chair and listened while I presented my case. He asked me a few questions, nodding at my answers. Then, in no uncertain terms, I laid it out. "Look, if I aspired to escape high school and get a job at Del Taco, then, absolutely deny me permission to graduate early. But, my vision includes so much more. I'm going to college to make something out of myself and contribute to the world and, with your help, my dreams can come true."

A sparkle twinkled in his eyes. And, when he heard the Del Taco comment, a smirk spread across his face. Other than that one smile, his reaction was poker-faced. But I must have won him over, because I skipped out of his office and into my hot pink Bug with his wholehearted approval for my early graduation.

I guess perseverance really does pay. Just because you don't get what you want right away doesn't mean it won't come to you. With a strong vision and a positive outlook, no challenge is insurmountable—but you might have to be willing to color outside the lines a bit.

Immediately, I launched my plan into action. I took Statistics and English 101 at the junior college, which made up the English and Math credits from my senior year. Things rolled right along until my junior/senior year started. Now that I knew I was getting the hell out of Dodge, it was all just a waiting game. My high school classes were pathetically easy, so I stopped going. I only showed up for long enough to ace the tests, so my grades wouldn't slip.

I had few friends left and those I did have were personally offended that I wasn't sticking around for year four of this absurdity. Eventually, they fell away too and I was left completely alone, skipping school. With nowhere to go, I spent a lot of days driving around aimlessly in my hot pink Bug, sometimes stopping at donut shops or gas stations to binge on junk food, then pulling off onto the shoulders of deserted roads to throw it back up again. I felt horribly guilty for missing school, but the more I missed the harder it was for me to go back.

I was still seeing Tom, but he was at the junior college and played on the golf team so he was busy during the day—and it was hard to spend time at his parents' house now that Carrie hated me so much. Sometimes, desperate to see him (and to get away from myself), I snuck away to the golf course and we hit balls together at the driving range. When I wasn't with Tom, my world narrowed to a pinpoint of focus: graduation. That was the light at the end of the tunnel—the only thing that kept me from sinking into complete lethargy.

Because I was able to keep my grades up, the school didn't tell my parents at first how many classes I was missing. But by the time April came around, I had more than one hundred recorded class absences. When the principal's office finally called, my parents were in shock.

Cindy, the straight-A student, who was graduating early, had stopped going to school? What? Carla was so taken aback that she forgot to cut me down.

"Is everything okay?" she asked, seeming genuinely concerned. "This just doesn't seem like you."

I just shook my head. She had no idea who I was or what I wanted. She was the primary reason I was leaving, after all. She was like a dark cloud I couldn't wait to get out from under. Maybe if I left her—and my childhood—behind, I'd hate myself less, too.

As the year went on, my mom seemed to get more and more concerned. The less I cared, the more compassionate she seemed to become. It was an odd dichotomy. She even bribed me with gifts to try to get me to go to school. Her way of showing me she cared.

Life got even more challenging at home when my parents kicked Tim out. He and my dad had never gotten along. It was assumed that Brian would follow my dad in the family business (which he eventually did). But Tim was expected to do something else—maybe become a lawyer or a doctor, since Carla was always going on about how smart he was. He was *not,* apparently, supposed to be living like a rock star in the Hollywood clubs, skipping school, staying out until all hours of the night, and sneaking his girlfriend in through his bedroom window.

"When are you going to straighten out and get a real job?" my dad demanded. "What the hell is the matter with you?"

It wasn't hard to appreciate the irony here. Bob Glickman, passing judgment on someone else's career choice? And yet, in their typical fashion, while my parents never really wanted any part of governing or disciplining us, when it came to our futures, they had very definite ideas. Bob expected Tim to go to college and make something of himself, while I was supposed to marry rich, settle down and keep my mouth shut.

Spouting conventional wisdom, based on what his parents taught him, my dad directed us the best he knew how. Following your passion wasn't something normal, successful people did. In Bob's world, Tim needed to think *realistically.*

Tension built between them and finally everything came to a head.

A suitcase full of Tim's things waited at the curb for him with a note attached, directing him to leave his house keys in the mailbox and get lost when he arrived home from school. He then crashed on friends' couches but more often he lived on the street or in his truck.

Some nights he slept on the roof of the school. Between his gigs and his job at a body-piercing shop, Tim must have earned enough to eat and make the payments on his truck, because he never asked Brian or me for money. In fact, we didn't hear a word from him for months.

The house felt empty now. And I worried about him. No one told me what was going on, or why my dad was so furious at him when he hadn't really done anything. Carla withdrew even more into her own world, worried sick about her favorite boy. She asked me a few times if I'd heard from him—which, of course, I hadn't.

And then one day he came back. His long, dark hair, shaved close to his head, and his heavy-metal rocker duds were gone, replaced by a conservative shirt and jeans. An ad for the Army on the street—"Be all you can be"—captured his attention in this come-to-Jesus moment. Upon meeting a recruiter through one of his friends, he decided to enlist. But there was one catch: He stopped going to school when he got kicked out of the house and the military required a diploma. So, he enrolled in Bowman Continuation School and, immediately after earning his high school diploma, he headed off to basic training. While he loved his music, he said that lifestyle just wasn't what he wanted anymore.

A Jesus moment, indeed.

He and my dad had a long talk, and I guess they worked things out, because Tim moved back in the next day. A serious, shaven-headed person had replaced my carefree brother—someone who was just as lonely and focused as I was. We had both found a way out; now, we just had to kill time until the day came.

My parents treated Tim like a prisoner and didn't trust him in the house. He ate dinner with them at night but, after that, they locked him in the garage. He moved into Brian's old room—now devoid of furniture except for an old, smelly couch. He had no television, no books, no musical instruments—just that couch. He didn't even have a bathroom, only a trash can to use like an old-fashioned chamber pot.

After he'd earned his high school diploma, Tim went to see about Army jobs. He ended up talking to a Navy recruiter, who analyzed his test results and offered Tim the pick of three jobs that were available immediately. Not willing to wait around and deal with the uncertainty of jobs in the Army, Tim decided to work with acoustics, so he took a job as a radio man in the Navy.

And that's how my rock star brother began his twenty-year career in the military. He went on to become an air traffic controller and earn two bachelor's degrees. He has a lot to be proud of in transcending all of his childhood struggles.

By the time all of this was happening, I was already gone. I'd graduated just days before my seventeenth birthday. Less than a month later I left to spend the summer in San Luis Obispo with my friend Clarissa, who was at school up there, before continuing on to my new college home in Santa Cruz. I packed up my car with a laundry basket, a computer, some clothes, and a few packs of instant coffee—and just like that, I was off.

The last thing I did before leaving town was to send a copy of my acceptance letter from the University of California at Santa Cruz to that snippy guidance counselor, Mrs. Flaherty. Just so she knew she hadn't beaten me.

Going to College

YIPPEE! *Finally*, I was getting out of Valencia. I was so excited and felt so free, exhilarated by the adventure ahead of me—leaving home and off to college.

Going to college didn't really matter to my parents, since my mother had never attended and my father hadn't finished; besides, why would a girl have to learn anything if she could marry wealthy? My father wanted me to go to college in L.A. but I opted to go to UCSC. I was going to consider some others but, after visiting the UCSC campus, I knew that was where I had to go.

After staying with my friend in San Luis Obispo for about a month, I headed further up along the coast to my dream school. Yes, I was a slug—a Banana Slug, our big yellow mascot.

Not that it was easy. My dad hadn't wanted me to go away to college. He often joked that I needed to live at home until I was twenty-five and not go anywhere. I guess this was his way of saying he loved me and wanted me to stick around—but, to me, it felt like he was trying to be my jailer. In his mind, a girl should want to be a wife and have kids, and college should take a back seat to those things. With Bob Glickman as my agent, it wouldn't have been hard for me to find a nice, rich husband. After all, now that I was throwing up half of what I ate, I was pretty darn attractive.

I don't know why he thought he could hold me back. I hadn't waited until my mom got to the hospital to come into this world, and I certainly wasn't going to wait on a man to get what I wanted out of my life.

Once he finally accepted that I was not going to forego an education in favor of marriage and babies, Bob suggested that I go to the local community college or Cal State Northridge, so I could live at home. But I needed my freedom, and the fresh air of Santa Cruz seemed like just the thing. Because he didn't like my choice, my dad chose not to support it. Basically, he cut me off.

In the end it was my Uncle Al who made it possible for me to go to college. Thanks to him, I had the support I needed to assist me through school. Al was a big believer in education, and he gave me a stipend of sorts to assist with tuition and books. To him, this was a business transaction; I'm sure he got some sort of tax deduction for it. But more importantly, he was a generous man and he loved doing well by others. Knowing that I had his support made life bearable when I was really struggling.

Regardless of the small amount of "face time" I had with my Uncle Al as a child, he was a powerful force in my life and his influence upon me was invaluable. He contributed to making me the woman I am today.

He was one of my first role models. I didn't even know what a role model was until I grew up. I certainly didn't want to grow up to be like my mother—who couldn't keep a job, made promises to me and then broke them, told me she tried to abort me, and taught me that being a sex object was okay and that all I needed to do was land a good man and have his children.

Uncle Al also instilled in me the concept of "pay it forward." He never wanted me to repay a cent of what he gave me—but I have reflected his kindness by donating money to the college where I used to teach and creating scholarships for students in need.

At one point later on in my career, I worked with a young woman named Sara at a real estate office. She was going to college at the time and paying for it herself. Her story resonated with me, since I knew how challenging it could be to do it all on your own. So I gave her a "scholarship" and paid for her books. When she wanted to pay me back, I told her, "Just pay it forward." It was wonderful to be able to do for her what my uncle did for me. And I hope to be able to do it for many more young women in the future.

Despite Uncle Al's assistance, college wasn't all fun and games. I was too confident after blowing off my last year of high school and found myself totally underprepared. The classes were much harder: I had to take Vector Calculus three times before I passed it—and I was a math major! I also had to get a Pell grant and take on student loans to pay for my room and board, and I worked the graveyard shift at Denny's to fill in the rest. I had little time to rest, and I felt worn thin, as if some of my solidness was leaching away.

Going home and taking classes at the local community college was the easy way out, but giving up was not an option. I didn't want that life anymore.

Due to his huge interest in golf, Tom had decided to attend the College of the Desert, a few hours south of Valencia, to study golf course management. When he graduated, he'd be certified not only to run a golf course but to manage pro shops and give lessons. He loved the game and the lifestyle that went with it. He golfed early in the morning, went to school during the day, and went out drinking with his buddies at night. Truly, it was a bachelor's dream.

I clung to Tom, not knowing how to find the strength within. When I moved to Santa Cruz, we were seven hours apart, and finding time to see one another was hard. We talked on the phone, but it wasn't enough. At least once a month, Tom flew me down to Palm Desert to visit him. He was busy with school, golf and work, and I wasn't allowed to have boys in my dorm room, so he rarely came up to Santa Cruz. When he did, though, it was special. I left an hour early for the airport, to be sure I made it there in time to see his plane touch down. Watching the passengers disembark, I bounced in anticipation. When I finally saw him, my lips turned up in a big smile and I ran to him pressing myself against him. Drinking in his comfortable, familiar smell, I kissed his lips and tasted alcohol and peppermint gum.

This was my man and I loved him.

His presence was like a drug to me. We had an intense physical relationship and, after we made love, we snuggled all night long. My body was screaming for affection. He drank a lot, but I didn't mind. When he wasn't drinking, he got so tense he grinded his jaw and would snap at me whenever I opened my mouth. Instead of being put off, I'd jump in and try to serve him. Anything to keep him close to me.

My parents were hardly talking to me by that point. My mom never took my calls at the office. On the rare occasions when I talked to my dad, he threatened me and my relationship with Tom. (Yes, he was still on that kick.) I don't know why he wanted to break the two of us up so badly, but at one point he actually threatened to have the police come and collect me if I didn't do what he wanted, since I was still seventeen and technically a minor.

"If you paid attention to your brain, instead of the fire between your legs, you'd listen to me," he said.

This, from the man who used to hand me condoms and say, "Have fun, honey!"

My dad called me a loose girl, a slut—even though I was anything but. He threatened to come up to Santa Cruz and pull me out of school—which scared the crap out of me. (I even made an appointment with the guidance counselor to see if this could legally happen—which she assured me it couldn't.) Eventually, I stopped picking up the phone, and let every call go to the answering machine, for fear of hearing him yell and scream at me for something. I felt like I was constantly walking around under a raincloud of guilt.

When I made plans to go skiing for a weekend with Tom in Mammoth, somehow my father found out. I ignored his calls for a week. When he finally got a hold of me, he threatened to take away my car—a Chevy Spectrum I'd gotten when the Bug finally took its final gasp. . He'd been making the payments up to that point.

"But I love him, Daddy," I said, crying. "I'm in love with him. He's the only one who's there for me. Can't you understand that?"

But he couldn't. If he hadn't been my dad, I would have said that Bob was consumed with irrational jealousy. The fact that he *was* my dad made the whole thing even weirder to me. Looking back, I guess any father would have been upset to see his teenage daughter with a man he didn't like—but my dad really laid it on thick.

The emotional pressure escalated my bulimia. Whereas before I'd made a concerted effort to hide what I was doing, now I was so tightly wound that I just didn't care. I had to control that part of my life. I'd set a limit as to what and how much I could eat. If I passed that limit by even the smallest morsel, I'd start to panic. The pressure built until the food just came back up. It didn't matter if I was at someone's house, in a restaurant, at a bar. I ran into the bathroom, praying no one else was in there, and threw up all my anxiety into the bowl.

I knew what I was doing wasn't healthy. I had other friends who were going through similar challenges, and I saw how destructive this behavior was for them. But I couldn't stop. Eating was the only thing that distracted me from the mountain of stress and fear I was carrying around. Plus, if I got fat and ugly again, even Tom would stop loving me, and then I'd really be in trouble.

CHAPTER 19

Who Am I?

I am Sam, Sam I am –
That Sam I am, That Sam I am.
I do not like that Sam I am.
Do you like green eggs and ham?
I do not like green eggs and ham. Sam I am. – Dr. Seuss

Searching for who I really was, I started with my roots. Rather than just deciding I didn't like something (like the green eggs and ham), I wanted to try everything.

I got involved in Hillel, a Jewish community for students, during my freshman year. My cousin, Jeffrey, was a rabbi and my other cousin, Brenner, was studying to become one; so I figured maybe it could offer me something. Even if I didn't become a full-fledged practicing Jew, I should still know something about my heritage. Plus, Judaism fascinated me.

The Jewish experience hit home, since I could identify with feeling like an outcast myself. But the crowning jewel came from my grandmother, whose penetrating words a decade earlier about the Holocaust had really gripped me, compelling me to discover more about my roots and truly understand who I was. Even though our interactions were minimal, the woman who gave me corn chips for birthday presents had planted a seed that sprouted a forest. This endless desire to know who I am became paramount in my life and is still constantly expanding. So I could see Mildred's contribution in that.

In addition to my regular college classes, I studied Hebrew at the Hillel center located in an old house right on the main street in Santa Cruz. Tapping into this community felt right. Students from the university held events there, and everyone offered a traditional dish for the holiday celebrations.

My friend, Brian, and I would saunter into the house, blasted with the smells of baking onions and matzo ball soup. Once the food was ready, we all sat in a large circle around the table, eating off paper plates and drinking from paper cups. Since I was only half-Jewish and not well-versed in the traditions, I remained quiet, observing rather than being the life of the party. Awkwardness overcame me due to not knowing the prayers and traditions—so I made the most of my time absorbing everything I could.

Unfamiliar with Judaism, Brian felt awkward, too, and like a fish out of water. I was only beginning to explore this heritage—but after just fifteen minutes of it, he was ready to run for the hills. I didn't ask him to come again; he clearly did not like green eggs and ham.

During my Hebrew classes, we sat with our teacher around that same dining room table, learning the alphabet. The other students knew so much about Judaism and Israel, and I found myself questioning my father for not making his culture part of our upbringing. I felt like I had lost out on an entire history, simply because he hadn't liked being teased—and now, I was somehow less than what I should have been—a half-Jew, bumbling along and trying to figure it all out at the ripe old age of eighteen. The lessons were uncomfortable for me, since I never like feeling like the class dummy. But I had a genuine interest and had committed to it, so I stuck it out.

A few months into my lessons, I decided to take that commitment one step further after seeing a flyer posted about a study abroad program in Be'er Sheva, Israel.

I was fascinated. This sounded so exotic and unique—the perfect way to get away from it all and discover for myself how my father's people really lived, by total immersion in the language, the customs, the culture and the history.

I tore off a tag from the bottom of the flyer and tucked it carefully into my pocket.

In a few short weeks, I'd set up the whole thing. I got scholarship money to help me pay for the semester at Ben Gurion University in Be'er Sheva. Uncle Al helped me out with additional expenses. While my parents thought I was crazy for taking this trip, Uncle Al understood the importance of this experience for me, both as a Jew and a student, and supported me unconditionally.

I was expanding my horizons on every level now. I was no longer just the daughter of a porn king. I was a now the prodigal daughter, with a long history and rich culture.

Sorority House

During that same period, I joined a sorority. Yep, I am a Gamma Phi.

How many chapters have you read?

And if I told you, I'd have to kill you.

Um…what?

Yes, a secret society with underground questions and secret handshakes.

I rejected the idea initially. After all, sororities were elitist organizations—fabricated groups of women whose sole objective was to conform to outmoded societal ideals and look down on other women.

Why would I want to be a part of something that caused so many problems?

Withdrawing more into myself by the day, that outgoing, loud, chubby Cindy from junior high—the girl who was voted Most Popular and Most Intelligent was no longer in evidence. Less sure of myself and my place in the world, I got lost in the sea of students.

The UCSC campus was huge, making it hard to find people to identify with. Being a mathematician doesn't exactly win you Brownie points, not to mention being a woman in a male-dominated field! No one understood me—but, at the same time, I didn't *want* to be understood. Because I didn't feel that I was cut from the same cloth as those around me, and I didn't want to become like them. In many ways, I left myself out in the cold.

Invited to a chapter event, I opened my mind and gave it a try. I discovered something completely different from my pre-conceived notion. A group of women, who also wanted to feel a sense of belonging, brought me in. With a mission committed to providing women the opportunity to achieve their potential through life-long intellectual growth and service to humanity, I was sold.

So, I joined Gamma Phi Beta, and moved into the seaside sorority house. Suddenly, I had a built-in group of friends. Looking for connection, I thought maybe this—again, something outside of myself—could fill my void. My roommate, LaTifa, was very sweet and cute, a tiny little thing with a blonde bob haircut and delicate, almost elfin features. She was the kind of girl I'd always wanted to be. In addition to her perfection, she was very kind to me and became a good friend.

For solitude, I strolled to the ocean and sat among the rocks with my toes in the sand, pondering my life. Listening to the waves crashing on the coast and feeling the mist on my skin, I talked to

God—or whoever in the Universe might have time to listen. I asked questions like, "Why am I here? What's the purpose? And, what is my purpose?" More than anything, I just wanted to understand more about the world and what I was supposed to be doing in it, not yet realizing how close it was to the Gamma Phi Beta creed: Love, Labor, Learning and Loyalty. Spreading world joy— that came close. But, I did know there was something huge inside of me to give to the world. And I just didn't know what or how to harness it.

A heavy burden weighed on my shoulders. I had a big job ahead of me. It was overwhelming and I was nowhere near completion. Seeming like I stood at the base of a staircase with a million steps and had merely only taken one, I felt exhausted by the journey ahead. Not having any clue how I would get up all those floors left me feeling inadequate. This feeling pressed on me. There had to be a point to this whole dog-and-pony show. There had to be some reason we were all here. Something inside of me always said I had a bigger job to do, but I had no clue what that was supposed to be.

This wasn't the first time I'd asked these questions. As a child in the house on Plaza Gavilan, I swung on the swing set at night, staring up at the stars, asking God why the kids at school always teased me. "Do we go around more than once? Am I more than just my physical form?"

There had to be someone out there who knew the answers.

Even when chilling with my friends or hanging in the garage with my brother and his buddies while they smoked the ganja, I questioned, "Why do you think we're here? What do you think the point is?" Of course, the answers varied greatly, depending on who I was asking. Some had grandiose ideas; others felt as small and confused as I did. Some just snickered through their smoky haze, laughing it off. Besides, wasn't that why they were getting high—so they didn't have to think?

One of them would inevitably say, "Oh, little Cindy always asking deep philosophical questions, man. You must have a contact high, dude." Brian, ever practical, would mostly say, "Who cares, Cyn? Why do you ask so many questions?"

Out there on the rocks in Santa Cruz, I came to the conclusion that the answers I sought, like all deep truths, were both simple and profound. I just couldn't seem to put my finger on them. I was convinced I'd find at least a piece of what I was looking for in Israel. If I didn't learn why I was here on this planet, at least I'd learn a little more about my heritage and who I was as a person.

Then, just before I was to leave, the Gulf War broke out. I was scared, but I'd already secured the scholarship money and been accepted, so there was no backing out. Besides, I wasn't going to let fear hold me back.

Bombs and Gas Masks – A real war-zone

No Internet booking back then! I actually had to go into the travel agency, where they wrote out my airline ticket *by hand*, pressing really hard so it would go through the carbon backing. I still have that plane ticket. And then, passport in hand, I set off for my latest adventure.

While changing planes in New York, I met another girl on the flight who was also going to study at Ben Gurion University, and—through no coordination on our parts—we ended up sitting right next to one another. Her name was Laura, and she was of Indian descent, with beautiful toffee-colored skin and wide, tilted black eyes that peeked out like jewels under her curled bangs. We hit it off right away.

Someone from the college was supposed to meet us at the airport so, after we collected our luggage, we went out to the curb to wait. And we waited, and waited… and waited. It started getting dark, and I was scared to death. We walked around the perimeter of the terminal at least twenty times, but there was no one holding a sign for us. We couldn't even use the phones, since they required tokens, and neither of us knew where to get them. All we could do was pace back and forth, sweating and panicked, lugging our enormous suitcases behind us, asking everyone in earshot, "Can you help us?"

People looked at us like we were speaking Martian. I don't know why, but I'd figured Israel would be like Mexico, where nearly everyone speaks at least a little English.

"What should we do?" I asked Laura.

"I guess we'll keep waiting," she said timidly. But we needed to do something more than that, or we were going to be stuck at that airport all night.

"Can we call someone at the school? We could call collect," I suggested. "Do you have a contact number for someone there?"

"No."

Neither did I. But (thank God) my Aunt Judy's brother had given me the number of one of his relatives who lived in the area, in case just such a situation arose. I hated to admit that we'd been so underprepared, but we were stuck. Neither of us had traveled out of the country on our own before—how could we help but assume that someone would be there to get us?

My contact through Aunt Judy was an American woman. It was such a relief to hear a voice speaking English! Since we didn't even know where on the Ben Gurion campus to go, she gave us step-by-step instructions about how to take a cab to her house. When we got there, she had food and hot baths waiting for us.

The next morning, she called the school and helped us coordinate with the admissions office. We had to take a bus from her house, then another cab, and when we got to the school there was a young man waiting for us who helped us connect with our roommates, get our keys, and get situated.

My roommates were great, and they really made me feel welcome. But, what I remember most about those first few weeks were the gas masks. No one knew whether Saddam Hussein was going to attack Israel, as he kept threatening to do, so everyone had to get suited up.

Omigosh! What was I doing in the Middle East in the middle of a war? I had to go to the distribution center and get fitted for a gas mask. It came in a cardboard box with a long black plastic strap that let me carry it over my shoulder. Inside was also a wicked-looking syringe full of some anti-toxin; I was supposed to inject myself with it, in the event that I got gassed. If I didn't have the kit with me at all times, I could be ticketed, just as if I'd parked in a tow zone in Santa Cruz.

This experience certainly broadened my perspective. Every night, holed up in my little cubicle of a room, I would listen to BBC News through the radio static, praying that I would hear those magic words: "The war is over!" Then, President Bush gave the Iraqis a deadline to cease and desist, and give up Hussein, or he would have to take action.

Of course, the Iraqis didn't give up, and Operation Desert Shield became Operation Desert Storm. Bush and the Allies went in full-bore, with the largest assembly of land troops and air power since World War II. I didn't know whether I felt more or less safe. I could only brace myself for an attack—and pray.

But as terrifying as the gas masks and the sirens and the constant vigilance were, the situation was also beautiful, in a way. The people of Israel took patriotism and community to a whole new level. I'd never seen anyone, not even a family, band together like that. And this was an entire country!

Don't Kiss and Tell

REER REER REER. The sirens would roar!

Bombs? Who cares? It's life. Get on with it.

Jamie was an artist and a little strange, but brilliant. Her striking abstract paintings were hung all over our walls. She taught me how to wrap our windows in preparation for a bombing attack, and held my hand through the first few drills. She approached everything with total nonchalance; this was just a way of life— fear never touched her.

Like all Israeli women, Jamie served two years in the military before going to college. Some young people with special skills go to college first and serve later; Jamie's brother,

Ben, was one such person. He was only a year older than me, and we became close friends. *Really* close friends—kissing friends.

Yes, shame on me. At the same time I was calling Tom every day on the pay phone, crying over the receiver about how much I missed him—and I did—I was cheating on him. That deep internal desire for connection took over, trying to fill that void, still from outside of myself.

Ultimately, my understanding of love was only so deep at the time; it wasn't the soulful love that I embrace today. I needed affection and Tom was too far away to give it. Childishly not think-ing about how I was affecting others and just serving my own needs,

I wasn't really into Ben that much—but being with him made me feel wanted. And if I was wanted, I was special.

Of course, I could try to blame Carla for this pattern showing up, which I am sure had some effect. But the truth is: Who hasn't been young and made choices like these that are not in total integrity? A more compelling question would be: Can you look back at past behaviors and let go of the judgment that you may have of yourself? I have. No justifications, just learning.

I was still trying to fill that void inside myself. But in the end, this didn't fill it either. Kissing Ben only served my ego. Even at the time, I knew how superficial it was. I was digging myself into a deep hole with the bulimia, the depression and the fear. Kissing Ben, as wrong as one might judge it to be, gave me the boost I needed to keep from sinking even further. At the time, I too was just doing the best I knew how. Looking back, is that the person I want to be now? Absolutely not, so now I get to change it.

Sick of the sirens and the wrapped windows and tired of jumping at SCUD missile warnings every day, after about two-thirds of the semester, I decided that I needed to go home. Tel Aviv was already being hit, and people were evacuating. A good portion of the credits I was earning at Ben Gurion University weren't going to transfer back to UCSC. And my fiancé was in Palm Desert, playing golf in the bright, safe, California sun.

Yes, fiancé. Did I forget to mention that?

My engagement to Tom wasn't exactly a romantic occasion. We were at the mall one day, before I left for Israel, and I dragged him into a jewelry store. I chose a small diamond solitaire, nothing too flashy, so as not to be too hard on Tom's wallet. I told him I wanted it, and he bought it for me a few weeks later. There was no getting down on one knee, no thrilling proposal in a crowded restaurant. It was more like, "Okay, here you go. Happy now?"

But, at the time, I still thought it was exceptional. I liked the way it made me feel "taken." It made me feel special.

Six months later, here I was in Be'er Sheva, making out with my roommate's brother and not feeling very good about myself. It was time to go home. Sweet, gentle Ben saw me off to the airport and kissed my forehead before leaving me at the security gate. He never knew that I was going home to the arms of another man—a man to whom I'd been engaged for the entirety of our short relationship—or that I would make no effort whatsoever to see or speak to him again.

CHAPTER 20

Sleeping with the Enemy (or his best friend)

Following the "fire between my legs" — according to my father, who was furious that I bailed on my experience in Israel (yes, that expression again, which he loved it.)—I jumped right back into the arms of my fiancé. Sweet little Cindy was a whore, selling it cheap to that cheapskate, Tom. So my dad made it clear he would not support me and that I was on my own.

I responded by clinging to Tom even more passionately than ever. I never told him about what I'd done in Israel. I figured that, since I hadn't actually slept with Ben, it didn't count as cheating. But there was a little place inside me that knew and flinched whenever I thought about it. I couldn't entirely ignore what I had done—and, if I could do such a thing when I loved Tom so much, couldn't he do it as well?

As much as I wanted to forget it, I knew that I had let my father down by coming home early. I couldn't escape the guilt and the fear. I'd let myself down, too. My father and I stopped talking, but it didn't alleviate the blame I harbored toward myself for not doing the *right* thing.

Wherever I went, there I was.

When I came to stay with Tom, he was living in a house in Palm Desert with his friends, Dave and Bob. Since it was an older home with only two bedrooms, Bob slept on the couch. Wall-to-wall green shag carpet packed with dust filled the rooms, no matter how much we vacuumed. I was only staying there temporarily until the fall semester started at UCSC. But the addition of another person made for a pretty crowded living situation.

Still feeling like I had a million-step staircase to climb, I bumbled around the bottom two steps. I felt like a failure for leaving Israel, even though I knew it was the right choice. I had no studying to do until the next semester began, so I got a job waitressing at an Italian restaurant.

It was like being in purgatory. I was stuck, with nothing to do but wait.

Since I worked evenings and Tom worked during the day, I didn't see much of him. By the time I got home from the restaurant, he'd be stumbling around drunk after an evening at Señor Frog's, the local watering hole. We had a highly physical relationship, but I felt like I always wanted more. Physically I was with him, but his attention wasn't on me. We didn't talk the way we had when I was in Santa Cruz or Israel. Sometimes I felt like he barely remembered I was there. And the longer I stayed, the worse it got.

So I did what I had done before. Dreadfully needing to fill the emptiness, I took what I needed from someone else outside of me.

I don't remember how it actually happened with Dave. One day we were talking, and the next day we were in bed. I didn't even really like him, in that way. I certainly didn't love him the way I loved Tom. And I wasn't even attracted to him physically since he was overweight, had acne scars all over his face, and smelled awful when he sweat. But he was there—and what he wanted, I needed. I wasn't special to Tom anymore, but I was special to Dave.

Yes, I slept with Tom in one room and Dave in the next. And the whole time I heard my dad's voice in my head screaming, "Whore!" When the guilt threatened to tear me to bits, I found myself agreeing with him.

I'm no longer ashamed of my behavior and I've forgiven myself for it. At that point, I hadn't realized that, just like my mother, I was operating on auto-pilot—a victim to the situation—and not knowing that what I really needed had to come from inside myself. I had a burning desire to be loved but didn't know where real love came from or how to distinguish it from intimacy. I could only look without and blame the men around me for failing to fulfill my expectations.

It was Dave, not Tom, to whom I confided my struggle with binging and purging. It was Dave who confirmed for me that, yes, Tom was an alcoholic. It was Dave who stayed up all night with me, talking about everything and anything, sharing ideas and dreams and hurts. I leaned on him for so many things, and he always took my side. When he told me he loved me, I said I loved him too. When he asked me to leave Tom for him, I reluctantly told him I would. But even as I said it, I knew I couldn't. I was just playing along, certain that I was a helpless victim.

Guilt-ridden and ashamed, I would order mountains of food on my way home from work. The void was getting bigger, deeper and harder to fill. Speeding down Fred Waring Avenue at midnight, I drove with my knees so I could eat with both hands. When I was full to bursting, I pulled over at the nearest gas station. I knew by heart which ones would have a private stall for me to take care of business. Red-eyed and shaking, I looked with disgust at myself in those dirty mirrors and told myself everything was okay.

Just rinse your mouth out, Cyn, I'd tell myself. *Just chew some gum. You got it out fast enough. You're going to be okay.* By the time I got home to my drunken fiancé and my secret lover, no one was the wiser.

When I lived with my parents, I sat out in the back yard at night and talked to God. In Santa Cruz, I sat on the rocks by the water with my journal, thinking and writing, taking time alone to process whatever was going on in my life. But in Palm Desert, I had no outlet. I didn't drink or smoke anymore, and I had no real desire to touch harder drugs (although I can't say the idea of that escape didn't tempt me). I had only one vice—but it was getting worse by the day. The only way I knew how to distract myself from the pain in my heart was to stick my head in a bag of potato chips, attempting to satiate my appetite.

One terrifying question kept coming up over and over: Was I becoming my mother? After all, she'd cheated on my dad with Brian B. She'd made excuses about it, claiming that my dad didn't give her the love and affection she needed. She'd done exactly what I was doing with

Tom and Dave—playing them off one another and manipulating them. She looked outside herself for happiness but never found it and never took responsibility for it.

The more guilt and shame built up in me, the more I tried to purge myself of it. Hanging over the toilet, I could release all the wickedness inside me. Sometimes I stayed late at the restaurant and had drinks with the rest of the staff. Alcohol wasn't really my vice (I wanted to eat my calories), but I didn't really want to go home and neither did they. So I'd sit and sip a Diet Coke while they hit the harder stuff.

One night, Barbara, who waited tables with me, was sitting at the bar in her black slacks and white blouse. She was a tough old thing, leathery and dry, with her scotch on the rocks in one hand and a cigarette in the other. I think she was a lot younger than she looked, but life had worn her away.

She looked at me and said with a little slur, "Well, Cyn, life sure dealt me a bad hand."

Tony and Jennie raised their glasses to that, swallowing their poison in wholehearted agreement. I listened as the three of them commiserated about the lives they'd been given. Jennie was cute and sweet, the kind of person who's impossible not to like, but her marriage was suffering and her weight was skyrocketing. She'd always wanted to travel but would never get to do it now. Tony, a six-foot-two surfer dude with long, dirty-blond hair, didn't express himself too much. But he, too, seemed to have lost his aspirations and night after night he drowned his sorrow in his beer.

"I wouldn't be working here if I had been given a better shot at life," Barbara continued. "This place is like hell's asshole."

"Yeah. Cheers to that," Tony muttered.

In that moment, I took my own swallow of reality. *Wow*, I thought. *Are things really that hopeless? If you don't like the hand you were given, can't you ask for a new one?*

This was one of those earth-shattering realizations that come when you're least expecting it. I looked at the three of them and knew that they didn't have to remain stuck in their misery. They could choose at any moment to leave it. They had given up on their dreams and passions because they sadly didn't believe in themselves. But they were so immersed in their current reality that they didn't even know what they wanted, never mind how to shoot for it.

I drove home that night thinking about my coworkers and wondering how I could help them. But I never thought to apply this newfound knowledge to myself. Unlike Tony and Barbara, I had goals. I was going to finish my education. I had a fiancé who loved me (sort of). I had a bright future to look forward to (filled with binging and purging and constant searching for something to fill the emptiness). My life was fine the way it was. And, anyway, this place was only a temporary stopover for me.

Finally, the summer was over. Dave had wised up to the fact that I wasn't going to leave Tom for him and got himself a new girlfriend. I moved back to Santa Cruz to start my junior year, and things pretty much went back to the way they had been before Israel.

A month or so after I left, Tom and Dave moved to a trailer park with Bob and whoever else decided to crash out there. Tom, still drinking like a fish, finished off at least a 12-pack of bottled beer every night, and the other men in the house were definitely partiers too. The first time I came back to visit, Tom and I went to the movies. I don't remember what we saw—but I remember very clearly what I saw when we got back.

We walked in the door to find Dave and his girlfriend sleeping (or more likely, passed out) on the living room floor. This girl was wearing nothing but a thong, and her ass was hanging out from under the blue blanket like a little white whale breaching the surface of the ocean.

At first, I was so stunned that I couldn't even move. Then, I spun around to face Tom (who looked as startled as I felt) and asked through gritted teeth, "Is this what you come home to every night? Sluts with their asses hanging out?"

He tried to explain that this was not his fault and that he had no control over what Dave did when he wasn't around. But that wasn't good enough for me. In full-blown Carla style, I started ripping into him, swearing and screaming. I was absurdly jealous. He was completely confused.

We took the fight into the bathroom. I don't think he would have engaged me at all if he'd been sober—but of course, he wasn't. We slammed each other against the walls. I slapped him; he slapped me back. I tore his face with my nails. He grabbed my shoulders and shook me like a rag doll. It was horrible and dirty and shameful. And yet, it felt all too familiar.

I finished that semester at UCSC and the next. Tom and I saw each other less and fought more. My parents cut me off, and my father wasn't speaking to me at all. My brother, Brian, with whom I planned to stay for the summer in Las Vegas while I made up the credits I'd lost in Israel, pushed me to break off my engagement. In Brian's mind, Tom was a no-good drunk, and it was time for his little sister to get out.

Tom was no good for me, it was true. But Brian didn't know I was no good either. I never knew for certain whether Tom was loyal to me—but I knew that I wasn't to him. A two-timing whore in Israel and then I did it again, right under his nose, with his best friend. Tsk, tsk!

And yet, I wasn't yet aware enough to understand that my behavior wasn't Tom's fault. I could only blame him for his shortcomings. I'd run to Ben because Tom was so far away. I'd run to Dave because Tom didn't pay me enough attention. That night at the restaurant, I'd grasped the idea that I could create my future—but I didn't realize that, through my actions, I was creating all of my current circumstances too.

At the time, the only lesson I could say I learned from the whole experience was: *Don't date a guy with a drinking problem!* I broke up with Tom over the phone. If text messaging had been invented in those days, I probably would have done it that way. I just didn't want anything to do with the situation anymore. I felt that he'd done me wrong and so he didn't deserve an explanation. A smaller, silent part of me knew I had failed.

My last year at UCSC was lonely. I was still battling my weight and still looking outside myself for happiness. My parents had split for a second time. Only my mother and Brian came to Santa Cruz for my college graduation.

The night before my graduation, Brian and I sat up all night talking and laughing. I told him that I saw myself speaking in front of large crowds. Here comes that huge staircase again that I don't know how to climb. It was something so far off that I couldn't see who the people were or why they were gathered. But Brian didn't laugh at me; instead, he confirmed it.

"I can see you doing amazing things, Cyn," he said.

I knew that I had far more education ahead of me if I wanted to earn my Ph.D., but I needed to take some time off to sort things out and follow my spirit. Part of me was afraid to apply to grad school and worried that I wouldn't get into the program I wanted. I researched the Peace Corps and other travel abroad programs and finally decided that I would teach English in Spain for a year.

As long as I was in Europe, I could ignore the massive staircase and escape the fear of my own imminent failure.

CHAPTER 21

Life in a Box

Bye-bye little car.

In order to fund my trip to Europe, I sold my silver car for $2200 and bought a plane ticket to Paris, with a return flight a year later out of Madrid. This left me with around $1500 to get a place to live and a job. It was going to be tight, but I was sure I could make it work. I had to.

I started this journey with my friend Monica, who was one of the only other female math majors I knew. We decided to explore a little first before settling in Spain. This way I would have a chance to brush up on my Spanish before I started looking for a teaching position.

We traveled up to Belgium and then took the train back through Paris, down through the beautiful south of France and finally stopping in Madrid. We'd decided that we ought to go to Madrid because it was a big city and it would be easy to find jobs there.

Not as easy as we'd hoped. I struggled to find someone who would hire me and Monica wasn't having much luck either. And, we were getting low on funds.

While I was interviewing, we came across a woman who rented out rooms in her flat to foreigners. As we found out later, she systematically brought people in, took their deposits, and then kicked them out—which is exactly what she did to us. After that, one bad thing after another came our way. I'd gotten a nanny job, or so I thought, but, after the first day, the mother handed me one day's pay and sent me on my way. Guess, I wasn't really meant for children.

I only had $180 left to my name and no place to go. But I set out to do this and I was not quitting, especially after coming home from Israel early. I had to follow through on this one or I would never be able to live with myself.

The last straw for Monica was when she had fifty dollars stolen from her in a table game on the street. She was betting on which nut the ball would go under—and the next thing we knew, the guys were folding up the table and scooting away with her money. Somehow, her passport was also stolen in the chaos. This was the end of the road for her. It was a Friday, which meant we had to stay in a hostel for the weekend until the embassy office opened on Monday, giving up more of our already limited funds.

By Monday afternoon, Monica was on a plane back to the States. And I was alone in a foreign country with almost no money, no job and no place to sleep. I went straight to the student travel office to buy a train ticket on my credit card. Clearly, I thought, the Universe did not want me to live in Spain. I'd done some research about other places in Europe where my money would go much further. In the end it came down to a choice between Western Russia, Poland and the Czech Republic.

The notion of living in Prague seemed mysterious. Something mystical about that city—even though I'd barely heard of it before coming to Europe—struck a chord.

When I changed trains in Germany, I transitioned into the Twilight Zone. The train headed toward the Czech Republic, traveling eighty years back in time. Everything was so old! Naïve as I was, I didn't realize that in many ways the Eastern European countries had been left in the past, stranded decades behind the West by Communism and war.

I found a car that had cabins rather than forward-facing seats. I always preferred those cabins because, if no one else came in, you had the whole space to yourself—and if someone did, it was more convenient to talk. On this leg of the journey, a man from the Czech Republic sat across from me in the cabin. When he discovered I was an American, he was so anxious and excited. He really wanted to communicate with me, but my command of Czech was nil at that point, so he did his best with a few key English phrases. It got a little hard to follow him, but I kept smiling because he was trying so hard. What I gathered from him was that his son spoke English—and when we got to Prague, he invited me to his house for something to eat and said his son could translate.

I wasn't sure what to say to this man. Only twenty at the time, I figured that waltzing into the house of a strange man might not be a very safe idea. But he was so excited that I couldn't help but agree. I could always back out when we got there, I figured.

When we stopped in Prague, I had been on the train for more than sixteen hours and was ready for bed and a shower. My new friend's family was there to pick him up, so I got to meet his wife and two sons right away. They seemed like nice people and I had no reservations anywhere (not to mention the fact that I only had $180 to my name), so I decided that keeping them company wasn't such a bad idea after all.

I soon realized that, while the Czech people may have very little, they are more than generous. When we arrived at their home, my new hosts showed me to an extra room with its own adjacent bathroom. The house was small but immaculately clean, and I felt right at home.

When I explained my situation, my hosts were incredulous. What was a girl like me doing on her own in a foreign country, with no money and no job? I simply couldn't be left to wander the streets of Prague on my own.

As it turned out, my new friends knew another family in the neighborhood who were looking for someone to teach them English. Before I knew it, I was a live-in tutor. This was a very fortunate arrangement for me, since it afforded me a safe and free place to live. My new employers also cooked meals for me and took care of almost everything. I felt incredibly blessed to have stepped into such an ideal situation.

This second family, the Novaks, had two daughters. The elder one was away at college, so I was able to use her room. The younger daughter, Ludmilla, was nice enough at first, but soon she started to have issues with me. The only thing that could explain the way she acted toward me was that she was jealous. Certainly she wasn't enjoying my stay—but since I still didn't speak much Czech, I wasn't sure how to broach the subject with her.

One day I came home to find that I'd lost the key to the front door of the house. I have no idea how it happened and felt horrible about it. I pulled out my new Czech-to-English dictionary and found all the words for "I'm sorry," and kept repeating them as I tried to explain what had happened.

"I lost the key," I told them in my broken Czech. "I'm so sorry."

The three of them kept shaking their heads and looking at one another. Then, the daughter pointed at the piano.

I couldn't imagine why she was doing this. It made no sense to me at all until they lifted the lid and pointed directly at a piano key. Apparently, I had been telling them how sorry I was that I had lost their *piano* key.

I scoured the dictionary for the word for key to the door and when we discovered it, we all fell out laughing once we figured out the miscommunication. Or, at least, the parents and I did. As I was wiping tears of mirth from my eyes, I looked up to find their beautiful blonde daughter giving me a horrible, dirty stare. Ludmilla clearly did not find as much humor in this as the rest of us.

I knew I couldn't stay with this family forever, no matter how kind they were. So I went to the post office, borrowed a phone book, and started calling English schools in Prague to see if they were hiring. I heard "no" a few times but, when I called Culturní Stredísko, Hanna said "yes."

At the time, I was just living life without recognizing the divine intervention I was experiencing. I was in the flow and everything was unfolding beautifully for me. My salary at Culturní Stredísko would be about four-hundred dollars a month, which as far as I knew was plenty to get me by. I shook Hanna's hand at the end of my interview and dove right in.

I had no idea where to begin, so I began to study the curriculum book, which actually had instructions in the text about how to get the students actively involved. This was helpful, since I didn't really have any prior experience.

My students were adults who were paying out of their own pockets for classes. Since the fall of Communism, they were dealing more and more with the West, and it was important for them to learn English—just as the older generations had learned Russian and German. I was amazed at how quickly these people were adapting to an entirely different social and economic environment. They believed that, if they worked hard and educated themselves, they would rise above the substandard living they'd been provided under Communist rule and be able to create something better for themselves and their families.

Being in Prague really broadened my perspective on life. When I walked down the street with a smile on my face, people literally moved off the sidewalk to get away from me. I guess they thought I was crazy. My students saw hope in their futures, but too many others had a bleak outlook on life and seemed to have a hard time finding joy.

As capitalism began to take hold in the Czech Republic, there was some resistance to Westernization, despite the fact that many people seemed to consider America the Promised Land—a place of opportunity, freedom and wealth. Usually, I kept out of the debates, not wanting to be seen as "pushing" my Western viewpoints on my students.

In one class, a student asked my views on the U.S. president. At the time, Bill Clinton was in office. I declined to answer—that was one argument I wasn't willing to start—but, as this student talked, the others joined in. Soon the whole class was involved, talking about how much everybody loved Bill Clinton (who had apparently just received a sixty-percent approval rating in a national poll). As I listened, I realized how generalized these people's perceptions of America and the American way of life were. They were based entirely on what they heard in the media—understandably, since the media was the only real link to Western life for most of them.

This student went on to state, totally matter-of-factly, that in America people were so rich that women didn't have to go to work at all—and wasn't that wonderful? I really had to take a deep breath on that one. As someone who'd struggled to put herself through college and who'd fought for the right to excel in her chosen field, I wasn't sure what to do with this. The life my students were idealizing was the one I'd run from the night my dad set me up with Rob, the Israeli millionaire.

I had to remember that, in Socialist countries, the women worked right alongside the men; it wasn't a choice. The Czech women were scientists, engineers and skilled laborers. I had one female student who was a physicist. Yes, they were still discriminated against because they were women—but this level of success and education was expected of them. Yet, while I saw their achievements as something to be admired, to them staying at home with the kids was the real indicator of wealth and luxury.

What a difference experience and perception makes. What a huge eye-opener it was to think that the feminists in America had fought for the life these women lived as breadwinners and, yet, these women only dreamed of the life they believed most American women lived—at home with the kids and taken care of.

This was a piece to that puzzle that had started to take shape when I sat at that bar in Palm Desert. Do we create our reality based on our perceptions? Whose rules are we living by anyway? Are we really stuck in our circumstance or do we have the power to change it?

When I left the family that I had started off with, I was invited to stay with a couple who had a home in the mountains—literally. After a twenty-minute train ride out of town, I had to climb a mountain to get to their house. It didn't matter how cold it was; I still sweat my ass off getting home at night.

Mikel and his wife, Anna, invited me to stay so I could help her study English, but the situation was far from ideal. I wasn't at all comfortable in their home and stayed in my room most of the time. They laughed with me a lot, but something felt off about the whole thing. When bald, pasty Mikel started to put the moves on me—

standing too close, making lewd comments about my body and all sorts of other icky stuff—I knew it was time for me to go.

Another one of my students, Vlăda, found me a place in the Kolej (college) dormitory for just twelve dollars a month. I shared a room with Shărka and Iveta, two chemical engineering students in the doctoral program. Shărka was a tall, dark-haired girl with long, beautiful hair and big brown eyes. She was a very smart young woman, but all she really wanted to do was finish school and follow her husband-to-be to America. Peter, her fiancé, was living in Texas, doing a residency at one of the universities. As soon as she was done with her studies, she would join her man and start living the American dream. (She did, in fact, do just that.) Iveta was more serious about her studies but she, too, dreamed of a life outside the Czech Republic.

My year in Prague was a life-changing experience. Spending time with amazing women like Shărka, Iveta and Monika, and learning about the experience of the Czech people changed me forever. I may not have experienced their lives or their obstacles, but hearing their stories helped me to see the world through a wider lens.

Getting Out of the Box

As much as Prague taught me, I thirsted for more. I voyaged out of the city at every opportunity. One of the most profound trips was the journey to Amsterdam I took with Monika. One of my students, she'd become a good friend. She was close to my age—twenty-three to my twenty—but it always seemed to me that she was younger than me; the chronology didn't really have much to do with it.

Amsterdam seemed like such a cool place to be and I wanted to get there before I left Europe. Plus, Monika's twenty-fourth birthday was coming up—and what better place to celebrate than the party capital of the West?

We took the bus and, being a big spender, I paid for our tickets (the fare was only six American dollars); Czech money was nearly valueless to the dollar at the time. Monika's family didn't have a lot (the average family income at the time was somewhere in the neighborhood of fifty dollars a month) but they gave her some funds they'd been saving up and told her to enjoy herself.

This was Monika's first trip out of the country, and she was a little scared. Up until this point she had led a very sheltered life—living in the box. But I was right by her side, and so off we went into our grand birthday adventure.

What I remember most about our arrival in the city were the Ferris wheels. They were everywhere! Amazed by this, I thought, *Wow, it is a bit of a party town being Amsterdam and all.* But, as it turned out, it was the queen's birthday. We couldn't have picked a better time to visit. The entire city had taken a vacation day. People dressed in bright colors and funny hats thronged the streets, drinking beer and snacking on foods from all over the globe served up by street vendors. The sun was shining; everyone was laughing and talking at once. It was such a marked contrast from gloomy, overcast Prague, where everyone wore gray and black and frowned more than they smiled.

There were groups of Americans in Amsterdam. They seemed to have come there because it was cheap and fun and because the lifestyle was a far cry from "real life." While they were there, they didn't have to make decisions about their futures or move forward with their goals. At first, this reluctance to grow up sort of disgusted me—but then I realized that, in a way, I was doing exactly the same thing. I knew that I'd eventually go back to complete my doctorate, but I hadn't applied to a single graduate school. What would my focus be? What was my passion? Did I really want to continue in mathematics or the sciences? Or did I want to shift my focus to social or behavioral studies and explore the various gender issues and different male/female roles I'd been exposed to in the Czech Republic? I had no idea.

I tried not to let my questions bother me too much. I told Monika that, since we were in Amsterdam, we should smoke some pot. After all, it was legal and everyone had it.

We didn't have a pipe, so we bought a joint from some people in the park. We found a quiet spot under a tree and lit up. Monika sat with her back against a tree, facing a huge Ferris wheel and some bumper cars. We could hear the children screeching with joy. I started giggling—and Monika started to cry.

I totally didn't get it. Her reaction stopped me in my tracks.

"Wait a second, what's wrong?" I asked. "What's going on?"

She looked up at me. Her stylishly long bangs fell over the rim of her glasses. She sniffled, and then said, "Imagine growing up in a box. The box has white walls and a white ceiling. And everyone tells you from the time you are born that this is all there is. So you live your entire life only knowing and understanding this box. And then, one day, someone opens the lid, and you discover that there's a rainbow."

The entire world around me stopped. Her answer affected me so profoundly that I knew, even as she spoke, that she had changed me at my core level, as I had changed her. We had both been raised in our own boxes. Mine might have had Technicolor walls, but was it any less a prison? And here was a young woman who was brilliant and poetic and courageous, seeing color for the first time.

I took other trips while I was in Prague—to Italy, which was amazing, and to Poland, which was heartbreaking. I visited Krakow and toured the concentration camps. I thought it was important for me to see these things since they were part of my own history. As I looked at the collection of shoes taken from people who'd been thrown into the camp at Auschwitz, my stomach started to churn. They had a whole collection of eyeglasses, too.

Somehow seeing these everyday items was more powerful than seeing the site itself. Every one of those things had belonged to a living being. What horrible things human beings could do to one another, in the name of race and faith! When I stood in one of the closet-sized rooms where the Germans had crammed dozens of people for days on end, I started to get dizzy and nauseated. By the time we reached the incinerators, I had to leave the tour. I'd seen cruelty in my life, or so I thought—but this was beyond my reality.

Poland as a whole was pretty heavy for me. The country seemed to be struggling more than the Czech Republic with the transition from Communism to capitalism. I felt the pain. Old men were drunk in the streets of Krakow, numbing their sadness with alcohol over what had happened to their country.

There were some bright spots on the trip. I met a guy from Holland who traveled with me to Gdansk, a beautiful port city and far more tourist-friendly than other parts of Poland. I had some fun trying to speak Czech to the Polish people. The languages share a common root, but it was like I was trying to speak Spanish to an Italian. The locals understood maybe one word in five.

As the school year drew to a close, I started making plans to head back to the U.S. I'd been talking to my mom, and she said that I could stay with her in Las Vegas if I wanted. I decided to take her up on it.

I helped Hanna hire a new teacher and got a train ticket back to Madrid because that was the departure point on my return ticket. As I retraced my steps from a year earlier, I realized just how much my perspective had changed. My understanding of the world was so different now. The rickety old trains I rode in were simply what I had become accustomed to. When I made the transfer in Frankfurt, I was astounded at how luxurious everything seemed. This was no longer the world I knew. It was all so clean and bright, so soft and sleek.

After a brief stop in Barcelona, I boarded my plane to Las Vegas. I had mixed feelings about coming back. Life in Europe had certainly been much harder and more drab in a lot of ways and maybe that had distracted me from my usual binging and purging, without the usual catalysts. But now, I was going back to it all.

On one hand, I had had enough of Eastern Europe—but I wasn't sure if I was ready to pick up where I'd left off. I was nervous about what the future would bring. I felt as if I'd taken a major detour, and I wasn't sure I could get back to the starting point again. I'd gotten back on the Ferris wheel, but now, the view was entirely different.

CHAPTER 22

In the Closet

Eight years later, I woke up on the floor in a dark closet.

Sitting cross-legged on the floor, surrounded by shoes and clothes, a sharp pain emanated from the center of my chest—an aching hole in my heart so compelling, so incredibly empty, that I couldn't ignore it any more. The door, slightly cracked open, allowed in a small column of light from the bedroom, which fell across my favorite pair of black boots. I stared at the boots in a daze, trying to figure out why they seemed so entrancing to me. Then, like a skipping CD, that old Nancy Sinatra song started playing in my head. "These Boots Are Made for Walking..."

Shaking my head, I took a deep, shivering breath. "What am I doing here?"

I was married to a man named Joe, but he wasn't my soul mate. That deep, connected and enchanting feeling of being in love had never been a part of our relationship. Our connection wasn't spiritual; it was situational. I had been with him for seven years, but our time was up. As the song continued in my head a chill came over me and I realized, as surely as I've ever known anything, it was time for these boots to go walking.

Yes, that was my wake-up call. The beginning of my internal journey, literally and metaphorically, for I had been in the dark and in the closet.

213

How did all this happen?

Grungy and wiped out, I had been traveling for days with no shower and little-to-no sleep. First there was the long train trip from Prague to Frankfurt to Madrid. Then I had to traipse through tunnels, lugging a cumbersome backpack for what seemed like miles, to get to the flight from Madrid to New York, changing planes in New York for the final flight to Las Vegas. I wearily stepped off the plane at the end of my year abroad and there was Carla with her new boyfriend, Jimmy. Oooh, boy! Back to familiar territory.

Jimmy was tall, skinny and red. Over baked by the sun, he wore a button-down shirt with only the bottom three buttons fastened and one thin gold chain. My mother had offered me a room in her house and, not knowing what I was getting into, I'd decided to take her up on it while I got back on my feet.

Exhausted and grimy, I crammed my body and luggage into the back of my mother's red hatchback Corvette. "Let's go out!" Carla said.

"*Oh, brilliant!*" I thought to myself. *Are these people crazy?*

As If I had a choice in the matter. What I would have done for a hot shower and a clean pillow in that moment. With total disregard for my extensive journey and overwhelming culture shock—a stark contrast between a colorless former Communist country and the glitz, glamour and lights of Las Vegas—Jimmy sped off to the local pub. My head spun from the sounds of bells and whistles of all the poker machines at the bar.

After just a few drinks, Jimmy got down on one knee with a small black box in hand and asked, "Carla, will you marry me?"

Wait... *What?*

Carla turned to me with a big smile. "Well, what do you think?" she asked.

Are you frigging kidding me?! I thought to myself. *Now I am certain these people are out of their minds— geez, just get me to bed! Heck if I knew!*

I had no idea who this guy was. The only thing I had to go on was the ring, which was a carbon copy of the one Tom had given me two years before: a quarter-carat, marquis-cut solitaire. The Carla I knew appreciated larger flashier jewelry. Either Carla had changed in the year since I'd seen her, or Jimmy didn't know her all that well.

"Are you happy, Mom?" I asked her.

"Yes, honey. I'm really happy."

"Then that's all that matters."

If my year in Prague had taught me anything, it was that happiness is something to be treasured. The more I thought about it, the more I realized how desperately my mother wanted to feel special. It didn't really matter much who Jimmy was, or what kind of person he was. He wanted her, and that was enough.

I was reminded, sickeningly, of my relationship with Tom's roommate, Dave. Never underestimate the power of mutual need.

My dad and I had not spoken since he asked me to leave, so I had no idea what had transpired between my parents while I was in Europe. It had probably been the same ol' carousel of fights, jealousies and power struggles between them.

Immediately, I started looking for jobs and researching graduate schools. I didn't want to stay with my mother forever. In fact, the faster I got out of there, the happier I'd be.

Jimmy, who'd seemed all right at first glance, turned out to be an abusive, co-dependent alcoholic who suffered from Post-Traumatic Stress Disorder, thanks to his years in the military. He had horrible nightmares about his experiences in Vietnam, and booze was the only thing that could keep the bad dreams away. On several occasions he swore to my mother that he stopped drinking, but really all he did was find new ways to hide his addiction from her.

A few weeks later, still without a job or a plan to get to graduate school, I decided to go to California to help my brother, Tim, move from Long Beach to a new home on a different naval base. Since Jimmy had a truck, he offered to drive out there with me. It was pretty clear that I couldn't say no.

While stopping for gas in the desert, Jimmy went to the restroom. I reached into the cooler where he kept his stash of Dr. Pepper, hoping to find some Diet Coke. Under the ice, I found a nearly-empty bottle of vodka.

He'd been lying to my mom all along. Apparently, he'd discovered that the combination of vodka and Dr. Pepper doesn't make your breath smell.

I became enraged and more than a little frightened for my safety. This man had been driving us at breakneck speed through the desert while draining an entire bottle of Smirnoff. Since we were nearly there, I just held on and prayed. When we got to Long Beach, I pulled Tim aside to make sure I wasn't overreacting. He confirmed for me that it was, in fact, a really bad idea to be driving anywhere with this man.

I bought a return flight on my credit card. Better a little debt than another six-hour ride with Jimmy and his bottle of vodka.

When I landed in Vegas, I took a taxi to where my mother worked, since I didn't have a key to the house. I told her everything that had happened, and that I simply didn't feel safe around this man. Oddly enough for Carla, she didn't freak out at this declaration. I waited a little while before going home. I wanted to make sure my mom was there.

When I got back, Jimmy—who'd been down the street in the Jacuzzi—came marching up behind me. Thank God I had the keys in my hand, because he lunged at me. I screamed, and slashed at him with the keys, leaving a big bleeding gash across his chest. As he staggered back, I dashed into the house and bolted the door behind me.

A moment later, Jimmy launched himself at the door. And again. And again.

"You spoiled brat! You stupid bitch! This is all your fault! How could you do this to your mother? How could you do this to *me?*"

When the cops arrived, Jimmy was still screaming like a madman. They cuffed him and put him in the back of the car, then came back inside to finalize the report. They could take him away for now, they said, but we'd have to file a restraining order if we wanted to keep him away for more than one night.

I took all of this on myself. Maybe it really was my fault. After all, my mother had been happy with Jimmy before I came along and ruined it. I knew I couldn't stay in Carla's house any longer. Especially when morning came, and she let a (momentarily) sober and shaky Jimmy waltz right back inside like nothing had ever happened.

And that's when Joe stepped into my life.

We'd met at a singles gathering. He was quite a bit older than me—thirty-eight to my twenty. At the time, I thought dating an older man made perfect sense, since I was (in my mind), a "mature" twenty. In retrospect, I still had so much growing up to do that the gap was pretty significant.

I wasn't particularly attracted to him but Joe was reassuring and solid, and I needed a bit of that in my life. He was working on his master's degree so he could be a school counselor but had no aspirations beyond this career. For him, both work and life were about establishing security, and a job in the school system provided that for him. His parents had left him some money after they passed. He used it to buy a condo and still had enough left over he didn't have to work for a couple of years while earning his master's, as long as he lived carefully.

The day after Jimmy got arrested, Joe called to invite me to an Eagles concert. I didn't really have any interest in going, but I couldn't very well stay at my mother's house and I had no car. So I agreed to go.

When he picked me up, Joe seemed to sense immediately that something was wrong. Ashamed and emotional, I poured out the story of the last few days. "You should stay with me," he said. "It's not safe for you there."

And there it is— relationship by default.

Miserable, I felt a little like a caged animal, restless and frustrated. I can't imagine I was easy to live with. Joe never got angry with me, or raised his voice to me—even when I threw screaming tantrums, in the beginning. But despite his calm demeanor, I always felt trapped with him.

Oh, surprise. Joe, like all of us, had some issues of his own. A child of alcoholics and in recovery himself, Joe suffered from what seemed to be Obsessive Compulsive Disorder (OCD), which meant he was overtly methodical about everything. The whole shebang, including intimacy, had to have a place and time.

No joke! You read that right—sex on a schedule. Sex during the week was blasphemy! We wouldn't want to ruin our sleeping schedule on a work night. And on the weekends, the cars got washed and waxed first, receiving a full detail down to a Q-tip swabbed in the door jams, a workout at the gym. And *if—only if*—it was on the schedule—then intimate relations took place. But it had to happen directly after we got home, so he only had to shower once.

Deep down he was kind. But he was trapped in layers and layers of rigidity and fear. The only thing Joe was really passionate about was his red BMW 325i convertible. I used to joke that the car was his real girlfriend. He gave that thing more time and attention than he ever gave me. He lavished hours on it every weekend. I think it was his way of proving to the world that he was worth something— eerily *familiar*. The Glickman tradition , right?

Why did I stay with him for so long? I had no idea what a "normal" relationship was supposed to look like. The only model I had to go on was my parents' marriage. I had no memory of them saying loving things, or cherishing one another. I didn't feel Joe in my heart—but was I supposed to? Alone in the world, with no money and no car and only a vague sense of purpose, I felt I didn't have any other options. After a while, we both just got distracted by other priorities and settled into a comfortable— passionless—partnership, marching unconsciously through our respective lives.

Not long after I moved in, Joe got me an interview with the Dean of Sciences at the University of Nevada Las Vegas, a man named Ernie Peck. When I spoke to Dr. Peck, he easily reached the conclusion that I should consider a graduate assistant position in the mathematics department. Right then and there, he picked up the phone and called Dr. Peter Shuie, the department chair. With my transcripts and degree from UCSC, there were virtually no questions asked; the position was mine if I wanted it.

I actually hadn't intended to stay that long in Las Vegas. I was settling in with Joe, but I hadn't yet made the decision to stick around permanently. Then again, a master's degree in mathematics wasn't something to sneeze at—and, if I studied statistics, I would be able to put my knowledge to use anywhere I wanted.

So I took the job and lived with Joe in his condo. We were close enough to the UNLV campus that I could ride my bike to school. My assistantship paid only about $8,000 a year but I was buying all the groceries and paying the utility bills at the condo, since Joe had already taken care of the mortgage. It wasn't a grand life, but it was the easiest choice for me to make at the time—the path of least resistance. Instead of creating my life, I was simply taking what was handed to me and telling myself that this was the way it was meant to be. After all, I wasn't being given a whole lot of other options.

Two years into our relationship, Joe and I bought a house. He had finished his education and secured his dream job with the local school district. I was just about done with my master's as well, and would soon be making more money in the foreseeable future. It was time to take a step up in the world.

Our home was in a new neighborhood, and the builder was only releasing six to ten properties a year. We had to put our names in a lottery and hope we got in on the first release before the builder raised the price. Once the deal was ours, we'd have to wait six months for the property to be built from the ground up.

On the day we paid our deposit, Joe was ecstatic. We drove out to our patch of desert, envisioning our home resting on this lot. He wrapped his arm around me, and said, "Well, we're as good as married now."

Those words, to me, sounded like a prison gate closing. *Oh, God,* I thought. *My life is over, and I'm only twenty-two!* I felt like I was losing control of everything—like life was just going to keep *happening* to me. I had no one to turn to, nowhere to run. I was going to have to deal with disappointment after disappointment, because that's the way life was. And, if that was the case, wouldn't it be easiest just to go along with it?

With my heart sinking down to somewhere below my knees, I turned and smiled up at him. "Good as married," I said.

Years later I found an old journal from that time. In it, I cursed Joe out in the most vivid terms I could think of (which, considering the way I grew up, were pretty raunchy). I hated him. I hated his personality and his OCD bullshit. I hated his BMW and his Rolex, because he was more proud of them than he was of me. In every way possible, he disgusted me. Funny how these feelings didn't affect me strongly enough at the time to force me to change things. I just poured all my anger onto the pages of this journal, and tried to let it go.

We moved into our house the following summer. We each had our own office space, plus a spare bedroom in addition to our master bedroom. It might have even been comfortable, but the more time passed, the more controlling Joe became. He gripped on to me more and more tightly, because the fear of my latent departure haunted him.

When I started my doctorate program at UNLV, things got tense. While Joe had been supportive of me earning my master's, he wasn't so thrilled about the prospect of me surpassing him in education. It didn't matter that he had no desire to earn a doctorate. It was about maintaining his superiority—about staying "bigger" than me, so that I couldn't outgrow him.

I was working full-time, going to school full-time, and sleeping very little. His lack of support really cut me, because I could have really used a bit of help at that point. But he wasn't stepping up.

Instead, he decided to marry me.

That morning I was sitting at my desk, working on my dissertation. A stack of papers sat at my elbow, waiting to be graded. I'd had about four hours sleep a night for the last month. My only focus was getting through the day. I certainly wasn't in the mood to talk about the future. I could barely lift my head to look up when he barged into my office.

"We're getting married," he said.

"No way," I said. "No, we're not."

"Yes, we are. And here's how we're going to do it."

True to form, Joe had the whole thing planned out. We embarked in L.A. and cruised through the Mexican Riviera. Simple, easy and quick, the ceremony transpired on board before we set sail. To him, there was no romance in the idea of marriage. It was just the next logical step in his obsessively organized life.

With Joe stuck on this idea and me too exhausted to argue, I passively submitted. What would marriage change about our lives, anyway? We cohabited for years. In the end, who cared?

"Fine," I replied. "But I'm not changing my last name, and we're not inviting anyone."

And that's how I ended up married to a man I wasn't in love with.

We selected an obligatory ring: a cubic zirconium set in eighteen-karat gold that felt as fake as our relationship. I barely remember our cruise or our vows. What I do remember is that Joe spent most of the cruise in the toilet, having somehow acquired E-coli.

"Thoughts are things." And Joe, so petrified about scary "south of the border" diseases, cautiously vaccinated himself for everything. And, sure enough, he fell ill the moment we stepped on board. Memories of my old coworkers at the restaurant in Palm Desert flooded my mind, hearing them complaining about the bad hand dealt to them. Trapped in their prisons, bringing on their own bad luck and perpetuating it, the connection solidified in my head.

You get what you wish for, I thought, standing alone at the railing of the cruise ship.

Driven to earn a doctorate, pay off my student loans, and rise to tenured professor status, clearly I manifested my destiny. At the same time, I unwittingly failed to apply this wisdom to my relationships, and a healthy, loving union eluded me.

Once the cruise was over, everything regressed back to normal. Joe spent hours on his car, and I worked myself into oblivion.

Romantic, not *so* much. Dull and boring captures it. But at least nobody shot his head off in the front yard like Jimmy.

Oh yeah, did I mention that Carla told me that after she filed for the third restraining order against Jimmy, he went off the deep end and shot himself... I guess he couldn't live without Carla— codependency at its worst. Of course, Carla's response to the whole thing was the usual high-drama major production. I guess she still couldn't see how she was calling in the familiar but unconscious script of her father. And, while I still wasn't completely out of those deep dark woods myself, at least I was starting to search my soul and listen to my gut.

Meanwhile, despite all of that and the stresses at work, I eased up on my cycle of binging and purging. I sort of cut a deal with God that if I won a car... Well, that didn't exactly work out, but I stuck to my end of the bargain and stopped the destructive behavior for years. Joe's OCD created a stability that eased my anxieties and subdued my disorder. Besides, you can't keep bulimia a secret when your partner overhears hacking sounds of puking in the next room. The vision of the man of my dreams faded, but at least Joe stuck around.

Without my usual outlet, everything started bottling up. And I let it. Part of me thought, *Just lose yourself in your work— it's a healthy distraction*. In the midst of writing my dissertation, teaching classes, and compiling my tenure file to become a full professor, the weight of my responsibilities overwhelmed me.

So, I decided to take a Sunday afternoon off and go look at some houses. I just needed a break and a chance to let my mind roam in a fantasy realm. Joe offered to come with me, and off we shuffled to tour the homes at Red Rock Country Club. The billboards intrigued me. The high-class, guard gated, luxurious living exemplified a life I dreamt about.

We arrived at the massive wrought iron gates surrounded by colossal-sized palm trees. Totally intimidated, Joe stopped the car dead, and said, "Forget it! We could *never* afford to live here."

Instantly, I started bawling. Tears gushing down my face, I had suddenly realized my dream—and, just as quickly, he crushed it.

"I wasn't thinking about moving," I told him. "I just wanted to look. I am a dreamer. Who said anything about can or can't?"

Obviously confused, surviving in this world meant practicality, working hard, and being organized, not lofty pie-in-the-sky ideas.

"Just take me home," I sobbed. "I want to go home."

"No," he said with one of those deep, frustrated sighs. "We'll look. As long as we're just looking, okay?"

In we went, me with my eyes swollen and still in tears. As we drove up to the models, he started to pull back again. "This is a bad idea," he said. But we were already there, so what was the harm?

Touring the models opened my eyes to the possibilities in life. So inspired, I started running numbers in my head. With both of our salaries, I conjectured, plus the proceeds from the sale of our current house, our budget covered it. Shocked at this realization, Joe flip-flopped and immediately contacted his Realtor, Doug, to sell our home.

We would be selling it, but not for the reasons we thought...

Two days later, in the dark of my closet, the light came on. My soul shouted and my ego quieted. Brushing it aside was no longer an option, as it said, "These boots were made for walking..."

For years my inner guidance spoke but I ignored it, busying myself, earning my doctorate, paying off my car, applying for tenure, and focusing on controlling my food intake all distracting me from the truth. I didn't really want a bigger house in a nicer neighborhood. A part of me was dying; I wanted a new life.

My heart was dying inside living this lie of a passionless marriage.

On the surface, it fit: This is what people do, they get married and settle down. An entire month passed working up the courage to tell him and to go against the societal grain. I feared his reaction and still didn't trust my own. I felt obligated to him—after all, we *were* married—and this was going to crush him. *All in all*, I told myself, *he hasn't been a bad husband. He doesn't scream at me, or hit me. I can't hurt him. He loves me. But, above all else, I had made a commitment to him.*

On the other hand, I didn't love him in *that* way. Which voice was I going to listen to—the one serving him or my true inner voice that had been hiding in the closet all these years?

For those four weeks, I sickened myself with worry and fear. I had stopped purging for nearly four years, but now my bulimia kicked right back into high gear. The familiar cycle kept me from directly facing my worst fear. I dropped twenty pounds in four weeks. Even without sticking my finger down my throat, nothing stayed down. I hid this from him as well, eating when he wasn't home and smuggling junk food in the house in my work bag.

Eating me alive, the anxiety worsened. I decided to see a counselor. I thought maybe I was in an early mid-life crisis. Why should I be going through this now? Why should I be questioning myself in this way? Maybe something in me needed to be fixed.

As for Joe, I offered to go to therapy with him, as a last-ditch effort. Since he worked as a school counselor himself, I thought he'd be open to the idea, but he wasn't. For my own well-being, I set an appointment.

"You've outgrown him." the counselor stated matter-of-factly, with nothing more than a shrug. In an instant, everything clarified in my mind and those words rang in my ears. "Yes, I *have* outgrown him." I contemplated. A sense of freedom came over me, like a butterfly emerging from a cocoon. I now had permission to fly— something I denied myself—and now there was no going back.

As soon as I dropped the bomb on Joe, he wanted me gone. I believe a part of him knew this day was inevitable and he instantly shut me out, subconsciously knowing I would one day outgrow him and leave, just as his previous fiancé had done too. His rigid mind required a pattern re-order immediately. Everything in its place—and I had no place anymore. But at least these patterns were really starting to become apparent to me.

The divorce only took three days. Turns out, the wedding hadn't been properly witnessed (thanks to my decision not to invite anyone), and therefore it was never really official. In my mind, I never really married Joe. I never legitimately gave that piece of me away. A marriage of situation and naivety, it didn't really count.

When Doug initiated the sale process, he came back over to put the lock box on the door on a day Joe was at work. He joked that this was rather like the movie, *Sleeping with the Enemy*, in which a woman plans her own death in order to escape from her obsessive-compulsive husband. Doug commented that it was inevitable that I was going to grow up, become a woman, and fly out of the nest. My life wasn't much of a horror movie—and Joe was no maniacal killer—but it clarified for me just how much dysfunction I'd been living with.

Breaking Free of Prison

"I'm free!"

Dropping the top on my white convertible and speeding off for the last time from the house we shared, I blasted the radio, raised both arms in the air and gleefully bellowed, "YAHOOOO!!!" Twenty-eight-years old, a single girl in the City of Sin, and I had just lost 185 pounds and was feeling as light as a feather. Released from my prison, I finally realized, I had locked the prison gate. Although naïve, I manifested my own unhappiness. I stood at the foot of my spiritual path. Now, my real life was about to begin, and things were going to be different.

The world opened up to me. Living in Las Vegas provided a sensory overload like nowhere else. As a girl who had her nose to the grindstone through college and then found herself trapped in a loveless marriage with every detail planned— I was like a kid in a candy store who had never seen candy before. After I left Joe, my heart told me a soul mate was out there, but I ran from being caged again anytime soon.

Because my car was paid off and I had no debt, I was able to get one-hundred-percent financing for my townhome. Thank goodness, since my professor's salary didn't allow for a down payment or furniture. Despite some hassles with the builder, I ended up with a great deal.

Leaving Joe with all the furniture except my computer desk, I ended up sleeping on the floor. Thanks to a former student, who donated a mattress and a small kitchen table, I was in business.

Emptiness stirred within me, starting back at square one like this—
but willing to sacrifice for the sake of freedom was every bit worth it.

Girls Gone Wild

Breaking free from prison has a way of unleashing someone's
inhibitions.

When the tension is finally released, along with all the oppres-
sive restrictions and rules, it opens something in people that can
make them go pretty wild. Such behavior is typical after graduations,
divorces, leaving the roost or, in my case, a split-up and the end of
the grindstone.

Just like so many college kids, set free from their parents' home
and finally able to let their hair down and do what they want and
when they want with nobody watching, I found myself suddenly
without limitations. Completely sheltered for seven years after going
to college, working my way through school and then pursuing my
master's and doctorate, I didn't really stop to smell the roses. My nose
remained glued to the grindstone, plowing through the next step to
reach my next goal. Add to that all of the oppression of living with
Joe—I was ready to burst at the seams!

The closest I ever came to feeling like a porn star was my weekend with Jeremy. Just as I was making my transition out of the house
and sleeping on my office floor so that I didn't have to share my bed
with Joe, I started talking with a former high school classmate,
Jeremy. We hung out with different friends at school, but we had
honors math classes in common and shared our favorite teacher, Mr.
Mansfield, who fondly called me "Chainsaw," because I still had
braces and I talked a lot.

Jeremy was sweet and innocent. Apparently, I was the one who
corrupted him by introducing him to parties. He was an only child

so, unlike me, he didn't have the chance to get into trouble with the influences of older siblings like mine.

What a huge gift he was at the time. Jeremy helped me to make this awkward and scary transition, while the rug was already pulled and I was trying to find my footing.

I remember when I saw the picture of Jeremy in the high school reunion book that he looked exactly the same. But there was one difference: He was now a man—a very handsome man. He even resembled David Duchovny (who in my estimation is a sexy-looking guy). As I checked Jeremy out, I thought to myself, *Omigosh, I have to see him.* The reunion book had e-mail addresses and phone numbers of all those who had attended. Since, at this point, I was already on the outs with Joe, I figured it was ethically okay to start flirting with another guy.

I immediately emailed him because, at the very least, I wanted to tell him how handsome he had become. As the dialogue began, everything started to evolve. I think we were both fascinated with the developments in each other's lives and what we had made of ourselves. And, sure enough, he was single. Wow, I was connecting with someone my own age who felt familiar to me and was entirely different from Joe. Strangely, it felt like we both understood each other.

Eleven years had passed since we had last spoken; I was intrigued and wanted to discover more. I didn't realize until now that he had gone to college in Santa Barbara and had studied software engineering. And he was living in San Francisco during the dot.com boom. I loved and missed Northern California and the ocean. Exchanging e-mails for nearly a month we planned a trip. The first weekend when I was living in my new townhome, and was officially free of Joe, I flew to San Fran to meet Jeremy.

He picked me up and we went to dinner. I was really nervous and wearing a little pale blue spaghetti-strap mini dress. Unlike the gregarious, confident woman I am today, I shyly hid sideways behind him as we checked in for our reservations. Shyly, I held his hand, peeking out behind him. I had never actually been on a real date! Going out with Joe certainly never seemed like a date and, prior to that, what experience did I really have with a "dating"? Not to mention, I had been with only one man for seven years who I was comfortable with—versus suddenly being with a guy I had known from so many years ago who had become so handsome while I felt like an awkward little girl.

We sat down to dinner and, as I let go of the fear, I yearned to connect with something I had been missing for so many years. It didn't take us long to feel comfortable together. By the time we got back to his place, we started kissing and the rest was history. That entire weekend was about making up for so many years of drought with Joe. We tried every position under the sun and some we didn't even know existed. As I lost all my inhibitions and kept asking for more, every room got christened, including the hallway. Leaving no room untouched, we finally emerged on Sunday for breakfast.

I chose Jeremy not only because he was, of course, handsome to me, but also since I liked how he was sweet and gentle—not controlling and very different than Joe. I chose him because we had some history together and I felt safe

So—maybe not too wild, but for me this was totally out of character. I had been totally loyal to Joe because I considered marriage a solid commitment and had grown beyond it. So I thought searching for a man to fulfill me was the answer.

Tears welled up in my eyes the afternoon he took me back to the airport. My time with him actually mattered. Part of my heart was with Jeremy, but the other part was shut off, knowing that this would never work. I had a life in Las Vegas; he lived in San Francisco. And, after a marriage that felt suffocating and stifling, the last thing I wanted was to lock myself in another relationship, because I had a belief that all relationships would somehow chain me down, keeping me from flying like the butterfly I always knew I was.

Everything happens for a reason. I believe that Jeremy had been meant to travel on this journey with me. As little as we have known each other and as long as our time together has stretched, beneath it all I have always seen him for *who* he is and not *what* he does. He did me a huge favor and saved me, revived me and gave me the confidence to date again.

There are those certain people in life, amidst dramatic change or upheaval, who towel you off, rub you down and fill you up so you can go back out into the ring again. Jeremy was one of those special people and remains a good friend to this day, twenty-five years after we first meet in school.

Bursting My Joy Bubble

Ella, a former stripper and the on-site sales agent for my townhome, set me up with Jim because he was wealthy, handsome, experienced...blah, blah, blah. Jim fit the bill nicely, on paper. After our first date, I thought he was a bit abrasive—but really, what did I know? I was so inexperienced, and the only people I really knew were the educators I worked with.

On the Fourth of July, Jim threw a pool party at his house. Actually, it was a "pools" party, because his enormous custom-built home included not one but *three* resort-style pools. For weeks beforehand, I obsessed about my body and purged everything I ate. If I just stayed skinny enough, if I just looked beautiful enough, maybe Jim would decide he loved me. And I would have a successful, handsome man who could provide the finer things in life—the things my professor's salary denied me.

Internally conflicted, I appreciated the irony of these thoughts. Wasn't this exactly what my dad had wanted for me—and what I'd sworn I didn't want? Well, the difference was that I truly wanted both, not just one or the other—a man to love, someone who loved me dearly, and the financial freedom to do whatever we wanted, without using coupons every time we went out to eat.

The day came for the pool party and I sported the itsy-bitsy bikini well. Ella and I floated on a raft in the pool with Jim and a few "dancers" (a.k.a. strippers) and, suddenly, I just started laughing. This was surreal for a nerdy math teacher.

"What have you been smoking?" Jim asked irritably. "What the hell is so funny?" "They're joy bubbles," I told him, laughing even harder. "I'm just enjoying the moment."

He wasn't digging this at all and started shouting at me. I don't even remember what he said; the words didn't matter. I forced myself to stop and stifled my own laugh. After all, if I wanted him to love me, I had to conform to his wants.

Looking back, I am reminded of all the times my mother tried to burst my joy bubbles when I was a little girl. Happiness just isn't a comfortable state for some people, I guess.

Later that summer, Jim invited me to another pool party. I guess that, despite what he called "crazy cackling," I was good enough eye candy that he wanted me there. This time I made sure not to laugh out loud. I just smiled prettily and showed off my flat abs and tan legs. It wasn't anywhere near as much fun as the first time.

Needless to say, Jim and I didn't last. As the saying goes: "Dance like nobody's watching!"

Obviously, back then I hadn't yet embraced one of life's most important lessons: Always listen to your own voice, focus on what you makes *you* (and not other people) happy, and be who you really are—a divine child of God—without conceding your true self and becoming what somebody else wants or expects you to be. [See the back of the book for more about this in my book and course, *Finding Your J-Spot*, where I share how to live in the Joy Bubble. Go to www.yourjspot.com today to download your free 101 Joy Tips.]

CHAPTER 23

Year of Debauchery

O ver martinis, my friend, Doug, and I discussed my dating foibles. And, goodness gracious, did I love those mandarin martinis! Yum! We rated guys on an A- to-F grading scale and he schooled me. I marked Jim an A-minus and Doug said he would be lucky to get a C. Amazing! He was so brilliant and how green I was. Clueless in the beginning, what did I know about dating? After being locked away for seven years, very little, I had so much to learn in every way. Life is just that way isn't it?

After I ended things with Big Jim, I went on a full-fledge dating binge. Liberated, I wanted to try all thirty-one flavors—and did. It taught me a lot about myself: what I liked, what I didn't; what I wanted, and what I didn't. It also brought out all my worst fears. I had visions of my dad's porn stars, with perfect bellies and arched backs, parading around in their lingerie. Despite all my achievements, experiences and newfound ego, a part of me still felt I had to be a vision of perfection to get a man's love.

On the surface, it was all fun and games. I went to all the coolest pool parties, spent hours at the gym, and drove "topless" (the convertible top, of course) all over town, letting the sun kiss my skin. I stayed out all night on the weekends, going to after-hour clubs, where the real fun began, and reclaiming the college party years I never really had.

I hadn't touched a drink in seven years, since Joe was a former alcoholic, but I started indulging a bit just for fun. But food was another story. I'd binge by grabbing greasy junk from drive-through windows on my race home from the clubs and then throw up the whole masticated mess of fries, cake and booze into the toilet. I knew I was on a bad road—but I was convinced that, sooner or later, I was going to meet the man of my dreams and he'd restore me.

Because of him, I would want to be more than what I already was. He would fill the void I was pouring food and booze into and bring me the happiness I craved. In order to appeal to him, when the time came, I just had to stay thin and perfect enough. In the meantime, I was always dating five guys at a time. This was all new to me—getting the attention of men, keeping them on rotation, and working it.

My bulimia might have made my case extreme, but what I was thinking wasn't really all that different from what many women think: If we can just be pretty or sexy or perfect enough to land the right partner, we'll be happy. But the truth is, if we're not happy without a man, we're not going to be happy with one, either.

Love Burns

A year of binge dating came to an end and I finally realized how shallow and unfulfilling this venture was. I wanted something more, something deeper.

Things changed for me when I decided, at a friend's suggestion, to try online dating. It was easier than the whirlwind of blind dating and, after my initial hesitation—online dating? I thought that was only for people who ran out of options… I realized that there were a lot of interesting people out there I wasn't likely to connect with at swanky pool parties or rowdy bars.

My criteria were as follows: He had to be tall, have at least a master's degree and be "spiritually aware." He also had to earn at least as much as I did, as well as be a light drinker and non-smoker. Obviously, I still hadn't learned the difference between conditional love—what I was looking for at the time—and authentic, soulful love, or the kind I really needed and wanted.

Several hundred disappointing e-mails later, I found Mr. Burns.

His eyes were what got me. They were a bright blue-green and practically jumped off the screen. He was a graphic artist, successful and communicative. After exchanging a few e-mails, I gave him my phone number and we agreed to meet for drinks.

I didn't know it was him until he walked up to me. He was stylishly dressed in nice jeans and a black shirt. Taller and leaner than I'd expected (*Maybe too lean*, I thought; *I'll feel fat next to him*), he was balding but carried it well. All in all, he was a very attractive man.

We talked and talked, and the more we talked, the more we flowed together. (Or maybe it was the margarita bomb I was drinking. When in doubt, blame the booze!) We moved to the fireplace and got cozy. I felt like we understood one another.

At the end of the evening, he walked me to my car and landed the most magical kiss ever on me. I tingled all over and my heels lifted off the ground. I knew I just *had* to see him again. Swept off my feet like Cinderella, our next date was a black-tie event at the Turnberry Towers. My prince for the evening spun me on the dance floor, while I was dressed in a beautiful gown, like a fairy tale. We couldn't keep our hands off each other.

Encapsulated in an immense joy bubble, my whole world sparkled. This was as real as it had ever been for me. I'd never felt quite like this—even with Tom. When he took me home, I didn't want him to leave. We didn't go all the way (a girl has standards), but we stayed up all night, and he made me laugh so hard I thought I was going to pee in my pants.

Soon after that, we planned a trip to California to see my family.

"I want you to meet my daughter while we're there," he said.

Wait a minute. His *daughter?*

"Your profile on the dating site said you didn't have kids," I said. "How come you didn't tell me this before?"

"Well," he replied smoothly, "She's nineteen and in the military. Since she doesn't live at home anymore, I didn't think it was important to put it online."

Well, maybe not. But *honest* and *important* are not the same thing.

So, I met Brian's daughter, who lived on a base near San Diego, and his grandson, who was only a year old. It seemed so strange to me that Brian was a grandfather at the ripe old age of thirty-six—but it happens that way sometimes. And by the time we were done with our weekend on the beach at the Hotel Coronado, I'd forgiven him for lying to me.

Laughing so hard that I fell over in the grocery store aisle while we were buying chocolate, strawberries and whipped cream (cliché, I know), we were like little kids, totally unabashed.

A month later we went to New Orleans. Since Brian bought the tickets, I agreed to pay for food and drinks once we got there. We stayed on his friend's couch—which to me was just as good as the Coronado because I was with him.

One night, while his friend was out, Brian wanted to take some provocative photos of me. I wasn't entirely sold on the idea—but I let him snap a few shots. After all, I was in love with him, and he was in love with me.

Or so I thought.

His daughter was the first secret. His salary was the second. On his dating profile, he'd claimed to earn $100,000 per year but he actually made $40,000. I didn't really care whether he had money or not—but why had he lied?

When he got home from New Orleans, he asked me to pay him back for my plane ticket, which hadn't been the arrangement. When I said no—after all, I shelled out the dough while we were there—he charged outside with a golf club and threatened to put it through the windshield of my BMW if I didn't give him the cash *right now*. Oh, and not only would he smash up my car, he'd take those racy photos and e-mail them to all of my colleagues at the college.

As it turned out, he was desperate. He owed a lot of people a lot of money and wanted me to bail him out. I guess my profile made me seem like prime pickings—but the truth was, on my academic's salary, I didn't have a lot of extra money outside of my retirement savings.

If I'd had the money to give him, I might have done as he asked. After all, I was in love with him. But I was forced to take a step back and really look at what was happening. He might have gotten caught up in my joy bubble for a little while, but the truth was that he had ulterior motives from the beginning. Our whole affair seemed like one big lie.

Things cooled off after that and, thankfully, he never followed through on his threats to spread my naughty pictures around. When he had to have an operation on his knee at a V.A. hospital in California, I went with him, thinking that no one should have to go through a major surgery away from home with no one there for support.

He made some advances the night before the surgery, but I turned him down. My soul told me it was right that I should be there to support him, but I wasn't his girl anymore. His eyes just weren't as bright to me. (He had also Photo-shopped his online pictures to make them brighter. Another lie to add to the list.)

I was no longer in the joy bubble. When he came out of the surgery, I didn't just see anger and rejection in his eyes: I saw hate.

And still, I missed him when we parted ways.

Five years later, I bumped into him at a wine-tasting event and asked him how he was. He just shook his head, and I could feel his unhappiness. After a few awkward words, we both turned and walked away. But my heart still remembered that fairy tale and how many smiles he brought to my face. When I actually met up with him again ten years later, I discovered that there was a piece of me that had not totally put him to rest in my heart, which ultimately I had been measuring every other guy after him by.

It occurred to me how a synchronistic pattern was emerging in my life with men's names, such as Bob—my dad, Carla's father—and all the Brian's too—my brother, my mom's lover Brian B., and now Mr. Brian Burns. And, not only did my Brian have a brother Tim, like I did, but, incredibly, both Tim's have daughters named Chelsea. Was there a prompt here calling for my attention or was it all just coincidence?

As I sat and wrote out what I loved about Brian Burns and why I left him in the first place, I sat with four pages of negatives compared to only four lines of positives. That day I finally closed the chapter on my beloved Brian and totally released him from my heart for good and opened that space for my true twin flame.

If you're reading this, Mr. Burns, know that I loved you. I wish you the absolute best and hope you find your own J-Spot too.

CHAPTER 24

Praying to the Porcelain God

Since I'd become the Dean of Distance Education at the college, my boundaries had been tested in more ways than one. The lifelong academics weren't exactly thrilled at the prospect of having a twenty-eight-year-old woman as their superior, even if my "power" over them was mostly perceived rather than actual. Every time I met people outside my circle, I had to contend with their disbelief that a female dean with a Ph.D. could also be a sociable, fun person. And while I certainly wasn't opposed to hard work—I'd been working hard all my life—there were limits to what I was willing to put up with for an academic salary. I didn't want to become my job.

Doug planted a seed in my mind about a career in real estate and encouraged it to grow.

So I decided to make a change. I networked and asked questions all over the place. My brother, Brian, put me in touch with an old fraternity buddy who, in turn, referred me to some guys from Colliers International who were (coincidentally) going to be in Vegas for a convention in the very near future. If I was really interested in a career in commercial real estate, I could meet all of the key players in one weekend.

That's how I met John Green.

Hunched over a table in the Palms hotel bar, he was drawing a picture: a Gothic study of a man in torment, with a bleak cityscape in the background. As I studied it over his shoulder, the image confused me and even frightened me a little; it was so dark and sinister, like something you'd see in a horror flick. But when he turned around to look at me, I knew that what was on that paper wasn't inside him.

He looked so young. He wouldn't have gotten a second glance in any high school hallway. Small-boned, he was several inches shorter than me, with freckles across his nose and bristly brown hair. With his round glasses, he reminded me of Harry Potter. This couldn't be the big-time commercial real estate agent I was supposed to meet—could it?

"Want to sit down?" he asked.

I certainly did. He intrigued me, and not just because he was a big player in my potential field. When he smiled and I saw the tiny lines around his eyes, I realized that John was probably in his mid-thirties. And when we spoke, I don't even remember most of our conversation—only the amazing exchange of energy between us, like a tornado had blown through my body, leaving my molecules rearranged in its wake.

The only person who'd come close to making me feel this way was Brian Burns. But now I'd stopped dating altogether. No more thirty-one flavors; no more blind dates or Internet matches. I wasn't going to be with anyone else until I found *that* feeling again.

Brian had been a lover—but John was a stranger, a little boy-man in a hotel bar. How he conjured that *fullness* in me, I will never understand. But in the Bible, John the Baptist was the one who purified people before God. What John Green brought me, I can never repay.

"Who are you?" he asked, watching me curiously.

"I'm Cynthia Glickman, of course," I replied. I'd told him that when I'd introduced myself.

But he continued to stare at me, and I reconsidered the question. Who *was* Cynthia Glickman? Did I even know?

I was calling out for help every day. No, I was *begging* for help, on my knees before the porcelain god, purging myself into oblivion. I was getting beat up at work daily, coming home to my lonely townhome every night. Since I wasn't going out drinking every weekend anymore, eating became my only escape—and yet, I was finally beginning to realize just how much of a toll this destructive behavior was taking on me physically, emotionally and spiritually.

And every night I huddled over the toilet, cringing at the disgusting mess in the bowl, I promised myself that I would stop and that I would never be in this moment again. And yet, night after night, there I was, thinking the same thoughts.

This is stupid. This is disgusting. I am disgusting. I hate this. I hate myself. Please, God. Help me!

Hollow and emptied, with bloodshot eyes and that horrible taste in the back of my throat, I would wander out to my patio and have conversations with God as I looked up at the stars in the dark sky. I asked the questions I'd always asked but had always ignored the answers to.

What am I doing here? What is the point of this life?
Who am I?

"I'm Cynthia Glickman," I said again, more firmly this time.

John didn't accept my simple answer. He narrowed his eyes at me a little, and I felt like I'd failed an exam. I left in a bit of a huff and, as I drove home, I could feel my frustration building. Over and over, I asked myself that question, looking for the answer I should have given—the answer which, I reminded myself acidly, I would have known right away if I'd only been smart enough or connected enough.

That night I dreamed up a storm. And when I woke up, I knew with absolute certainty: *I am Cynthia Glickman.*

An amazing revelation, I know. But what did it mean?

Next time I saw John, he asked me again: "Who are you?"

"I am Cynthia Glickman," I said. And this time, I meant it.

"Okay. Do you think you are alive or dead?"

I wasn't falling for a trick question this time. "What do you mean?" I asked, thinking I could buy some time to come up with a good answer.

"What I've discovered," he said, looking at me over the tops of his round glasses, "is that we're already dead."

That one left me a bit baffled. At first I'd seen light in him; now I saw that there was darkness, too. I'd gathered, in our prior conversations, that he'd had some sort of near-death experience but when I asked him to tell me about it, he got very tight-lipped.

When I was with John, it was like we existed in a parallel universe. I think I fell in love with him a little. It wasn't romantic love—it was more, on my part, like the love of a child for a really cool older sibling. When we were together, he would tell me things like, "Slow down. Pay attention to the details. Everything has significance."

One day, when I was visiting him at his house, he pulled me into his roommate's bedroom. Above the bed hung a crazy painting of men walking with chains around their ankles. All the figures looked gray and distorted, like they'd been dead a long time, but just hadn't realized it yet.

"What do you think this means, Cynthia? What's the significance?"

I thought for a long time. Then, as I slowed down my mind and paid attention, the answer came. "It's how people live their lives. They're chained. They're sleepwalking."

He smiled at me, and I knew I'd passed his test.

A month or so later, he asked me again. "Who are you?"

I blurted out the first words that came into my head. "I am a loving, giving being. I am a child of God."

"Yes, that's exactly who you are." Those mesmerizing, little-boy eyes sparkled at me, and I giggled. I was a child of God, and he was a child of God, and we were okay, just the way we were.

And then, he said, "You asked for me, you know."

I thought about it for a minute and I realized that I the truth of his remark. Hanging over the toilet, praying for someone to come along to show me a better way... Was John the answer to my prayers?

He may have had a dark side, but John Green awakened me to my light. He helped me find so many of the answers I'd been searching for. After I met him, my whole world began to shift. Suddenly, my urge to binge and purge was gone. Poof!—like magic. I was a child of God, and there was no need to harm myself any longer. John had baptized me with his questions, crystallizing my thought—and, as my soul cleared, my body demanded purification as well. I began to eat more in alignment with what my body needed: no more chips and cake and cookies.

I went from drinking a twelve-pack of Diet Coke every day to drinking only water. You could say that I lost my taste for things that destroyed me.

I'd like to believe that I have always been connected to the universal flow. I may not have been aware of it—but, after my conversations with John, I gained the sense that everything that happened to me in my life and everything I'd created had been preparing me for this moment, right now. After all, *now* was all I had.

Show me where you want me to go, I told the Universe.

And the Universe answered in no uncertain terms: "You are done with academia."

I'd been dealing with the stress and doubt for years, but what really pushed me over the edge was what appeared to me to be some sexual harassment on the job. I was only age twenty-nine to his fifty, and I'm sure he felt it was his right to say whatever he pleased. You know, the usual "he said, she said" type of situation. It didn't help that, when I brought the issue to my superiors, they told me that I should dress more modestly and get over it.

After that, I was done. I'd worked my whole life to be more than a sex object. I wasn't in the porn industry; I didn't take my clothes off for a living; and I wasn't going to be treated this way The time had come to walk out the door gracefully with my head held high and never look back. I felt a lot like I'd felt on the day I convinced my school superintendent to let me graduate early. There was a new path in front of me: I just had to have the courage to step onto it.

I had six months and just enough severance pay to make my real estate career work. I already had my license: I'd worked on that while I was talking to the commercial real estate people the year before. All I had to do was choose the right company and dive in head-first.

I ran into my gym buddy, James, in the bookstore one day. He found me browsing in the self-help section.

"Why don't you read something real?" he asked me teasingly, drawing me toward the real estate section.

The book I ended up with was about how to become a millionaire in real estate in three years or less. That night, as I started reading, a picture came into my mind. I could do this. I could be wildly successful on my own terms. I learned about land acquisition, rentals and residential properties. In addition to helping other people buy and sell property, I could do some buying and selling of my own.

The company I'd chosen didn't have a training program for new agents, so I had to do my own research. I also used the connections I'd made in Vegas over the last couple of years to get the word out about my career change. People I'd met at pool parties, at the gym, waiters and waitresses, former academic colleagues—they all heard about Cynthia Glickman's new venture.

Although I was excited, this transition wasn't easy for me at first. I had to get over my ego. Even if it didn't pay that well, a dean's position was a prestigious one and not easy to attain—especially for a woman under thirty. I'd worked for years to earn my Ph.D., and now I was throwing away all that education to be a Realtor. Sure, my math skills would be useful, especially when consulting with clients about investments and returns, but it wasn't like I needed a doctorate to do the job.

But soon I realized that I wasn't just any old agent; I was a real estate professional. I didn't just sell houses; I helped people become wealthy through smart investing. As my pride and confidence grew, I shifted my perspective. Tapping my raw skill and savvy, within just a few years, I was worth millions. I owned my own realty company and had more than thirty agents working for me. I had finally created the level of success and security I'd been looking for.

In this process, I learned that we have the power to create our realities. Just prior to launching this career, I wrote on my mirror that I was going to earn $300,000 in real estate, which was ten times my academic salary. The first year I earned $298,000 and the following year I went beyond, reaching my original goal by tripling that. We can train ourselves. It was a hell of a ride and it wasn't always easy, but once I'd decided to be successful, success came to find me. I felt like I was living proof of the Law of Attraction.

I just wasn't as successful in love.

Never Date a Client

Three years into my real estate career, Bob was referred to me by a lender I knew from the gym. He was pre-approved and wanted to start investing. When I spoke to him on the phone, he was all over the place and had no idea where he was going with his investment ideas. He only knew that he wanted to buy a condo.

We agreed that we should meet in person. I usually asked my clients to come to me but since the properties he was considering were close to his home, I agreed to meet him out in Green Valley. I'd gotten into the habit of chugging down a big bottle of water before work in the morning, so by the time I arrived to pick him up I really had to pee. At ten o'clock sharp, I knocked on his door. It took him forever to answer, and I was doing a little dance on his doorstep.

When he finally opened the door, Bob's eyes bugged out of his head. I don't know who he was expecting, but I don't think it was me. The visual effect for me was startling; his eyes were already sort of protruding, big and nervous in his face. But they were also a deep blue, and contrasted nicely with his dark, closely-trimmed hair.

"I'm Cynthia Glickman," I said. "And I need to use your bathroom."

He pointed in the general direction of the toilet and may have stammered something.

I dashed through the house. *Definitely a bachelor pad*, I thought, processing the barrenness and sterility of the place. *Maybe that's why I make him nervous.*

We got in the car and drove out to the property Bob was considering. He told me that he sold cars for a living, had a daughter and two sons and wasn't married. (Well, that much was obvious!) I remember thinking that he was pretty immature for a forty-something-year-old man.

At one point, his phone rang. He'd gotten this woman a good deal on a car, he told me; now, she wouldn't leave him alone. He kept glancing over at me as if he expected this to produce some sort of reaction.

I didn't care: I was there for business. But, hey, if he wanted to talk, I'd listen.

We looked at a few condo units in the development. Sitting on a couch in the first unit, he told me he was planning to invest with two of his friends. "That's great," I said. "Investing in real estate is almost always a smart thing to do." We joked about guys we both knew from the gym—especially the guy with a big fish tattoo on his arm. He was a Pisces, and so was Bob.

At the next condo, he told me that the reason his buddies wanted to buy the condo was so that they could bring girls there without their significant others finding out. "But that's not my style," he assured me. "That's just them."

"Whatever you three do is your business," I told him. "I'm not here to judge. The bottom line is that this is a good investment opportunity for you, and I'm here to facilitate that."

But what I was really thinking was: *Whatever, buddy. If you're hanging out with guys like that, you probably have something in common.*

On the way back to his house, he pulled out his phone again. "Oh, isn't that cute," he said. "I just got a text message from my daughter. 'You are the best daddy in the world!'"

I never found out if he really got that message. I *did* find out, later, that his daughter wasn't allowed to send texts on her phone. I think maybe he staged the whole thing, in typical sleazy car salesman fashion, to make me like him.

When we pulled up to his house, I asked his opinion about the properties we'd seen.

"I'll have to run it by my boys before I do anything," he said.

I drew him a picture of the houses, and showed him how he could become a millionaire by buying condos.

"Yeah, that's exactly what I was thinking."

After that day, we talked often. He had all kinds of grand ideas about where and how he wanted to invest, only some of which made logical sense. When he would try to tease and flirt with me, I would joke right back. I didn't think too much about it, because I'm generally friendly and outgoing, and I didn't get to where I was by being rude to clients. He talked too fast and still seemed sort of nervous. He jumped around in the conversation. In retrospect, he might have been on some sort of drug.

The weeks went on. Now, when he got me on the phone, he didn't want to let me hang up. When it came to business talk, I liked to be direct and to the point and then move on. He required a lot more than that, but I didn't really mind, because he was kind of funny in his weird, nervous way. He wasn't at all my type—a body builder and a car salesman? Not my usual taste—but I didn't push him away. I had just come out of a painful breakup and the attention was a welcome distraction.

By the time we arranged for me to come back out to Green Valley and show the condo units to one of his buddies, I was pretty sure Bob was interested in me. I met him and his friend at Gold's Gym and we set off. I sat in the front passenger's seat, so it only seemed natural that I should chat with the friend who was driving.

"What do you think would be a good offer on the first property?" the friend asked, after we'd seen the condos.

I gave him the figure. "But we're getting multiple offers on this property, so if you're interested, we should submit your offer as soon as possible."

"I need to talk about it with my girlfriend and explore a few more options, but it sounds like this might work. Give me your number, and I'll let you know."

I rattled off my numbers, because that's what you do when you want potential clients to be able to reach you. Apparently, Bob didn't see it that way. He got quieter and quieter the longer we drove. When we got back to the gym, he jumped out of the car without saying goodbye.

"What was that about?" I asked the friend.

"I don't know. I think he had to go to work."

I called later to check on him, and he said pretty much the same thing. "Had to get to work early." But I had a terrible, anxious feeling that I'd done something wrong. I reviewed the day in my head, looking for possible mistakes. The only thing I'd done was try to stop the two of them from dragging their feet. Had I been too pushy? Why was this bothering me so much?

Later, I found out that Bob had been jealous. I'd been talking to his friend instead of him, and in his mind, that was intolerable. But then, I'd called to check on him, so I must really have cared.

And so the drama began.

Lost Fortune

While all of this was happening, I lost my dog, Fortune, an adorable Shih Tzu. He was a bit of a free spirit; given the smallest chance, he would dart out the front door and take off. He'd often be a mile away before you could catch up to him.

Most of the time, I kept Fortune on a leash. But one day I met my friend, Jeff, for a hike at Red Rock Canyon and, once we were far enough away from the road, we decided to let the dogs off their leads. We roamed around chatting, soaking up the sunshine and watching the dogs play. We might have stayed out there all day, but the clouds rolled in and it started to sprinkle, so we headed back toward the cars.

Prosper, my Pomeranian, came trotting right back to my side. But when I called Fortune back, he just stopped where he was and looked back at me as if to say, "I'm outta here, Mama."

Then, he turned and sprinted toward the road.

There was no way I could catch him. And in my heart, I knew he was gone—even before the eighteen-wheeler came roaring toward us. But I ran anyway.

The semi managed to swerve out of the way—but the smaller truck behind him thumped right over my little Fortune.

I turned my back. I couldn't even look.

The guy driving the truck skidded to a halt and jumped out to apologize. "It's not your fault," I sobbed. "It's okay."

Jeff was crying, too. It had been his idea to take the dogs off the leashes, and he felt responsible. We were both silent as he drove me to the vet's office. Even little Prosper was quiet. We dropped off Fortune's body, and Jeff (still feeling guilty) paid for the service. Then he brought me home, and I sat on my bed in the quiet.

The way Fortune had looked back at me... He'd known he was checking out. It had been his time to go.

I called my assistant to tell her I wouldn't be coming into the office. "Oh, my God," she said. "I wish I had read you your horoscope earlier. This might never have happened!"

"What are you talking about?" I asked.

"'June 19, 2005,'" she read. "'Money is important, but it isn't everything, and what happens around the time of Wednesday's full moon will remind you of this fact in a way you cannot ignore.' I wish I would have had time to read this to you before you left!"

I'm not sure this would have stopped me from taking that hike with Jeff. But my dog's name was Fortune, and I couldn't ignore the parallel. I was pretty sure I knew that money wasn't everything, but apparently the Universe thought I needed another reminder.

That night I had a dream. Fortune came back, running toward me, tail wagging—but once he was standing at my feet, he transformed into a little boy. I wasn't sure if that was his soul coming back to show me that he was in a better place, but when I woke up, I felt totally at peace. I could move on, because it was destiny. And, even if it made me sad, this was the way things were meant to be.

From that day on, Prosper would cry when I left the house. He would dart out the front door between my legs and stand beside the car, begging me to take him along. It was heartbreaking and, after a full week of this, I decided it was time to find Prosper a buddy.

I found a beautiful girl at the pound. She was supposed to be a Pekinese, but I think she had some Shih Tzu in her. She was just about Prosper's size and had the most beautiful little face. I figured her crankiness was just due to the fact that she'd been living at the pound for a while—but when I took her to the groomers a week later, she started snapping at Prosper for no reason. When I tried to intervene, she sank her sharp little teeth right into my hand.

I started to cry. Part of it was pain and shock—but mostly, I knew what this meant for her. I couldn't keep a dog that bit people or might hurt Prosper while I was gone. She would have to go back to the pound.

I'm not sure why I called Bob. At the time, I guess he seemed like the one to turn to with this.

"You have to take her back," he said. "And you have to file a report."

I cried harder. Once I signed that report, the poor girl was marked for death. But I couldn't risk her being adopted by a family with small children, either.

Needless to say, this was not my favorite day.

A few days later, Prosper was crying again. Rather than take another chance at the pound, I decided to find a puppy. Bob told me he wanted to buy the puppy for me, but I didn't want anyone else to choose Prosper's new companion. I found a woman selling Shih Tzus in the Green Valley area. Bob met me at her house.

"You're really lucky that I was able to do this today," he told me. "I'm missing the gym for this."

Yes, Bob was a bit anal about his schedule. For a moment, I was reminded of Joe, and his rigid time management.

When he opened my car door and saw Prosper, my ten-pound fluff ball, for the first time, he said, "That dog is *so* you." "Umm…? Thanks.

The breeder's house was incredibly dirty (I guess that's what you get when you have dozens of dogs running around), but the pups were beautiful and healthy. I was playing with the rambunctious ones, but Bob picked one of the smaller, quieter ones.

"You'll see," he told me. "This little guy will be full of personality."

I named him Happy Pants. It was a reminder to me that it doesn't matter how "prosperous" you are, or how much money you have; ultimately, you have to be happy.

Once I got Happy settled in the car with Prosper, there was a bit of an awkward silence. Bob just stood there, like he was waiting for something. He'd chipped in a few hundred dollars for Happy, which

I hadn't asked him to do. Maybe he wanted some further of expression of gratitude?

"Do you want me to take you for coffee or something?" I asked.

"No. I'm on a schedule. I have to get to the gym." He took a few steps away, and said over his shoulder, "Glad you like the puppy."

I wasn't sure what he was trying to tell me. Somehow, I'd offended him again and I had no idea how or why. A week later, we were talking every day. On a whim, I stopped by the gym to say hello on my way home. We sat outside on a bench. It was the first time I'd seen him in a muscle shirt. Oddly, he was a little shy about it, like there was something he didn't want me to see about him. Or maybe I just didn't react the way he'd expected. He had a nice physique, but I wasn't into the bodybuilder look. He didn't really do it for me.

I didn't move when he put his hand on my knee, and I guess that was all the encouragement he needed. We chatted for a few more minutes, and then he kissed me.

He isn't the one, I thought. *He just isn't the one.*

"Wow," he said when he pulled away. "That's magic. Don't you feel the magic?"

I didn't. I knew what magic was; I'd felt it when I kissed Brian Burns. This wasn't even in the same ballpark.

But Bob seemed like a nice guy. How many of us have mistakenly qualified Mr. Wrong as Mr. Right with that simple presumption?

But Bob had also helped me buy a dog. And he called me every day, even if he wasn't following through on his real estate purchase. He obviously liked me. But was that enough to start something? I didn't know. With my earlier upbringing, I still remained unsure of myself in relationships and lacking in confidence as well as feeling loved. Despite my career success, when it came to love I was still looking in the wrong places, or maybe just with the wrong perspective.

After that, I started getting text messages every night. "Sweet dreams, Peaches. Thinking of you." It didn't make a whole lot of sense to me, since he'd never asked me out on formal date. There was no courtship at all. He just started acting like we were together. Soon, "sweet dreams" had progressed to "I love you."

There was the next red flag. How can somebody profess love when he doesn't even know you? It seemed ridiculous. But knowing that someone loved me warmed my heart. I mean, who doesn't want to be loved?

I told Bob that if he really felt that way, he needed to take me out somewhere. Dinner, drinks…Something. We made plans, which he canceled. He showed up out of the blue while my assistant and I were having lunch, which was awkward, since I didn't know whether I should hug him or shake his hand. When we finally went to Claim Jumper on a Friday night, he was so nervous and awkward that I wished I'd never insisted on a date. Rather than solidify our relationship, it reminded me of all the reasons he and I didn't match up.

I should have known then that something was up. My instincts were still screaming, *He's not the one, Cyn!* But I couldn't see any real reason not to test the waters despite all those warning signals. After all, he was obviously into me, and the attention was flattering. I was just being silly.

Like so many women who ignore their intuition and make similar wrong choices, I craved the attention and needed to feel loved and appreciated and even adored and desired— you know, like all those babes and the little girl at the porn convention. And how many people of both sexes make foolish choices for the sake of love? Sure, we've all done it, but the important thing to remember is the underlying reason *why* we do it.

I went to visit my mother in L.A., where she'd been living for the last few years.

"I met this great guy, Mom. He's really been there for me. Isn't it great that there are still nice guys out there?"

My mother looked at me, and her eyes went a little unfocused. "I see him with another woman. He's married, or has a serious girl-friend. He's not for real." Carla was now a seer!

I was furious. I thought my mom was just being her usual negative self, projecting her dislike of men, in general, and men who liked me in particular.

On my way home, I called Bob and told him about the conversation. "You are single, right?" I asked with a laugh. "Carla's just crazy."

Dead quiet. Then, he muttered, "Yeah. She's just crazy."

Again, I ignored yet another red flag—the eerie silence or dead pause. I should have listened to it, but I wanted to believe him. And I certainly didn't want Carla to be right for once. I wasn't in love with Bob, but the thought of him being with someone else upset me. *Maybe he isn't the right man for me now*, I thought, *but given the opportunity, he could become that man.*

So I asked him again. "Are you single?"

"Yes, I am. Of course I am."

Liar. Liar liar liar liar liar, shouted a voice deep inside me.

"I'm glad, Bob."

CHAPTER 25

Oh My God, I've Become My Mother!

I had stepped into the Abyss of Bob.

He claimed that he didn't want to introduce me to his kids because he wanted to be sure I would stick around. On the weekends, he could only come over after 7 p.m. on Sundays—but he didn't always show up. I would get prettied up to see him and then sit on the couch, waiting… and waiting. Sometimes I wouldn't even get a call, only a text message. "Sorry, can't make it. Sweet dreams, Peaches."

When I would finally talk to him, I would be so upset that I could barely get the words out. "I was waiting for you," I'd sob. "Why didn't you call?"

"You don't understand," he'd reply. "It tears me up to leave my kids. It's not you, baby. I just don't want to talk to anybody after I leave them. They want me to stay so badly."

And what could I say to that? That I needed him to put me first? Who could even think of making that demand?

I wanted to feel loved but all I was getting was pain. The back-and-forth was the hardest part. One day I was getting texts saying, "I love you," and the next I would get screamed at for being an insensitive bitch. There was no continuity; there never is in the passive-aggressive psyche. Sound *familiar*?

It got to the point where I only saw him when I made the effort to stop by the dealership, or when he came around on a Sunday night.

That's why I was surprised to get a call from his second cell phone at 7:45 a.m. on a Sunday, just as I was headed to my yoga class.

I'd never stopped to think that it was odd that he had one phone he used to call me and on he used to text me. I just figured one was a business line from the car dealership, and the other was his personal line. Why pay for text messaging if you don't have to, right?

I answered the call. "Good morning, Sweetness!"

A woman answered me in a tight voice. "This isn't Bob."

Oh, boy.

"My name is Michelle, and Bob and I are engaged to be married. He proposed to me in Hawaii." There was a pause. "Are you sleeping with him?"

I had no idea what to say. For a moment, I had the insane thought that I should lie, so he wouldn't get in trouble. Finally, I told her, "I'm so sorry. But if this is the man you're planning to marry, you really should reconsider. Because he's attempting to have a relationship with me, too."

Vamps, Tramps and the "Other" Woman

I remembered his trip to Hawaii. Bob said he was going with friends—but while he was there, he would only communicate with me through text messages. Not once in those two weeks did he pick up his phone. He was messing around on me. Worse yet, I was actually the other woman. Oh, shit! But a big part of me still refused to believe it was as bad as it looked. He loved me; he'd said so. And I so badly needed to be loved.

Looking back, I wonder how I could have been such a strong and successful woman, in so many respects, and yet have been so deluded and wrapped up in this man. From the start, my instincts told me he wasn't the right one. And yet, there was something so *familiar* about him and about the dynamics of our relationship. I settled right into it, like pulling on a ratty old pair of jeans.

Of course I didn't realize then that it was all a reflection of my parents' stormy marriage and the neglected little girl, so desperate for love, appreciation and attention. Little Cindy was alive and well in this adult woman, despite all her career and financial successes, still looking for some shred of affection. And I knew I wasn't the only person on the planet with this dilemma.

I didn't hear a peep out of Bob for a month. I deleted his number from my phone and tried to get on with my life. I had a multimillion dollar business to run, after all. And then, one night, my phone buzzed on the nightstand. I picked it up, and there he was: Bob K. Apparently, I'd forgotten to take him out of my speed dial.

I hung up on him. Five seconds later, he called me back. "You know you missed me," he said.

Arrogant bastard. But, of course, he was right. Why? How could anyone miss a liar and a cheat? "How's your fiancée?"

"I was never engaged to Michelle. That was a bunch of bullshit. I never asked her to marry me. She's a nut job. And it's over now, so it doesn't matter."

"Then why was she at your house at 7 a.m. on a Sunday, calling me from your phone?"

He was quiet for a few seconds. "She was dropping off a check for a car I bought for her under my name. We dated a while ago, but I ended it. She had bad credit, so I helped her out."

Yeah, I thought. *You're just that kind of guy.*

But my heart softened a little, because I wanted so badly to believe him. I managed to avoid him for a while, but he was persistent. I told him he'd have to step up and be a better man if he wanted me back. He promised that he would try.

Every day he made me cry. But I couldn't summon up the courage to kick him out of my life, because what if he really did love me? What if by saying goodbye to him, I was saying goodbye to my last chance at love? I hadn't exactly had great luck in relationships up to this point, and who was to say that things would ever get better? All relationships required compromise, right?

That I didn't need a man to be whole had never occurred to me.

In my mind, I wasn't enough all by myself: I had to have a partner, a "better half." I wanted my man to adore me, to recognize that I was special and wonderful. Most of all, I wanted Bob to love me enough to straighten up and become the man I believed he was capable of being. If he loved me that much, that would be enough.

But after our initial reconnection, he stopped making an effort. He would make plans with me and fail to show. He would disappear for days and refuse to pick up his phone. When he came back, he'd bury me in guilt for my suspicions. The worse he treated me, the more I began to care about him.

He became an addiction. The more he made me suffer, the more I wanted to win his approval. In some ways, he took the place of my bulimia. Instead of eating, I would binge on drama and unrequited love and then purge myself with tears.

One night, I made dinner plans with a male friend. It wasn't a date; he and I had done a lot of business together and, since I hadn't seen him in a while, we decided it was time to catch up. Bob hadn't tried to make plans with me (and if he had, he probably wouldn't have kept them anyway), and so I didn't tell him where I was going.

During dinner, my phone rang. I let it go to voicemail, because it's not only rude but also unprofessional to take personal calls during a dinner meeting. When my friend went to the bathroom, I sent Bob a text to say, "I'm at dinner with a friend. Call you later."

I don't know what set him off, but over the next hour I got a dozen voicemail messages and even more texts: "You fucking whore. You little cunt. You'll just give up the pussy to anyone, won't you?"

I was horrified. I had no idea what to do. Panicked, I cut my dinner short and literally ran out of the restaurant. I was dialing his number before I even got to my car.

"Dinner with a friend?" he sneered. "You're out with a guy. I know it."

"Yes, he's a guy," I said sheepishly. "But it's totally innocent. There's nothing going on. I swear to God!"

He wouldn't listen to a thing I said. He was so convinced that I was cheating on him that I began to doubt my own motivations. Had I really just wanted to have dinner with my friend? Or was I looking for attention?

He called me a few more awful names and then hung up on me. I called him back; no answer. I sent a text: "Please listen to me. I wouldn't be out to dinner with another man if you were around."

Wait—where did that come from? I'd just been having an innocent dinner! How was this becoming my fault? Why was I willing to make it my fault?

God, I was so sick of crying. Was I ever going to be able to have a healthy, normal relationship? Why couldn't I make him happy? I would love and adore and be loyal to him until the day I died, if he would only love me back. But I kept showing up to this party alone.

"What's wrong with me?" I asked my steering wheel with tears streaming down my face.

The steering wheel didn't answer.

"What the hell is wrong with you?"

Where had I heard that before?

Bob didn't speak to me for days—which was, of course, the worst thing he could have done to me. He dug the knife in deep and then left me there to languish. Every night I snuggled into bed with my dogs and cried myself to sleep. Even little Happy Pants seemed to feel my pain.

Part of me was disgusted with myself for putting up with this. It was stupid of me to love this guy. He was a creep, a liar and a cheat. I hadn't liked him the day I met him. How had I fallen into this mess? I felt like I was stuck on one of those spinning amusement park rides. I wanted to get off, but it wouldn't stop. When it finally did stop and when there was finally a break in the action, I would beg for one more ride, because maybe this time it wouldn't make me want to throw up. (Funny, that insanity has been defined as repeating the same actions over and over, expecting a different result.)

A few months later, I went out to dinner with a group of friends. I was dressed well, in a long black skirt, black blazer and a black lace top. It was a Saturday night, and I knew that Bob worked late on Saturdays, so I decided to stop by the car dealership once dinner was over.

When I got there, the main lights were off, but there was a light on in the showroom. I was excited and a little nervous. Bob had never seen me dressed up like this; he always saw me in my work clothes or my gym gear. Tonight, though, he was going to take one long look at me and fall in love all over again.

As I walked up to the side door, I saw him sitting at the manager's desk. When he looked up and saw me, I grinned from ear to ear, as if to say, *Here I am! Don't I look fabulous?*

He didn't smile back. As I approached, he glared at me with his eyes bugging out. "Who did you go to dinner with this time, you fucking whore?"

I froze. *Please, not this again.* "I went out with some friends," I told him, trying to keep calm. "I left early so I could come see you."

"Bullshit. You always say you're out with friends, but I know you're with another man."

My heart sunk into the pit of my belly. "How could you think such a thing?" I whispered. Most Friday and Saturday nights I spent alone, waiting for phone calls that didn't come.

I knew then that I'd made a mistake in showing up here. I'd wanted him to see me all made up and think I looked pretty. I wanted him to recognize that it wasn't fair that I spent every Saturday night alone. I was a little girl in her best dress, wanting the popular boy to desire her. I was that little girl at the porn convention again, thinking that, if I looked beautiful, I could feel adored like all those women the men fawned over.

"You tramp," Bob hissed. He stood up and leaned over his desk. "Get out of here. I don't fucking want you."

Everything seemed to stop. His words cut me to the bone. I wanted to be strong, to hide this hurt from him, but the tears just welled up and started streaming down my face. Finally, I got my body to move and turned toward the doors. I didn't try to get a last word in; I had no words left.

That walk of shame was excruciating. I could feel his eyes on me the whole time. But even that wasn't enough to send me screeching out of there. Shaking, I waited by my car to see if he would follow me out. Maybe he would come out and wrap me up in his arms and tell me he loved me, that he'd just had a bad day and hadn't meant any of it.

But that didn't happen and, once more, I was driving home in tears, asking my steering wheel, *What the hell is wrong with me?*

My brothers were both married with families of their own—but here I was, thirty-something and childless, chasing a man who didn't want me. I seemed to be able to do everything else on par with—or even better than—the rest of the world: I had a Ph.D., ran a successful company and made piles of money. But when it came to love, I didn't have a clue. I was broken—incapable of love, just like my mother always said I was. The final jabs that night were all mine, as if Bob hadn't beaten me up enough.

Sure enough, the text messages started up again a few days later. "Sweet dreams, Peaches."

Give me a break!

For weeks, I just deleted the texts and tried to move on. *One day, he looks at me like I'm a dog who just shit on his floor—and now he loves me? Is this guy insane?*

Yes!

I don't know exactly when I first started drawing parallels between my relationship and my parents' marriage, but it started when I realized that Bob was my dad's name. Well, of course, that was obvious—but knowing and *really knowing* are two different things.

I remembered the time my dad called me a whore because he didn't like me being with Tom. The feeling had been the same: utter shame and a panicked desire to fix whatever I needed to fix in order to be loved again. Just like Bob, my dad would stop calling me for days or weeks at a time when he was mad at me, leaving me to stew in uncertainty. Eventually, when I was in college, he'd cut me off altogether. He'd *abandoned* me. Just like Bob had.

Only now was I finally able to see a pattern showing up so blatantly that had stayed with me over all these years and that was one of being left behind… I had always felt totally ignored, neglected and even abandoned at times. So I kept drawing in relationships in which men would leave me to go on "vacations" and leave me behind completely... while they were off with other women!

That night at the car dealership, Bob really nailed home the point for me. I relived the pain of my dad's anger in living color. Just like Bob, my dad had been irrational in his judgments of me. I wasn't a whore; I didn't take off my clothes for a living, or have sex with strange men for a camera. I just wanted to be loved.

My addiction to Bob was a mirror of my parents' relationship. Most of the time, they hated one another—and yet, for the longest time, they couldn't break away. In this scenario, I was playing my father's role—sitting back, taking the verbal punches, trying to find a way to control the situation, or at least get through the day without an explosion.

Bob was my mother—unpredictable and irrational—switching back and forth between accusation, love, manipulation and distrust at lightning speed.

I was back in my childhood all over again. Once more, I was stupid little Cindy, who didn't know how to love or feel wanted, adored and appreciated.

And I still couldn't let him go.

As hard as it may be to believe, I held out for a few months after the incident at the dealership. But the more I tried to ignore him, the more he latched onto me. The text messages continued. Finally, I broke down and let him take me out for my birthday.

Still harboring bitter resentment, I asked him, "How's Michelle?" I was certain he was still with her. There couldn't be any other reason that he'd ditched me on so many Friday and Saturday nights.

"It's over with Michelle," he promised. And to prove it, he spent the entire weekend with me. At first, I felt triumphant. *We've been through some hard times*, I said to myself, *but now he's really with me.*

Still, I couldn't help but play detective while he was in the bathroom. I opened his overnight bag to look at the toothbrush he used. Sure enough, it said "Dr. Miller." There was an address as well, which I wrote down, all the while thanking God for dentists' marketing ploys.

I knew that Michelle worked for a dentist, because Bob's ex-wife, Sandy, had told me. For several months, I'd been tutoring their daughter, Krystal, in math, and Sandy and I had gotten friendly. Well, maybe not friendly, exactly. I think she felt bad for me, duped as I was by her obnoxious ex.

I went to Dr. Miller's office early in the morning, hoping I could catch Michelle before any patients arrived. The last thing I wanted to do was make a scene; I was already humiliated enough.

When I walked in, a tall, slender woman came out from behind the receptionist's desk. She had thick brown hair and warm brown eyes framed by stunningly long lashes.

I was instantly intimidated. "Could we speak outside?" I asked meekly.

She stared at me for a minute. "You must be Cynthia," she said.

Yes, that was me. Cynthia Glickman. But no longer the Cynthia who'd been revealed by John Green. No longer the radiant, empowered child of God. I'd stepped out of myself.

Michelle knew all about me—my real estate business, what kind of car I drove, the names of my dogs. According to Bob, I was a psycho stalker, an agent he'd refused to hire who now wouldn't leave him alone. I found that funny, since the Michelle he'd described to me had been a desperate customer who couldn't stay away from him. I was beginning to grasp the parallels.

"Are you still seeing him?" I asked her.

"What do you mean? We're engaged! He gave me a five-carat ring, you know, in Hawaii." I looked down at her hand, and she blushed. "I forgot to put it on this morning. I was in such a rush, I even forgot my makeup." Was that supposed to make me feel better? Even bare-faced, she was gorgeous.

"Honestly, I'm done with him. I'm sick of this bullshit. I was visiting my parents in Utah this weekend, and I knew something was up when he wouldn't answer my calls."

I was crushed. My birthday weekend was supposed to be special—but he'd only been with me because Michelle was out of town.

The tears were on their way again. "I'm so sorry," I said.

She shrugged. "Me, too."

Bob, of course, denied the whole thing. "It wasn't like that," he said. "We didn't really get engaged. She saw the ring in a store while I was buying a necklace for myself, and I got it for her. It isn't even real; it's just a cubic zirconium. When she put it on, she said to me, 'Well, I guess we're as good as married now.'"

Where had I heard that one before? Oh, yes. It was the same line Joe had used on me.

Was Michelle like Bob's Joe? Was she just a comfortable place for him to go? But the cat was out of the bag on the Hawaii trip and, if he could lie to me about that for so long, he could lie about other things, too.

The King of Disappointment

I felt sorry for myself—but I felt worse for Michelle. If they really had been engaged, he'd betrayed her by screwing around with me, and not the other way around. I wasn't as much a victim as she was because, although I wanted Bob to love me, we'd never actually made a commitment.

Both Michelle and I swore him off for a while. He started texting both of us that he loved us. "You are my heart and soul," he would tell her—and minutes later, I would get the same message. He was desperately trying to hang onto something, like a lost puppy chasing cars down the road.

Michelle and I were both hurt and amused by the whole thing. We checked in with one another periodically. We weren't friends— more like uneasy allies. But seeing "my" texts sent to her phone helped me keep my head clear.

"He really is the King of Disappointment, isn't he?" she asked me once.

The King of Disappointment. Now that was fitting. "He sure is," I sighed.

I told myself I was keeping in touch with Bob out of the goodness of my heart. But the truth was that I was still looking for reassurance. I didn't believe in myself enough to realize that I deserved better. I shrunk myself to fit him.

He didn't take away my power: I gave it to him, over and over. And, apparently, I hadn't been kicked around enough yet.

I had always wondered how a woman could stay with a man who abused her. What kind of person would subject themselves to that violence over and over, willingly? Even after Jimmy had attacked me on the front steps, my mother had taken him back. I'd been so disgusted with her, then—but now, I was beginning to understand. Sometimes, the need to be loved is stronger than any self-protective instinct and, when you don't value yourself, you're willing to put up with a lot more in the name of love.

I no longer threw up everything I ate. I no longer binged in the car at midnight. I'd gotten an inkling of empowerment during my association with John Green. But I didn't yet love myself enough to stand up for what was right for me. I still had some growing left to do in order to transcend the patterns.

Bob didn't get me back with text messages or phone calls; he got me back with tears.

He'd lost his job at the car dealership. The economy was on the downslide and, although he'd been their top salesman (or maybe *because* he'd been their top salesman), management decided they couldn't afford to keep him on. He went to another dealership but, after a few months, they had to let him go, too. He was anxious and afraid—totally uncertain of where his life would end up.

One day he showed up at my office. I don't know what he had taken—maybe Valium, or something like that—but he was sort of stumbling around, and his big blue eyes were all glassy. I took him to lunch, partly to get him the heck out of my office and partly because I was afraid for him to drive in that condition.

As we sat across from one another in the restaurant, he started crying. "I love you," he said. "I can't stop loving you. Please don't leave me."

And just like that, I was sucked back into the game. I had a white Mercedes and a burgundy Porsche. I owned more than a dozen rental properties and had a lovely home in the suburbs. But none of it meant anything to me without love.

I wanted so badly to help him. He became my project. We were together all the time. I had a vision of him in my head: the Bob Who Could Be. If I worked hard enough, if I was pretty and sexy enough, if I yelled loudly enough—*if I loved him enough*—eventually, he would see sense and become this person I saw in my mind.

By this point, Michelle had wised up and was finally out of the picture, but I just wouldn't fucking quit. Like a boxer in the biggest match of his career, I kept coming back for more only to receive debilitating hits. Punch-drunk as I was, the rest of my life started to feel unreal. Bob sucked me in; he consumed me. If he could just be loyal... If he could just be caring... If, if, if...

The Bob Who Could Be was the one I wanted to be with—but the Bob Who Was presented an entirely different being. I wonder now if he was bipolar, or suffered from some other undiagnosed mental health condition. Just like my mother, he snapped back and forth between personalities and extremes with no warning at all. His eyes would even change color! There was the Bob who loved me, the Bob who cried when he thought I would leave him, and the Bob with the bright blue eyes. Then, there was the Bob who shouted obscenities at me, who threatened and smashed things, and who issued ultimatums. That Bob had stormy gray eyes, like hurricanes, in his face.

It was so familiar. There was the Carla who loved me, and the Carla who hated me. The concerned Carla, the jealous Carla. It was what I knew. Maybe even what I deserved.

Two months after we got back together, Bob proposed. I didn't know what to say, so I didn't say anything at all for a good minute.

"Okay... Are you going to fax me the answer?" His face took on that puppy-dog look of hurt. I felt like I'd kicked him. Marrying him was a bad idea. I knew it, deep down. But I was still so attached to the Bob Who Could Be that I ignored my instincts.

"Yes, I'll marry you," I said, finally. "BUT you need to give me at least a year."

A year, I figured, would be long enough to find out if he really could change. A year would be long enough for him to prove that he could stay loyal to me and not go running back to

Michelle (or worse, find a new woman-on-the-side). Who he was at the moment was not the person I wanted to spend my life with but, if he really wanted to become a better man, then didn't he deserve a chance? *If, if, if.*

He did well with the ring: a square cut, tastefully designed, with four small stones in the middle. I knew that he was on a tight budget since he'd lost his job—but I was still a little disappointed. After all, I'd seen the ring he'd bought for Michelle, with its huge center stone. Once again, I was second-best. When people asked to see the ring, I held my hand out shyly, embarrassed.

The truth was that I wasn't really embarrassed by the ring; I was embarrassed by my relationship. I was ashamed of Bob, and I was ashamed of myself.

Back to Business

While all this was happening, the real estate market in Vegas took a nosedive. Suddenly, no one was buying. At the same time, Bob was kicked around from job to job as car sales plummeted. That's when I took pity on him and offered to help him get his real estate license.

I saw the parallels. My dad had brought my mom in to help him with his business, and it had been a nightmare. But, as similar as our relationships were, Bob and I were not Bob and Carla. Our experience would be different. We'd make it work. I was *determined* to make it work.

I bought a huge new office space and set about making it beautiful and inviting. After all, I wasn't just any old agent; Glickman Real Estate was a thriving business, despite the sudden downward turn the industry had just taken. My clients were demanding and classy, and my new space had to reflect their discerning tastes.

The Bob Who Could Be would have been a great fit for my business. He was a truly talented salesman and, after spending so much time with me, he knew his way around real estate. Fortunately,

I already owned the building two years before he came to work with me and ran a respected enterprise. But, unfortunately, I brought the wrong person on board. The Bob Who Was remained a jealous, volatile bastard who routinely lifted up his shirt in public to show off his ripped abs. He didn't recognize any difference between truth and fiction. "Integrity" wasn't even in his vocabulary.

And, yet, I made a place for him in our brand new high-end realty office and tried not to notice when he made a jackass of himself in front of my clients. I clung to the dreamy idea that he would grow into a conscientious and reliable partner.

He didn't have to do much: I gave him the title of "partner"—and it was just that, a title—but I wisely retained sole ownership and control of the business, a fact which he resented. He would brag to his friends about how he got a major salary for doing nothing—but then berate me at home because I made him feel useless. Why didn't I trust him? Why couldn't he make the decisions? Why couldn't he be the boss? I felt used, and told him so. He called me a bitch, and stormed out of the room. I burst into tears and followed him, apologizing for things I hadn't even done.

Sound *familiar*? *Ugh.*

Just like Carla, he stretched the truth, and told people it was his company. When asked, "Are you Bob Glickman?"—it would make me wince. ... No, that would be my father. Since the name of the company was Glickman Real Estate, people assumed it was his name.

My ship was sinking, and he was a dead weight on the stern. Revenues were drying up, and I kept telling him we needed to tighten our belts and ride out the storm. He would agree and nod his head like he knew what I was talking about—but he was still a sleazy car salesman and before I knew it, I was dropping money by the fistful into the black hole of Bob.

I paid for him to go to classes so he could get his real estate license. I paid him a salary of $10,000 a month for doing basically nothing. When Christmas came around, he milked another $10,000 out of me, saying that he always gave his kids a nice Christmas and couldn't disappoint them just because things were tough right now.

How living on ten grand a month was "tough," I had no idea. But I still cut the check.

Not long after that, he needed money again. I was literally down to my last pennies, trying to stay afloat in a market that was getting more unpredictable by the day. He literally dragged me to the bank by the hair. With tears in my eyes, I took out my last $10,000 and gave it to him, knowing that I would never see that money again.

I felt like a victim. Notice how I beat myself up; this was my own torture created by me. I spun myself into a dark cave. I was my own worst enemy and it was the meaning I derived out of it. So pay attention to the misery you bring on yourself.

But the truth was, like most people in victim mode, I *was* getting something out of this situation. I had the title of "fiancée," which was very validating for me. I had my dream of us as ideal partners. But now, not only did I have to wait for him to change, I had to wait for the real estate market to turn around—two things over which, I was beginning to realize, I had very little control.

Once again, I started to pull away from Bob. The more I tried to assert my independence, the more jealous he became. He wouldn't leave me alone in a room with my male clients.

When I threw a party at our new office, two lenders I worked with showed up to offer their congratulations. I'd worked with Rocco and Steve for years and had no interest in dating either one of them—but Bob didn't believe me. He threw a fit in the middle of the party and called me every name in his book. Then, he slammed out the door, and peeled out of the parking lot in the shiny red Corvette I'd helped him pay for.

I was mortified. This was the man I was engaged to marry and he was slamming me in front of my colleagues, the people who made my business possible. It was one thing to treat me horribly in private but quite another to do it in full view of the world.

How had I gotten myself into this mess?

CHAPTER 26

Taking Back My Power

How does the old adage go? "If it looks like a duck, and quacks like a duck, it's probably a duck."

So... If he talks like a jerk, and acts like a jerk, he's probably a jerk. No amount of work on my part was going to turn the Bob-Who-Was into the Bob-Who-Could-Be. No amount of kissing was going to reveal the charming prince under his slimy skin.

My heart was breaking. Not so much because I didn't want to lose Bob, but because I didn't want to lose my dream. I had invested every fiber of my being into him, revealed all of my vulnerabilities—and it had left me wasted, whittled down to nothing, and still starving for the love I wanted so intensely to receive. As much as I had moved beyond the pain of the past and my unloved childhood, I was still that unloved little girl, the daughter of a porn king. What would it take to turn things around and experience real love?

The stress started to show physically as well. I was too worked up to eat or sleep. When one of my employees quit unexpectedly, my mother came out from California to help. When she first saw me, her eyes got really wide and her black hair almost bristled. "You look like a concentration camp victim," she told me. "What the hell is going on?"

On a side note, Mom didn't last long as my assistant. I think she meant well, but naturally she wanted to do everything according to her own system of rabid disorganization. After just a few days, the office was in an even bigger state of disarray than it had been before she arrived. I love my mom, but the fact that I thought it was a good idea to bring her in at all is a pretty accurate testament to my mental state at that time.

Meanwhile, Bob was eating me alive. I began to see him as a mangy, rabid wolf. He tore me up without hesitation and then sat back on his haunches, licking his chops with that arrogant smirk while I bled. By the time I finally found the strength to shut him out, I couldn't feel any sense of redemption. In fact, it was like he'd planned the whole thing all along. He'd stripped all the flesh from my bones, leaving me as little more than a skeleton while he walked away with a full belly.

How had I ever thought I could tame him? What had I been thinking? No amount of love will ever turn a wolf into a lapdog. It wasn't his fault, really; he was simply showing his true colors all along. It was I who had cultivated the illusion.

All of this information was coming at me like a hail of stones, beating me up day and night. I was learning to let Bob go—but I was still writing him checks, which meant he was still showing up at the office every day to gnaw at me a little more.

One day, I'd had enough of the suffocating atmosphere. I needed fresh air, or a nice long drive through the desert. At the very least, I needed some caffeine.

Of course, Bob was at my side the moment I left my desk. "Where are you going?" "I just need to get out of the office for a minute."

"Well, I'm coming with you."

It wasn't the office I was running from—but I was too tired to fight, so I just shrugged.

"Okay. Whatever."

When we got in my car, he asked me again, "Where are we going?" "I don't know. Maybe for a cup of tea." Of course, I could have gotten tea in the office kitchen, but I felt a little better just being outside.

Leaving the parking lot, I turned left instead of right. I don't know why; I just felt that left was the way to go.

"Starbucks is the other way," Bob reminded me.

I just nodded.

A little way down the road, I turned left again into a shopping plaza. There was a coffee shop on one end—but my eyes went immediately to another sign that read "Yoga Center."

I yanked the wheel to the right, and screeched the Mercedes into a parking space. "I'm going in there," I said. And without another word, I leaped out of the car and pushed through the double doors.

Immediately, the soothing sounds of chimes and a waterfall washed over me. The energy of the space was completely contrary to what I'd been feeling for the last year and a half. Instead of feeling dark and heavy and trapped, I suddenly felt light. It was like I'd been running through a deep, dark tunnel and had finally emerged on the other side of the mountain.

I took a deep breath. And for the first time in what felt like forever, I started to laugh.

When the yoga master came out of the studio to greet me, I laughed even harder. She was tiny, standing no more than four-and-a-half-feet tall, and her tilted eyes held a wisdom I couldn't even comprehend. She looked at me, standing there in my heels towering over her with my perfectly fitted suit, cackling like a madwoman—and she started to laugh, too. It was like our souls recognized one another. I bathed in the joy. I had found my J-Spot!

By this time, Bob had come inside. He just stood there, totally confused, as I laughed myself into tears with this miniature woman. After what felt like a long, long time, the laughter died out and the fear set in. What was Bob going to do? Was he going to make a scene? Say something nasty to ruin the feeling of this magical place? Haul me out of here by my hair?

The tiny yogini took charge of the situation. "Hello," she said in a thick Vietnamese accent. "I am Tina."

"I'm Cynthia," I whispered.

Tina took my hand and led me away to a small room off the main foyer. She shut the door firmly behind her and motioned for me to sit on a mat in the middle of the floor.

Panic overcame me. No way would Bob stand for this. He couldn't even let me go for tea by myself! My back was to the door, and I kept glancing over my shoulder as the knot of terror tightened in my stomach.

Tina put her hands on her hips. "You are fine. Lay down."

"You don't understand! He'll be furious!"

"You need relax," she said patiently, like she was speaking to a child. "You lay down now."

She began to move her hands over my head in a clockwise motion. She didn't actually touch me, but I sensed her hands moving over my face, down my neck, and over my chest. When she reached my belly, she paused.

"What are you feeling?" I asked her. "What's wrong?"

"Hmmm… Your power, very low." She shook her head. "Very low."

I was shocked that she could know this from just a few waves of her hand. But what came out of my mouth was, "I know! He's a psychic vampire! He's sucking the life right out of me!"

Tina just nodded, and her hands kept moving.

After a little while, I started to relax. I was still worried about what Bob was doing out there since he could be trashing my car, harassing someone in the foyer, or walking back to my office to wreak havoc among my staff. But something was happening in my body. I felt the sensation of coming back to my center.

Tina finished the session with a short massage of my feet. Then, she helped me sit up and sat gracefully on the floor in front of me.

"Power very low," she said again. "More work, you need. Today, this just a little."

She was right. I *had* stepped out of my power, and I had a lot of work to do if I was ever going to get it back. Not totally convinced that this *hocus pocus* was the way to do it—maybe this whole thing was just a marketing ploy to suck me in and get me hooked—but I did feel profoundly different than I had when I'd walked in the door.

"I'll come back," I told her.

I wasn't sure what I would find when I walked back out into the foyer—but it certainly wasn't an empty room. I looked back at Tina in surprise and had just opened my mouth to ask where Bob had gone, when he emerged from another room with a staff member. Apparently, I hadn't been the only one getting energetically tweaked.

When we got back in the car, we were dead silent for a moment—and then he started jabbering. "That was so weird. She did this thing to me, and she was waving her hands around, and I couldn't move, and…"

I let it all wash over me. The more I tuned him out, the more deeply I sank into this strange state of peace. Over lunch, he might as well have been having a conversation with himself. I don't remember a word he said and, if I responded to him at all, it was with grunts and nods.

We headed back to the office, and I wrapped things up for the day. "I'm going to the gym," I told my staff.

Bob simply shrugged, and said, "Okay. See you later."

I was shocked. This had never happened before. After all, there were men at the gym, which meant I could get hit on, and there was no way he was going to stand for that.

Funny, how something as small as going to the gym by myself could feel so liberating. As I worked out, I mulled over what had happened. Had Bob experienced an energetic shift at the yoga center as well? What could this mean?

And the answer came to me, loud and clear: *Eliminate him.* He wasn't the man for me. And I wasn't the woman for him. What had felt so challenging and dramatic had suddenly become simple and matter-of-fact.

I went to my locker and grabbed my phone. My text simply read, "It's over. That's it."

He called me back right away, but his response wasn't heated, or volatile like usual. He simply asked, "What does this mean?"

I was quiet for a minute. This acceptance was totally out of character for him. "I am not paying you anymore," I told him at last. "I don't want you in my office, or in my house. I don't want to hear from you ever again."

I'd said those words before, but I never held my ground. This time, though, I put all of my power behind them. There would be no more chances, no take-backs and no arguments. The threshold of acceptability had shifted. In fact, it was in a whole different time zone.

"What am I supposed to do?" he asked. "Aren't we going to speak anymore?"

"This is the last call I will take from you. I need to move on, and so do you."

I smiled into the phone. I had my power back, and now I wanted my life back. For a long time, I was still dizzy from the impact of this enormous shift. I didn't take Bob's calls, but his text messages would bring on a wave of vertigo.

Cutting the cord was bittersweet. I was alone again, doing it all on my own—but I felt a bit like a kitten that had been rescued from drowning. Sure, I was on dry ground again, but my shaky legs weren't quite ready to hold me up.

I had no more painkillers, and the addiction that had been Bob left a void in my life. But rather than return to my self-destructive habits, I found myself drawn back to the yoga center. I took a yoga class almost every day. As I worked with the breathing exercises, I could feel tension releasing from my body. It was as if I'd been carrying a bag of rocks on my shoulders, but now I was dropping them, one by one. Once a week, Tina did her energy work on me, only now she started her work at my feet and moved gradually up to my head. I came to understand that she was balancing my chakras, which are centers or vortices of energy in the body.

At first, I couldn't believe that this stuff might actually work. How could working on my body make a difference in my brain? But the results I felt weren't imaginary. Every time I left a session with Tina, I felt as though a little piece of myself had been returned to me. At times, I would see visions while she worked: of my parents, of Bob, and of other traumas that had become stuck in my mind and body. When these things came up, I would start sobbing—and I would release them.

In one of my visions, I saw Bob's face, right in front of me. Then, the perspective widened, and I could see his arm and the tattoo he'd gotten while we were together—a devil's face with flames around it that seemed to pop off his bulging bicep. As I watched, the flames in the tattoo began to burn, higher and higher. They encompassed him, and he *became* the devil. He burned and laughed while I lay there on the mat in the yoga center.

So here was the devil coming to get me, just like those creepy stories that my nanny, Olivia, frightened me with as a child. Those fears had somehow manifested years later!

Tears streamed down the sides of my face, soaking my hair and the mat beneath me. I let the fear and pain flow through me, rather than fighting it as I'd done while Bob and I were together.

As I surrendered, the flames started to die away. Bob's face became his own again—and then, it changed once more. Instead of the rigidity I'd gotten used to seeing, he became softer, more innocent. It was as though he were aging in reverse. Finally, he ended up as a little boy with dark hair and big blue eyes.

Deep inside, that was what Bob had been: a scared little boy, doing the best he could to make his way in the world. The traumas of life had hardened him, but this child was still at the core of who he was. Maybe that's what I had seen in him all along: the Bob-Who-Could-Be.

In that moment, I was able to let go of all of my anger and fear of him and replace it with a deep and profound understanding and compassion. We are all innocent children of God, doing the best we can with the traumas and experiences we've endured, trying to find our way back to ourselves.

And if that was true of Bob, than it had to—it *had to*—be true for me, as well.

I feel that I owe Tina my life. Sometimes, we would practice yoga together, just the two of us, and I would find myself saying,

"Thank you, thank you, thank you," over and over in my head, like a mantra, or a prayer. "Thank you, God, for this amazing life. Thank you for giving me clarity. Thank you for bringing me back."

One day, as we were concluding our practice, I put my hands over my heart and burst into tears. "Thank you for giving me my life back," I told her. "Thank you for helping me to breathe again." She didn't answer but looked into my eye with a soul's understanding and smiled through her own tears of joy.

Oh My God— I Almost Married My Father

Like a blow-up doll that had all the air knocked out of her, I was flattened by that relationship. Being with Bob seized *years* of my life, and it required two just to get all my air (life) back. Dismantling all the layers of agony and the wounds from the Bob ordeal consumed me. For fear of losing myself again, I stayed away from men altogether.

My suffering hadn't just been caused by my refusal to accept Bob for what he was; it was due to my refusal to accept myself for what I was. I saw his potential, rather than his real self—but I also saw myself as flawed, in need of fixing. How could I possibly have been content with him when I wasn't content with me? How could I see his potential and fail to recognize my own? How can you help someone else when you're the one who is suffocating?

Eureka! Nearly five years later, I finally figured it all out—well, at least most of it. And, three guys later, I identified the pattern that Bob was, in fact, my father. Well, not in the real sense, but in the metaphorical sense. And, to add insult to injury, I was following my mom's choice in men. I became painfully aware of the uncanny parallels with my mother—my father's name was Bob, her lover was Brian, and then the guy she slept in my bed was Tom.

My first long-term boyfriend was Tom, the first guy I feel head over heels in love with was Brian, and—well, then there was Bob...

This is a crucial awareness for me because my mother married a Bob after having a very abusive father named Bob, while I had a hugely abusive relationship with a Bob. The pattern is now so clear to me, seeing that even the names are the same, with each of these men carrying a pattern for me to understand.

Darren and the Three Questions

Then *along* came Darren. It took me several years to comprehend all of these patterns and fully integrate them. After putting my dating life on pause for quite a while, I was destined to meet one more challenge.

For some time, I had been visualizing meeting my twin flame, the ultimate matching of souls, one's true other half. Through a series of coincidences, I ended up with a month-long house-sitting stint in Santa Barbara. On my last day there, I had a date with someone I'd met online.

I was so intent on meeting my twin flame that I had brought it up as a focal point for healing with a BEST practitioner, similar to the work that Tina did with me but using a different modality and done in a chiropractor's office. I had told the practitioner that I wanted to break through any obstacles I had to meeting my twin flame NOW.

So I posted my profile on an online dating site and was soon inundated with hundreds of e-mails from potential suitors, which I narrowed down to my top three picks.

Despite being ready to leave town, I booked three dates for my last day—one for coffee, another for lunch and the other for dinner. Based on these meetings, I would know if I had met the right one, or twin flame, and would then make Santa Barbara my permanent home.

After a brief screw-up in which one date named Darren had gone to a different Starbucks to meet me, he walked into the room. The beginning was inauspicious because he was nervous about the screw-up and I was a little irked since I had tried so hard to confirm the right meeting place.

Once things had cooled down, it became clear that Darren already had decided that we were going to be an item. I was unsure at first but, when he called me after our date, we talked for over an hour and I started to open up to him. The next day we talked again, and he told me he thought I was his twin flame. I was surprised he was even aware of twin flames, and struck by the coincidence of my visualization.

While Darren had not been my initial top pick of the three dates, the others did not work out. So, to my surprise, he turned out to be the twin flame I was looking for.

For the next several weeks we talked on the phone daily for hours. And I started to make plans to move back to Santa Barbara. Finally, my impatience got to me and I decided to go even though I didn't have a place lined up. I ended up renting a room in the Motel 6, while I looked for a place and got to know Darren.

Right from the get-go, and even during the drive back to Santa Barbara, Darren started to make the rules about our relationship. He had a little girl named Sarah and wanted to set some boundaries to protect her in case the relationship didn't work out. Essentially, that meant I couldn't be around when she was there. Hence, the Motel 6. It's like Darren had us set up for failure before the relationship even had a chance to get started.

After a month of anticipation, suddenly I felt like the brakes were on. I spent a couple days at the motel and then came to his house for the weekend. Darren met me at his office with a bouquet of flowers and we drove to his house.

Passionate lovemaking ensued but, at the end of the evening, he turned to me and said, "Oh, by the way, at seven in the morning you need to go out for coffee so that you won't be here when Sarah comes back." Sure enough, at seven a.m., Darren promptly wrapped the flowers in cellophane, literally threw them in my face and kicked me out the front door, without even giving me time to brush my teeth. My heart sank but there wasn't any time to talk about it. So I resolved to figure out what this was all about on my own.

Two days later, when Darren finally introduced me to his daughter, there was a new bouquet in the center of the counter.

"Oh, who are these flowers for?" I asked.

"Sarah, of course," he replied.

It felt like daggers in my heart. Suddenly, I was the other woman.

What?! The other woman to his daughter? This was getting creepier by the minute.

Sarah and I had met and were getting along smashingly well. Since Darren and I shared a common spirituality, I truly believed he might be my twin flame, but he kept pushing me away when it came to his daughter.

And, as if that wasn't complicated enough, then I also discovered he was going to Hawaii in just a matter of weeks with his daughter—and without me. Here we go again! Another man was leaving me behind—just like my dad did when I was twelve to move back to Southern California, and just like the King of Disappointment did when he went to Hawaii with Michelle to get engaged. A coincidence? I don't think so!

This deeply concerned me but, at the same time, it was also clearly an opportunity to shift this old pattern. I looked deep within myself to identify my beliefs that allowed this pattern to manifest so clearly and repetitively in my life again. It shook me to my soul when I came to the realization that I didn't want to be left behind and ignored again. Determined to shift this pattern, I discussed it with Darren and simply requested that he at least stay in touch with me while he was gone.

What was going on?

Apparently there was some strange dynamic here that somehow related to my experience of always feeling second best with my own father. Was I reliving my sense of being less than my cousin, Dawny? Or, being the other woman with Bob and now the other woman to this man's daughter? What was I creating?

This incident triggered a sense of being hidden and knowing also that I would never play second best—not to anyone. I was sensitive and understanding to his daughter but, at the same, time felt that we could all be loved. No one had to be pushed aside in order to keep another happy. "How about we all be happy?" I suggested.

Clearly observing this pattern and *soooo* ready to release it, I thought I needed to hang around a little longer to dance whatever tango was in store for me with Darren. Clearly there were huge dance lessons in this one.

Oh, but it didn't end there. The situation alone with his daughter issue might have been something easy to get over, but since it kept creating a huge point of contention between us, it was nearly impossible for me to be with him. Instead, it seemed like I was being completely ignored and my feelings regarding this situation were clearly being discounted.

So which piece of the puzzle was I in this? What part was mine to own?

I looked at my relationship with my mother and saw how she was always so jealous of me. And I shared this with Darren as an evolved man because I wanted him to know the baggage I was addressing.

But, in the meantime, I did a huge personal reflection and even went back to the BEST practitioner to see if there was something in me that was creating the situation. I quickly released anything that I may have been carrying that was my mother's and any part of me that may have felt jealous.

I then remembered how Darren would respond, "You just don't understand since you don't have children. You are not being sensitive to her needs."

Well, I suppose that is certainly one perspective, which is just that—one perspective. Yet I had another perspective to share that wasn't being considered. And isn't that what all my work over those last five years was all about—to come to a place where I could be with a partner who respected me and was sensitive to my feelings and for whom I could do the same? Couldn't we see each other's point of view and look to empower and raise each other up?

It had made me feel like I was being pummeled like a Hammer Head game at a carnival. I had long popped out of the box after I escaped my marriage nearly ten years earlier and now Darren was trying to hammer me back in that box. He wanted me to contort to his needs based solely on *his* perception of the reality, which I felt was based on fear—that if he introduced me too quickly and brought me in too quickly, it would cause damage to his daughter. He was so locked up in the fear of protecting his daughter that he literally locked me out of the equation and couldn't even see that.

"If you could only be more considerate and compassionate to my daughter, you would understand more." That's what he would say, after I had just gotten done sharing with him how I felt hurt that I was edged out, or that I felt out of integrity hiding things from his daughter.

In the past, I would have hidden my pain to put his needs above mine ignored my own inner voice and buried it all under the rug. For Pete's sake, anyone could see that it was just a white lie to "protect" his daughter and avoid any commitment.

Yeah, ten years earlier, he would have gotten me. I would have contorted to fit into that box—the one laced with fear and protection in order to "make" this relationship work. But he was convinced that I was the one who was screwed up because I didn't acquiesce to what fit into his box.

Denying my own internal compasses was not going to happen. It may have appeased him to tell little "white" lies to his daughter in the name of "protection." But, just as I picked up the vibration from my parents and just as I felt somewhere inside of me that something wasn't so good about those naughty girls at the porn conventions, his daughter too would see right through his side-stepping the truth.

In fact, she did discover things that forced him to bring up the truth, like my razor in the shower and my toothbrush. And, I began to wonder what subconscious pattern he was sending his daughter. That men would hide things from her just to protect her? Hmmm....

I do not judge Darren's behavior. I merely cite it as a point of reference and discovery for growth. He was absolutely well-intending in his motives, and I do not fault him in any way with that. In fact, I commend him for it.

However, I would have worked to elevate myself beyond that to a point where I can be in total alignment and integrity, or as the new catch phrase these days goes— total transparency. I believe from a unity perspective—being that we are all one—we could have risen to a solution where all of us were happy and united. The method of protection and fear keeps us separate. Why else would we need to protect?

On the day that I left, he and I had a final blow-out. We had an issue the evening before and, rather than address it, he told me that we would have to discuss it in the morning since his daughter was in bed. Why we couldn't have stepped outside or made some sort of alternative conversation is beyond me, but, ultimately, he did not want to discuss it. I thought we were never supposed to go to bed angry.

Well, the next morning after she had gone to school, we finally had our conversation, which escalated to a blow-out. Three statements penetrated me. First, he said, "You think I'm stupid; you just think you are holier than thou." That followed with, "You are really messed up, and it is all your baggage." Rather than accept any responsibility for the relationship not working, I felt he was putting it all on me. And lastly, "And now you are just going to run away."

As I drove off leaving Santa Barbara, I realized my time there was complete. For whatever reason I was there and for whatever the meaning of this relationship with Darren had, it was clear that I had danced the tango I was meant to with him and now it was time to head home. The only problem was that I didn't know exactly where home was at that point.

Interestingly enough, I had a gut feeling to call my mother and she welcomed me to stay at here place since she was leaving to visit Tim and would be gone for a week. Perfect. Since I didn't know where I was going to live, this offered an ideal situation for me to spend a week figuring out my next move.

Pondering over Darren's three penetrating statements, I looked at them from multiple angles. Do I really come across like a know-it-all? After looking at the situation from as many angles as I could find, I eventually dismissed it, since I could see no basis for it. Perhaps, this was merely a projection. I couldn't understand how he could feel or think he was in any way inferior, and I knew with every inch of me that I had no intention or thought of superiority to him.

Second, I was certain that I had baggage but no concern about addressing it. It was very clear where he was placing the blame. But, baggage or no baggage, it is for us to look at ourselves and not throw dirt on the other person. In the end, that is a lose-lose game.

And, sure enough, his greatest fear came to pass. In my experience, if you fear something strong enough, it is sure to happen. He feared me leaving and wanted to be cautious about bringing me too close to his daughter in the event I would leave. The fear was so strong that it edged me out and made me want to leave—in addition to the little white lies and deceit and, finally, our last communication. While clearly a valid concern, it brings up the issue: What do we do in life when people leave? Doesn't that happen in life? I wondered if she was always going to be so protected.

When I would express how I felt with him, he would try to make me wrong. Although it is a common male-female complaint, it was one that, when I was with Bob, I would just acquiesce and keep my mouth shut in order to avoid confrontation.

And it was a very common occurrence with my father. He would want to debate with me and I would generally just give him the point, concede, and ultimately just keep my own point of view to myself because I knew it wouldn't be respected anyway. But your feelings are your feelings. They may stem from past experiences, but there is no right or wrong and you have the right to feel them.

Oftentimes people try to rationalize or dismiss what others are experiencing. But emotions are not rational; they are from the heart, not the head.

Rather than being met with compassion and understanding, I was met with resistance as Darren tried to manipulate and coax me out of my feelings. Since that seemed strangely familiar, I made the connection that I had allowed this with Bob and, for the most part, just fell silent. But I was not about to do this with Darren. I had discovered one more piece about myself and, in order to achieve a relationship built on mutual empowerment, we had to be able to respect each other's viewpoint and feelings.

I remained dead-set on building a relationship that operated on a level of unity with my partner rather than a tug-of-war in duality—duality being two-sided—in this case, my side and your side and the battlefield of love that had been adapted to that. One person has to lose in order for the other to win.

Well, this is the short version, but I can say again that Darren wanted me to contort to whatever pleased his daughter. He felt that she should come first, based on his assumptions of what was good for her, which from my observation was not the same as what she felt. He was deciding for her and even denied his own truth, since what his definition as "safe" for her was based on his experience as a child, when his parents started to date after their divorce. It had been traumatic for him, so he assumed it would also be traumatic for his daughter—allowing his past to fill up his daughter's future. Some people might even perceive that as selfishly, overprotective behavior.

Darren's perception was clearly different than mine and for me it meant putting my own feelings on the back burner and going back into that dark closet where I lied to myself and ignored my own soul.

My release from prison had transpired ten years earlier and there was no way to stuff me back into that confined space.

One thing my life experiences have taught me is that it is time for us as a society to rise above the need to be right and focus on being happy. When we realize we are far more than two sides to a coin and the perspectives are endless, then life too opens and everyone gets to be right—rather than everyone being judged and someone having to win. Life and relationships are not football. We do not have to tackle one another in order to get to the goal. We can actually achieve it together and everyone can win. Hmmm… What a thought.

The Birthday Epiphany

After my Darren experience, I went to Valencia and spent my birthday with my mother and then headed over to my father's house to open cards and have some tea. Even though my dad and I had not shared much in recent years, we seemed to have reached a point in which we could respect on another.

After hearing my story, Bob launched into a dissertation about how I needed to go to a program that he had been pushing on me for nearly nineteen years. In this training, women are advised to date men who earn at least $100,000 a year, and it's all about money and power, not love. Based on what he shared with me, it was not in alignment with who I am and the relationship that I want to build with a partner.

From what I understand, it focuses on our differences as men and women and engages us to play into that. Now, I am all for doing whatever I can to understand my partner in every way and communicate better with him, but on the level of unity. Concentrating on our differences as man versus woman steps back into duality and separation, preventing us from connecting completely and deeply. Some women do want men for money and power, but this represents conditional love based on external circumstances, devoid of soulful, heart-centered love and a way of being that clearly is not who I have become.

What I am looking for and what I know I can have far surpasses anything that can be achieved by setting myself up for this ego-based form of operating. In fact, based on the relationship Bob has with his current wife, I would rather remain single the rest of my life, if that is what married life under those rules would look like. I have been there and done that with Joe and it is why I left so many years ago.

Again, feeling like I was in a squash game and being hammered back into a box that I had outgrown ten years ago, I expressed my disinterest.

Immediately, this triggered my father. He restated, at least five times, that since I am almost pushing forty and still not re-married, something clearly in his mind was wrong with me. And then, to my amazement, those same three penetrating statements from Darren came right out of my father's mouth.

"You think I'm stupid."

"You have baggage and are totally fucked up."

"And, once I tell you all this, you are just going to run away."

Aha!

I sat back as these three eerie sentences washed over me. Time completely stopped; everything stood still; and all I could hear were his words. As I breathed deeply, I felt myself rise above it on one level as I spoke to myself and sunk into my heart. I asked myself to listen to my father deeply, beyond the words, about what he was really saying to me from his soul.

As his screaming escalated and his face turned purple, I operated from multiple levels. I realized on the logical level that beyond what he was directly saying to me, it was really all about him. He was projecting his own insecurities and concerns on me. I even remember thinking to myself, *Wow, I wonder what his mother did to him to make him think he was stupid.*

In that moment, I felt compassion, while also sensing total humor in the moment too. For goodness sake, we all have baggage, as he was clearly demonstrating his feeling of being stupid with women. So, of course, I have baggage; he bought it! And helped me pack it! LOL!

As I went into the deeper expression of what he was trying to say on a heart level, I recognized that he was so passionate about this because, underneath it all, he really loves me and wants the best for me. In his world, having a partner would make me happy.

What he doesn't realize is that what has taken me all these years to discover and learn as I attract men who are better and better each time, is that I am *learning and growing.* And that what he wants is not necessarily what I want. The relationship he has would be like taking a pick to my eyeballs every day.

But, as I pulled back and really listened to his soul, he finally stopped to take a breath. He looked at me with bated breath, waiting to see what my rapid response would be. But I just sat there quietly in the silence. After about an entire 60-second pause that seemed like ages, I finally spoke.

"So, what you are really saying is that you love me and, by going to this program, you think I will be helped." I said.

"Yes!" he slammed his hand down on the coffee table beside him and said, "That's exactly what I am saying." Another long pause and he exclaimed, "That was my point; I won that one!"

Wow—I was speechless. A part of me found so much humor in this and it was just as if I had said, "Would you rather be right or happy?" My father was dead-set on being right, and sure enough, from his vantage point, regardless of my feelings, he was absolutely right! And it was all based on the assumption that I want exactly what he wants in his life and somehow that would make me happy.

Fortunately, along this torturous journey (at times), I have discovered for myself what makes me happy. I am so grateful to the amazing men in my life. First there was Joe, who meant well and showed me what the status quo was like —to get married and be roommates forever because it is safe. Next, Jeremy, who was sweet and helped to liberate me at the time by serving as a doctor nursing me out of prison and demonstrating that there was a light at the end of that dark tunnel, beyond just living a satisfactory life. Then, Mr. Brian Burns, who for a brief moment showed me what magical love could feel like. And, finally, Bob, for showing me what I absolutely did not want to create again, with the abusive arguing and self-destruction. They have all given me a point of contrast, support or lack thereof, but in all ways assisting me in my growth process so that I evolved. Thanks to them, I have become the woman that I am and getting better every day.

This birthday marked a huge turning point in my life and relationships. Reflected right in my face, I saw the pattern that I had re-created over and over: men who were like my father—controlling, demanding and having to be right.

And, having let go of those things, I also had to let go of the subconscious manifestation of men who would prove to me that all men were like my father. If there was any doubt, all I had to do was see the message behind the coincidental pattern of their names. I mean, is it any accident that my former fiancé, Bob, had a son name

Brian? Hmmm... I was learning to heed the signs now but, more importantly, the message behind them too.

This pattern included guys constantly leaving me behind, including Bob and Darren who both left me behind instead of taking me with them to Hawaii. Then, when I returned to Vegas after the Darren incident, I met a guy named Henry and—you guessed it—he had a trip planned for Hawaii that didn't include me. At that point, determined to learn my lessons and release my old patterns, I knew without question not to proceed with this relationship. Onward and upward!

So these epiphanies all started popping up around my birthday that year, which was a real turning point for me. That day my father gave me the greatest gift he could have ever given me: to see so clearly that I had drawn men into my life to be my partner who would wrong me for my feelings and want to convince me that their way was the right way. That day I got to release that and purify my being so that the men who come into my life now are loving, accepting, empowering and on the same team as one. And I, too, get to be sure that I am what I want to attract.

Plato tells the tale of man having been created as a "two-sided" being; male and female, he created them. God then split this two-sided creature in two and, ever since, the divided halves of the divine image seek and yearn for each other. And these two, seeking to balance the primal forces of creation, (the masculine and feminine energies) within themselves are not half-beings— but two full-fledged individuals. Each half of this being carries a primary charge of either the masculine or feminine energy and, yet, they each carry the seed of the complementary energy. You've seen this expressed in the symbol of the Yin/Yang.

We have, within each of us, these masculine and feminine aspects. Therefore, the key to balancing these elements in a relationship is to integrate them so that, together, we are one.

The journey to find the "one" has been the impetus for my spiritual growth and landing me back to myself, recognizing all is within me—I am the one; I am my own soul mate and twin flame. And the man outside of me is just a bonus and mirror of me reconnecting all of the parts within myself.

CHAPTER 27

Half-Naked Ladies

---

ho would have thought getting on a stage half-naked would be so empowering, especially when you ran your entire life from being on stage/camera as a naked woman being judged only for your physical appearance? Initially, I didn't have anything to prove; I just wanted to get into better shape. But I soon discovered this was one more piece of myself I needed to connect with.

A few months after I broke up with Bob, I entered a figure competition. Yes, you read that correctly. The former fat girl who had an eating disorder and who everyone called a chub decided to compete with dozens of other perfect bodies, on stage before a gawking crowd, and half-naked to boot.

The topic had come up nearly two years earlier, when Bob and I were going to the gym together all the time. Of course, he was totally dead-set against the idea; he had no desire to see me parade across a stage in front of hundreds of admiring audience members. (Despite the fact that he himself had competed as a body builder. He'd even won the title of Mr. Nevada not long before we met.) At the time, I didn't pursue the thought. If my lover didn't think I was good enough, how could I impress a panel of judges?

After Bob and our mutual insanity were finally out of my life, I went back to the gym more fiercely than ever before. I'd been working out steadily since I was thirteen—the summer I starved myself into a size zero. And, while my reasons hadn't always been the right ones, I simply didn't feel right without exercise. During the break-up, I'd slacked on my workouts for the first time in years and, although I was still thin, I felt flabby. I wanted to tone up—and the best way I knew to do that was to hire a trainer.

The first time I met with Michael, he told me, "I train competitors."

"Cool," I said. After all, if I was going hire someone, he should be the best at what he does. "Maybe, I'll compete." And what could be better than a competition to get me motivated?

"You've got to understand; this is serious. You have to be extremely disciplined. You have to train every day and stick to the diet. It's intense."

"Yeah," I said nonchalantly and shrugged my shoulders.

Michael only shook his head. I don't think he thought I could or would do it. In the three months that I worked with Michael, I trained five days a week and did cardio and yoga on my off days. I dropped a bunch of weight and built up some solid muscle. I looked feminine and healthy. My body fat went from twenty-six percent to seven percent. But the best part of the training was the diet. Even though I was no longer binging and purging, I had a tendency to eat sporadically and didn't always make the best choices.

Michael's plan helped me develop a healthier, more nurturing relationship to food. I ate in order to fuel my body in the best way possible, not simply to squelch my hunger pangs. I ate small meals all day long and, if I needed to tweak my calorie count, I simply adjusted the portions of carbohydrates. By eating more than I could have ever imagined I needed, I was transforming my body in a way I'd never been able to do before.

The competition I entered was one of the larger national qualifiers, held in San Diego. I knew it wasn't going to be easy. Other girls at my gym entered the same competition, so Michael and the other trainers taught us as a group to walk and pose properly on stage. About a week before the event, I walked into the locker room to find one of the other girls in her bikini, practicing in front of the mirror.

My eyes bulged out of my head, and my guts sunk to the floor. "You're beautiful." I told her. "I am totally intimidated."

If there's a pink elephant in the room, you might as well acknowledge it, right? She *was* beautiful, with nice rounded shoulders, a full muscle belly, a tiny little waist and curvy hips. And I *was* intimidated. I was so intimidated that I was nearly sick.

Suddenly, I didn't want to get into my suit. I knew I didn't look anywhere near as amazing as this girl. I was totally overcome with childish insecurity, feeling like I was transported right back to junior high—or even the porn conventions.

When we finished our practice, one of the trainers, Denise, came up to me, and asked, "What's going on? Are you okay?"

I burst into tears. "I don't think I'm a competitor," I gushed. "I'm not good enough."

"Oh, honey," she said, patting my too-skinny shoulder. "It's just the diet talking; don't worry. All my girls cry the week before a competition."

Easy for her to say, with her perfect, rounded muscles and four-percent body fat. Still, I thought, years of dedication had gone into developing that body, so she must have known what she was talking about.

"And, by the way, you're bloated." she proceeded to tell me, "I want you to up your cardio to ninety minutes per day and change your diet for the home stretch."

Ugh. Heading upstairs, I bumped into Michael's wife, upon whom I proceeded to dump a boatload more tears.

"Hey," she said, "You're doing this for yourself. Not for anyone else. Besides, look at all the progress you've made!"

All I heard, though, was "Blah, blah, blah." On a conscious level, I was totally over all of this stuff. But, apparently, some piece of fat little Cindy Glickman was still stuck inside me, because she was coming out in force. I couldn't shake the feeling that I wasn't good enough, and the fear threatened to consume me.

Still crying, I stomped on the stepper and started an intense workout, tears and sweat drenching my shirt. Michael called with words of encouragement; he was concerned that I might change my mind. He shouldn't have worried: I could no more drop out of this competition than I could have left Prague early or bailed on my Ph.D. program. I'd made the commitment, and I was going to follow through. What I needed to do was get to the root of this emotion and deal with it.

"Just give me a day," I told him. "I'll be fine. I just need to get my head right."

"Okay. Call me if you need me."

"I will," I said, but I knew I wouldn't. This wasn't something Michael was equipped to deal with. I called my friend and spiritual mentor, Jason, instead.

I knew this pain had to be tied to my childhood, but I didn't think it had to do with the fact that I'd been teased for being fat. I was thinner and more sculpted than I'd ever been in my life. No, this was something else.

I started to tell him the story. But, even as the words spilled out of my mouth, a vision flashed across my eyes.

"Flag team," I gasped. "My coach told me, 'You are the weakest link, Glickman.'"

The amazing thing was that I had experienced no memory of the flag team incident until this moment. Another repressed memory. I guess it was just one of those things I sucked up and moved on from. Only, I hadn't really moved on, because I could still hear that coach's words ringing in my head.

It all started the summer before high school, when I tried out for the cheerleading squad. I'd done the "we'll-take-everyone" cheerleading bit, but this was the high school team. I'd dropped a ton of weight by that point (thanks to starvation and ice cubes) but I still wasn't very graceful, and I wasn't as pretty as some of the other girls at tryouts. (I did get an award for "Biggest Mouth," because I could yell really loud. But it didn't get me onto the team.)

So, I decided to go for flag team, which, as everyone in high school knows, is where the girls who aren't good enough to be cheerleaders end up. It felt like second-best, but I wanted to be part of something. So I went for it, and I made the team. Barely.

I tried to practice—but since I couldn't always remember the routines and no one seemed inclined to teach them to me, I ended up just faking it most of the time, trying to follow the other girls. In retrospect, I probably really sucked.

I don't remember the coach's name, but I remember her face. She was a thin African-American woman with long, skinny braids that she wore tied up on the sides. And her voice was hard and gravelly, like a coal miner's.

"You are the weakest link, Glickman," she said. And as she said it, I felt it. I *knew* it.

You are the weakest link, Glickman.

Suddenly, as I relived that humiliation, so many things made sense. In every interaction with other women, I'd been operating based on the assumption that I was the weakest link; I believed, in the depths of my soul, that I wasn't good enough to have something better.

Any time I was in competition with other women, it caused me pain. I'd competed with my mother for my father's attention; with the women in my dad's porn movies; with Tom's imaginary girl-friends; and Bob's all-too-real fiancée. And now, when I'd healed so much and come so far, I was still trying to prove to myself that I wasn't good enough to make the cheer squad. I was always going to be on the flag team.

"Okay," Jason said, "Now we know what's going on, so let's shift it. What do you want this to look like?"

I wasn't sure at first. I wanted to win but, more than that, I want-ed to feel good about myself and have fun. I wanted to be able to be my joyful, bubbly self while wearing a bikini on stage in front of hundreds of people.

In my mind's eye, I saw myself as a little girl. I was wearing white shoes and a ruffled pink dress—the kind of dress my mother always tried to stuff me into and which I always detested because I was a tomboy. My hair was pulled into pigtails with big bows. I was on a stage, standing in the center of a circular pool of light, smiling from ear to ear. Just for a minute, I was the star of the show. I couldn't see the audience because the light was so bright, but I knew they were all watching me, because I was *special.*

I'd never seen myself like that before. I had no competition. I was dancing on a stage by myself, shining as brightly as I'd ever shone. *This* was what I wanted the competition to be like. *This* was what I needed to feel.

"Now," Jason said, "See yourself as you are now, in your competition suit. You're standing in that spotlight. How do you want this to feel?"

"I want to feel like I'm meant to be there. But I want to support the other women, too. I want us to support each other." I was crying again, but this time they were happy tears. I knew then that stepping onto the stage in this competition would be one of the most important things I'd ever done.

As my waxing lady, Priscilla, told me, as she systematically yanked out every single solitary hair on my body: "This is going to change your life. It's going to change the way you *are* in the world."

After I was waxed, I had my hair and nails done. Then, I had to find just the right shoes and practice walking in them. Who would have thought it would take so much work to be a diva?

The day before the competition, I flew to San Diego with Michael and Sara, another one of the competitors. After hanging on the beach for a little while, we had to get ready for our spray tans. I had never done anything like this: We had to strip down to nothing and present ourselves to be painted. Literally. The fact that one of the sprayers was a man made the whole thing even more awkward—but hey, after a while, all boobs and booties look the same, right?

If I'd had any inhibitions, they were gone after that, let me tell you.

I woke up the next morning after sleeping a grand total of three hours to find that I was going flat. Yup, flat. It turns out that if you dehydrate too quickly, your muscles actually flatten out. It might not have been so bad except for the fact that I was already really skinny.

"Eat a steak, and have some rice cakes and peanut butter," Denise, one of the coaches, told me.

"I'm a vegetarian," I said. "I haven't eaten cow in twenty years!" But I was ready to do whatever she said, because this competition was going to change my life.

There was something decadent about chowing down on a burger while everyone around me was starving. The whole makeup room smelled like meat. And after weeks of eating mostly fish and veggies, even the rice cakes tasted heavenly.

The meat took care of the flattening, but I was still bloated, because my period had, of course, picked this month to show up on time for the first time in years. Plus, my nerves had been so bad that I'd barely pooped in a week. My first competition and everything that could happen had happened—and yet, I felt great. Just as I'd envisioned while talking to Jason, I laughed and danced with the other competitors and told them how fabulous they looked. I was proud to be in their company and proud to be showing off the amazing body I'd worked so hard to sculpt.

The fear kicked in again seconds before the big moment, as I waited for my turn to go on stage. I even turned away for a moment, tensed to run—but I closed my eyes and had a brief chat with God. "Okay," I said, "It's just you and me now." This was the moment of truth; it was what I'd come here for. I kept taking deep breaths, just as I'd done so many times with Tina on my yoga mat.

Then, they called my name, and I stepped forward into the light. The moment I set foot on the stage, all my anxiety diminished. The intensity of emotion was still there, but it had shifted; now, all I felt was excitement. I was grinning from ear to ear, just like I had when I was little girl, tugging on strangers' pants legs. I saw myself again as I had in my vision, with my white shoes and ruffled dress—and, at the same time, saw myself as I was now , with my rhinestone earrings, matching belly ring and dazzling glass slippers.

In that moment, I was a goddess. I was the center of attention in a way I'd never been before. Everyone in the auditorium recognized me for my beauty and for my body, which was no longer a source of shame but a stunning work of art.

I walked proudly out to the center of the stage and struck my pose, as if to say, "Here I am, guys! I'm Cynthia Glickman! I'm the one you called!" I showed off my physique, turning slowly to show my back and my booty. I felt like I had to hold that final pose forever, but my smile never slipped. I held my head up high and let my gaze roam over the crowd.

Once all the contestants had made their appearances, they started calling numbers. I didn't know exactly what this meant, but I thought they were calling up the semifinalists.

"Number 60!"

Wait—that was me!

This was better than good. This was great! This meant that I was in the top ten—maybe even in the top five!

As I joined the small group in the center of the stage, I could feel the excitement building inside of me. This feeling was so huge that I thought I was going to explode. I struck my poses like a rock star, tensing my muscles and standing up as tall as I could.

Turns out that was only the pre-judging—but still, I was in the top five! Holy cow! All my hard work had paid off. I was a legitimate competitor. I deserved to be on this stage! I was pretty sure I wasn't going to win the title—but I didn't care. What was important was that I had done this at all.

In the end, it didn't matter what the judges or the crowd thought of me. I overcame my internal barriers, and I won. I subjected myself to intense scrutiny of my body by people I didn't even know, and I soared. I showered them with love—the judges, the audience, my fellow competitors—and let my light shine with all the glory I had inside me. And I won them over.

In the end, I placed fourth in the competition—despite the fact that the judges said I needed more muscle, that my butt was flat, and that I didn't know how to pose correctly. I won them and the audience over with my sheer audacity. They hadn't just seen a body on stage; they felt *me*. Denise told me later, "Wow! Who would've thought *you'd* be our star?"

"I know!" I said. "But guess what? I *am* a star!"

FINDING THE J-SPOT

After that day, being perfect no longer mattered to me. I am me, and that is good enough. By sharing love and giving love, I receive it in turn.

But I can't do any of these things unless I love the woman I see in the mirror.

When we are aware of who and what we are, it's easier to accept others. This is the gift that Bob gave me. He helped me take off the blindfold. Never again will I see a man for anything other than what he is—because I no longer see myself as anything other than what I am. Armed with this knowing, I can make healthier, more rational decisions about who I let into my life and whom I keep out.

In order to look at myself and really love what I saw, I had to shift my focus off the boys and onto me; I had to look inward, rather than outward. I couldn't count on my dad, or Bob, or the people at the gym, or anyone else to provide me with an experience of love and acceptance. Instead, I had to go deep within myself to find my soul's connection to all that is.

Love isn't just about being sexy and desirable like those vixens from the porn convention. It isn't a sexual exchange, offered in the hope of getting something in return. It isn't about molding someone to meet your needs—or letting them mold you to meet theirs. It is far deeper than a coy smile or a provocative outfit, and more profound than skin, muscle and bone. Love is about compassion, forgiveness and understanding the words, "*To thy own self be true.*"

The magical allure I saw in those porn stars as a child was potent, but no amount of sex magic can create real, lasting love. In fact, that kind of magic is a barrier to love, because it's a game of power.

If I hadn't experienced the porn industry as a child, I might never have come to know this so strongly.

Sure, the initial physical attraction is important, but it takes something deeper to create a relationship that endures.

What I discovered along this journey is that the most important relationship I can have is my relationship with myself. By loving myself—by being *in love* with myself, I am able to give love freely, without conditions. If I drive my car on empty, I won't get very far—but if I fill myself up through self-renewal, I can go anywhere I want.

I am self-centered—not *selfish*, but centered in myself. I no longer feel that I have to give myself up to make someone else happy. Just as I could not find happiness until I discovered it in myself, I cannot cause someone else to become happier, more confident, or more secure, because these things need to come from within. Yes, I am the center of my own universe—but like the Sun, I can shine out upon all the people around me, as long as I stand strong and centered.

In a lot of ways, I've come full circle. I began my life as a bubbly, joyful child who tugged on strangers' pant legs just to make them laugh with me. It was only when I absorbed programming and language that were not my own that I became heavy, depressed, fearful, and doubtful of myself. These things were like heavy winter coats, piled on one by one, over time. By the time I was going through my breakup with Bob, they were heaped on top of me so thickly that not a glimmer of my light could shine through. I couldn't breathe; I could barely move.

My years of healing were like a process of removing these ill-fitting coats, one by one, until I could see myself again. And while I don't tug on people's pant legs anymore, I do tap them on the shoulders and giggle, because I'm a joyful girl—the Joy Doctor—and that's what I do.

While I was writing this book, I had the thought that my story should end with a *bang*. Something felt unfinished. *Maybe*, I thought, *I should wait to write the closing chapters until I found my true love—my twin flame*. It would be nice to say that I finally manifested a healthy, stable, loving relationship. It would prove that all my hard work and healing had actually gotten me somewhere.

My lack of a partner was like a rock in my shoe. It irritated me. Then, I realized that I was looking outside myself again. The truth is, I've already found my true love—because *I am my own true love*.

I giggled over that one for a long time.

So, the journey of the porn king's daughter ends here—with me, at home within myself and my relationship with God, the Universe and the Source of all that is. I stand in the divine light of love and know that the wise beings in my soul group are looking out for me. I have forgiven my parents, my ex-boyfriends and my flag coach. More importantly, I have forgiven myself, because now I know the truth.

If someone is going to love me, it won't be just because of what I wear, or how flat my belly is, or how gorgeous my hair looks. It won't be just because of how much they desire me physically. If someone is going to love me, it's going to be because they see my joyful, buoyant, giggling soul, and find it irresistible. Ultimately, he will love me for every aspect of my divinity—not just one-dimensional, but both inner and outer beauty—with all my perfections and imperfections too.

CHAPTER 28

Forgiveness, Understanding and Self-Actualization

"A human being is a part of a whole, called by us universe, a part limited in time and space. He experiences himself, his thoughts and feelings as something separated from the rest... a kind of optical delusion of his consciousness. This delusion is a kind of prison for us, restricting us to our personal desires and to affection for a few persons nearest to us. Our task must be to free ourselves from this prison by widening our circle of compassion to embrace all living creatures and the whole of nature in its beauty." – Albert Einstein

A few years ago, I decided to visit my dad in Valencia. What are you doing on Father's Day?" I asked him. "Katie and I are going to visit her dad," he said. At first, I was disappointed that he already had plans with his new wife—but then it occurred to me that we might be able to go to breakfast with Brian and his kids.

Brian had followed my dad into the porn sales business for a few years, but then he got a job selling computer software. He's fantastic at it. All the skills he learned working the phones for my father have served him well. His two children, Joseph and Hannah, are the sweetest little souls. On the day Joseph, the oldest, was born, I literally felt his essence enter the world. I called Brian and asked him to tell me about his firstborn son. When he started to describe a healthy boy with ten fingers and ten toes, I stopped him. "Who is he?" I asked. "What's his soul like?"

My practical-minded brother was a little confused by this, but when he started talking about Joseph in this new way, I knew I'd been right on the money. Joseph was a special boy with a sensitive soul—he had to be, since I could feel his energy surrounding me from halfway across the country. I could almost feel him speaking to me.

I visited not long after, and while Brian's wife, Sarah, was upstairs in the shower, I laid baby Joseph down on the floor. He looked up at me with his big liquid eyes, and pointed straight at my heart. This was my first experience with him, and I knew that we had a special soul connection.

Six years later, on that Father's Day, Joseph and Hannah woke up really early and sneaked into my room. They wanted me to read them a story (at 6 a.m.? Really?) but I suggested that we make breakfast for their daddy. We'd have to be very quiet, so we wouldn't wake him up and ruin the surprise.

I asked what breakfast should be, and they opted for hot chocolate and waffles. Joseph explained to me the proper way to make waffles: You take them out of the freezer, put them in the microwave for a little bit, and then put them in the toaster. Once we had a little stack ready, we put just enough syrup and butter on them for his daddy.

Brian, needless to say, was very grateful for this spectacular breakfast.

Later that morning, I took Joseph and Hannah with me to meet my dad for a second breakfast at a great omelet place in the old part of Newhall. It was a perfect morning, so we sat out on the patio.

While the kids enjoyed breakfast number two, my dad and I got to talk—really talk—for the first time ever in my adult life.

Of course, we started out on his favorite subject, my mother. He has always been bitter about her and ultimately steers the conversation so he can make fun of her within the context of whatever subject we're addressing. But this was the first time I was able to connect with him on a heartfelt level about how he felt during the time they were married.

My mother was more intimidated by the women in the porn industry than I ever realized. Maybe even as intimidated as I was.

Years later, when I interviewed my mother about this, thirty-plus years after the fact, she had never forgiven herself for the choice she made that day.. She had never gotten over the impact that she may have had on her children's lives and the women in the industry. The truth was that she was just as much a slave to the business as the actresses. With no formal education and the only real business she had ever known, she didn't think she could leave. And she had become accustomed to fur coats, Mercedes, Corvettes, limo rides, travel and fancy dinners out.

Only in the last year I was able to share with her that I never held a grudge. Only in the last year I was able to share with her that I never held a grudge. So although she had never forgiven herself, I forgave her, even though I believed there was nothing to forgive. She made the best decision she could, based on what she knew at that time.

Still, many of my parents' screaming matches were the result of Carla's insecurities. She was jealous of the women on the video boxes. She was jealous of the women who worked for their company as salespeople. If my dad so much as looked at a poster the wrong way, it could send her into an all-day rage.

"Jealousy and the porn business don't mix," my dad told me. "It seemed so odd to me, her jealousy. It was kind of like, 'Yeah, hello! I'm in the business. I'm going to see naked women.' It's just going to happen, because that's the way it is. She should have known that from the beginning."

Dad went on to tell me about the rages Mom would go into after I left for college. When they went out to dinner, he would have to keep his head down and his eyes glued to his plate to prevent her from misinterpreting any accidental glances. But even that wasn't enough. One night, a young, attractive woman walked into the restaurant where they were eating. My dad saw her only peripherally; when he looked up, it was to make eye contact with Carla. The moment he did so, my mother started screaming at him.

Everyone could hear her. My dad was so mortified that he didn't know what to do. He could only signal the waiter to bring them the check and some to-go boxes so he could get Crazy Carla out of there before she wrecked the place.

Carla had the keys to the car, so she got in the driver's seat and peeled away from the curb, screaming all the while. "How dare you look at another woman while I'm sitting right there? What the fuck is wrong with you?"

When he didn't respond fast enough, she slammed on the brakes, threw the box of leftover food at him, and said, "Get the fuck out of the car, asshole!"

He did. And she drove off, fuming about what a pig he was for daring to glance at another woman.

Three miles from home, covered in spaghetti, my dad did the only thing he could do: He started walking. The next couple of hours gave him plenty of time to think about what a bitch he'd married.

When he finally got to the front door, she wouldn't even let him in to change or shower, so he grabbed the keys and slept in the van.

All in all, my parents were together for almost twenty-five years. As my dad spun out this story over breakfast, he had tears in his eyes. This might have only been his side of the story, but it was so real for him. I could feel the pain in his heart over what he'd gone through, and my eyes welled up, too.

I had experienced similar pain in my relationship with Bob. I feared him, and didn't know how to put up a fight. We would both scream and yell, but I never won a battle with him until the end. I guess in some ways I had to relive my parents' relationship in order to understand it and have compassion for it. I was able to gain understanding of the human struggle we all face and the binding prisons we build around ourselves.

As we sat there quietly for a moment, I realized that this was probably the first time my father had ever released the looming sadness he carried for my mother and their marriage. He'd been dragging it around like an extra piece of luggage—and now, he could set it down.

"When your mother finally came to me with the divorce papers," he said after a moment, "I was so relieved." By ending the relationship herself, she relieved him of responsibility. He signed the papers.

A few days later, in classic Carla fashion, my mother tried to change her mind. But the deed was done, and my dad wasn't going back. He'd put up with enough. It was time to end the pain they were inflicting on one another.

The thing he felt most sad about, he said, as his eyes welled up again, was the passion he'd had for my mother. They shared hate and anger, which they took out on each other daily, and which they sometimes mistook for passion—but underneath it all, they also had a true and deep love.

I had also confused anger and hostility for passion in my relationships. I'd done the same thing to Tom as Carla had done to my dad. I'd fed him crap about looking at other girls, because I thought this was how women were supposed to keep their men in line—but, all the while, I'd been the one who was cheating. And while my years with Joe had been comfortable (if repressive and passionless), Bob and I were every bit as volatile as my parents had been. Maybe more so, because, in many ways, Bob had been the worst of both my parents, all rolled into a big ball of craziness. I shared with my dad that I'd needed nearly two years of healing to fully realize the patterns my early life had set up—the patterns which had influenced all of my interactions with men and shaped my views of love and my Self.

I don't know if my dad understood all of what I was saying—after all, he hadn't had the benefit of all that yoga and energy work with Tina, or the spiritual seeds planted by John Green. But he didn't disagree with me, either.

He told me about meeting his current wife, Katie. After my mother left, he went a little wild again—back to his gold chains and open shirts. He got a toupee, and bought himself a Corvette. All hail, the Porn King of L.A.! He quickly discovered that, with his money and notoriety, he could get any woman he wanted. He fell in love with the chase, the game of meeting women and talking them into bed. It gave him a sense of power he'd never had before, and it was easy.

Then, he met Katie, who made him wait for a kiss, instead of falling into bed with him on the first date. "That's how I knew she was the one," he told me. "She wasn't as easy to catch as those other trout out there—but I had to win that game."

Katie is the complete opposite of my mother and, in some ways, that's what made my dad choose to include her in his life. She's far more emotionally balanced and doesn't get jealous, ever. Funny, that this actually rankles my dad. Sometimes, he ogles other women just to get a rise out of her—because, to him, jealousy still feels like love.

My dad is back in business for himself again, although this time he's picked a different industry. He's always been an entrepreneur and, while he never did stretch out as big as my Uncle Al, I have to give him credit for the risks he took in business. I learned a lot of my fearlessness from him—and, while he also taught me fear, a lot of that has been burned away.

There were times when my dad broke my heart, and there were times when I wished he was there for me and he wasn't. Although he is, at heart, a good man, he is run by his own set of programming. Business comes first. Fear is good because it motivates him to make money. Even now, at sixty, he still fears being poor.

Just as I'd seen the child part of Bob during that session with Tina, now I saw the child in my father. Everything he'd done over the course of my lifetime had been shaped by the fears and losses of his own childhood. His insecurity about not being good enough, the competition Mildred had created between him and Al, the abandonment of his time in the orphanage—all of these things combined to dictate the choices he made. Even now, he was still trying to find his way back to himself.

And because I saw that so clearly, I could forgive him.

The waiter dropped off the check, and my dad paid—because he always pays. We talked about endings and this brought us back to the subject of my mother. "How do you just dismiss twenty-five years together?" my dad asked.

"You don't," I told him. "But you have to accept it for what it is. You can carry that pain around with you like a bag of shit around your neck and keep complaining that it stinks—or you can take off the bag and let it go."

He grinned, and I could tell he understood.

That was a nice morning, out on that patio, with my niece and nephew playing beside us as we talked. I flashed back to my early childhood, when my dad still had his big belly and wore those enormous white T-shirts, and I would watch TV on his tummy. Later, as I drove the kids back to Brian's house, I wondered what their experience of their own dad would be. I hoped they found this kind of connection with Brian much earlier than I'd found it with my own father.

Just a few months before that meeting with my dad, I'd been driving with my mother. She was talking as she always does, mixing half a grain of truth with a whole bunch of bullshit and a sprinkle of imagination, making up her story as she goes along.

On this occasion, she was instructing me as to how I should conduct a particular real estate transaction. Some of what she was saying was actually correct, but some of it wasn't even close. It didn't matter either way to Carla.

As she talked, the anger boiled up inside me. By this point, I'd made millions of dollars in real estate and owned one of the most successful agencies in Las Vegas—and, yet, here was my mother, blathering on and on like she was Donald friggin' Trump. She was really pushing my buttons.

I took a deep breath, ready to start shouting at her. But instead, I found myself choking back laughter. The more I thought about it, the funnier the whole scenario seemed. Keeping one eye on the road, I turned my head and asked in my snobbiest voice, "Do you know who I am?" She looked right at me, and nodded. "You're my mother."

What? How could she say such a thing? Especially after I'd flown her out to Vegas to celebrate her birthday?

Maybe that statement wouldn't have been offensive to everyone, but my maternal grandmother is a fear-ridden, overweight, unhealthy, unhappy woman who isn't shy about sharing her bleak and negative outlook whenever the opportunity presents itself. So I didn't at all appreciate being compared to her. To this day, I don't think I've ever seen the woman smile. Even Carla, with all her craziness, couldn't possibly think that my grandmother and I had anything in common!

I took a deep breath, and asked, "Why would you say something like that?"

"Well," she replied, "You know this isn't our first trip around."

Time stood still. I remembered the time when I was little and she'd shoved her cold feet under my legs on the couch. Even back then, I'd had the sense that she was the child and I was the parent.

Carla hadn't been comparing me to my grandmother. She was telling me that I was right.

My soul, bouncing around in heaven, chose her as my parent. And if that was possible, maybe she had chosen me as well. Maybe she had as much to learn from me as I had to learn from her.

I smiled, and Carla smiled back. Then, her face settled back into its usual expression, and she happily resumed telling me all the things I didn't know about real estate. Only now, it didn't bother me so much.

At various points in my life, I have wanted a mother who wasn't my mother—a mother who loved me unconditionally and to whom I could confide all my problems. I didn't appreciate my colorful and traumatic childhood until years later. Even if I had the opportunity to do it all again, with different parents and a different set of circumstances, I wouldn't.

More than college or grad school, my life has been my education. Whether I recall the soul experience or not, I chose this path, and I take full responsibility for that choice. I believe that I came here to find my way back to myself—and spread joy in the meantime. And if that's true, what good would a vanilla life have done me?

My parents have done me a great service and provided me with great gifts in discovery; they have grown as I have grown. And, although at times, the way that I perceived the events that transpired in not such a good light for them, and even judged myself, I have arrived at a place where I have discovered compassion, acceptance and even responsibility for my part. I do not condemn them for anything, I love them unconditionally and recognize that thanks to them directly or indirectly, I have become the woman who I am today no longer looking outside of myself for validation, and sensory experiences to fill me up. No longer expecting people to conform to my wants and desires and no longer attempting to contort to others desires of me, I have been able to shift my focus to what I do want instead of what I don't want. The wellspring of love, joy and happiness all lies within me as it does with you.

The crown jewel to all of this is taking complete responsibility for yourself, which renders you powerful beyond measure. When we are victims to what is we give up our power to life, circumstances and others who we claim control us. Nobody can take you out of your own feeling of wellness—only you can.

CHAPTER 29

How I Chose My Parents

Whether there is such a thing as reincarnation and/or we consciously choose our life, belief in reincarnation is on the rise in our society today. More of the population is coming to embrace the concept that we just might have a choice in our parents and that there is a certain level of predestined postmarks along our journey in this life. Religions in India are known most to embrace reincarnation, such as Hinduism. However, there are also other religions that hold reincarnation to be true. Some of these other spiritual practices include New Age Thought, Esoteric Christianity and the Kabbalah. In addition, studies show that more than sixty percent of traditional Christians believe in past lives.

There's a school of thought that says we choose where, when and to whom we will be born. We decide, before we even set foot on this Earth, what lessons our souls need to be taught in order to grow and thrive. This takes taking responsibility for your life to an entirely new level. It eliminates the idea that your parents or your upbringing is to blame and something out of your control. This concept, whether it is an accurate theory or not, puts the control in your hands to shape the meaning of your life the way you wish. Rather than claiming, 'Well, this was just the hand I was dealt,' if I chose my parents, I choose to see the humor and the gift.

Wow! when i stood in line for a mission on this planet, I really got the hook-up. I was assigned the mission to spread world joy; what a job.

I stood in line, patiently and excitedly, with all the other souls that were getting the chance to return to Earth to assist in the next phase of the planet's evolution. There they were: All these childlike beings standing in their white-and-pastel-colored robes, in a light and airy atmosphere. They were all playful, joyful and excited in their glee about their upcoming journeys to planet Earth. All of us glowed like brilliant fireflies. My light was white, with a hint of yellow—just like the shining Sun. I was grinning from ear to ear, like a kid who'd been given a ticket to Disneyland. The most amazing ride of all—life—was just around the corner.

"This is *so* cool," I said.

They all talked and played as they stood in line and met with their wiser and even more evolved soul counselors in preparation for this journey. These souls were so pure right now; they had not yet been tainted by the day-to-day minutiae of living on a dense planet in physical form—the third dimension.

The journey to Earth was the ultimate ticket that they had all chosen to ride. This journey that the third-dimensional plane had in store for them represented a huge time of transition to a Golden Age by the end of the Mayan Calendar. These souls knew they were coming to Earth to assist in the planet's transition from the old ways of doing things to a new way. And they were so honored and thrilled that they were getting this opportunity.

I was the most excited of them all, smiling from ear to ear and bouncing up and down. I knew that I had a part to play and that it might be a small one. But, as we understand the butterfly effect, it would impact millions of lives.

I was in love with the idea of going to planet Earth with all of these wonderful souls who were my friends and cohorts. My excitement rose up from the root of my belly and beamed up through my eyes. My light surrounded me—white light, with a small hint of yellow appearing as if I were the sun itself shining out to the world. And that is when they decided, yes, I had a special gift of joy in her, kind of like the way you feel when your heart tickles. Yes, I had this light feeling that was a high vibration. Simply by being in my space, people could not help but feel lighter in their hearts, with their lips turning up into a smile.

So, my wiser mentors and I all decided: Let's make this a mission to spread joy and assist in transforming the planet into a higher vibration of joy and bliss. I was so exuberant that, by the time I reached my soul group to select my family, I could barely contain herself.

This was a small, loving group, all dressed in these angelic, loose-fitting robes. They were much older and wiser and, as they consulted with her, they could barely help to contain their laughter as well. Although this was a serious mission, they also had a sense of what was really important and that was being childlike in nature. That is the essence of joy that is a higher vibration than even love; it is all-loving.

They each had their own feeling of laughter. There was Don, who had a warm and loving laugh and who referred to me as "darling" and "child." He treated her with unconditional love and understanding, like a guardian of her soul, while he gained, in return, laughter that was like Santa on Christmas Day.

Two other females and one other older man, all warm and loving souls with a great sense of humor, engaged in a circle together. They all knew that this was not only going to be a time and place where they could do a lot of good, but they also knew that this would be a journey to remember. This was the ticket to ride! There was no more challenging and dense schoolhouse than planet Earth.

At this time, the Earth is going through the end of the 26,000-year cycle that was divided into five parts. We are passing through the final phase and we have choices: We can choose chaos and destruction, or we can choose joy and love. That's what made this trip, at this time in the world, such an amazing one. We had a powerful opportunity and a once-in-a-26,000-year opportunity to see the planet evolve beyond anything we have ever experienced there before. Special souls were selected for this journey and yes, that includes you. It was a gift to have the chance to be here at this time to be a part of this and have the opportunity to evolve our souls and this planet in a quantum leap.

Part of our duty is to wake up and see that the world is no longer based on hate and anger and duality. It is evolving into a higher level of being and that includes one of unity. We are all one. We have been, in multiple lifetimes, the perpetrator and the victim. We have been a man, a woman, black, white, Indian—whatever you choose to experience, you have been around and seen all of these aspects of life. And, with that, we have a chance to raise our level of thinking and recognize that our external differences are only in appearance.

Ultimately, we are made of the same energy and, therefore, all children of God. And all of us have God, Source, or whatever you would like to call it, within us. Even Jesus made it clear that the kingdom of heaven is within us. We all have the light within and now is the time to open up to it completely and experience the world through a new set of lenses.

We have all been given challenges and obstacles. And especially now, as we are moving into this new era, we have all been given the chance to straddle the two different realities and transition our souls into a new way of being in which we are aware of our experiences and use them to inspire us to become better people and wiser souls.

I figured that, with my soul group, what better way to learn how to do that—grow my soul and expand my horizons—than to have a father who was going to make his break into the pornography industry and a mother with a had a borderline personality? As they helped me select my parents, they all chuckled as I laughed so hard that I fell to the ground, rolling in laughter with the bellowing of huge belly laughs.

While we hung out and mapped this thing out, we just laughed our asses off. It seemed so clear that this would be an ideal challenge to find my way through an environment that would challenge me to my core being. I would have to come out the other side completely whole and secure in who I am. This background created a situation in which I would not have the same fostering and development in a family environment that would normally be cohesive for a girl; it would be something that would require inner strength and fortitude.

Hmmm, that sounds great... Can we also make the father a Jew? That will add some real flavor to the story.

A big Jew in the porn industry? Man, they sure were creative with this one, wouldn't you say? Then we will make sure that both the mother and father have long patterns with parental issues that affect them both and their ability to relate to each other in a loving way, because that will make for a great foundation to work around for growth.

And throw into the mix a grandfather as a survivor of the Nazi regime, for good measure? This was an experience he chose, an opportunity to endure this treatment so that he could develop a higher level of compassion for all people. If we accept that we choose our parents and our lives before we come here, we can also choose to take control of our lives, and strip away the diseases that are passed down through the generations before we become carriers ourselves, replicating those negative patterns. Instead of burying our hearts beneath a landslide of painful events, we become like oysters, filtering mountains of dirt in order to produce one perfect pearl.

In other words, if we realize that our souls are here to learn and grow, we can transcend the negative experiences of childhood and claim our purpose with humor and grace. We have to throw some challenges in there, right? How else do souls evolve if they don't get some resistance in life? It is like the pearl; it doesn't get created in an oyster without the dirt that gets into the shell. Then the oyster builds this protective shell around it that eventually becomes this beautiful stone of great value. So, it's like that—every life should have some of those pieces of dirt so that each soul can create a pearl of its own.

I gazed down on the three-dimensional plane and laughed like my heart was being tickled. I laughed so hard I might have peed in my pants, if there was such a thing in heaven. My excitement at being a part of the world just bubbled over, and I couldn't control it.

That's how I got my mission: to spread joy in a world that desperately needs a little more of it.

Brought into this crazy world with such a huge job, I just happened to forget it when I arrived. And, to add insult to injury, I chose these parents with all their baggage for the lessons to be learned and, *of course*, some entertainment value. Sounded like lots of laughs before I got here; my soul group and I all thought it was *real* funny. Sort of like looking at the Matterhorn at Disneyland, it looks like lots of fun until you get in and your screaming at the bears jumping out of the mountain at you. Little did I realize how intense that decision would be in the "real world"—the third-dimensional plane.

I guess I was ready for the ride of a lifetime!

CHAPTER ⬛⬛ ⬛

Epilogue

We Are One

From the depths of hell and back again—would that be a true way to describe what I went through? I don't think so. I didn't have such an awful childhood, did I? You can be the judge but, in the end, it is up to us as individuals to judge situations for ourselves. Whatever our story, we judge it; we create the meaning out of it that we want.

While one might presume that our upbringing would lead me and my brothers to troubled lives as adults, the fact is that we are all leading fulfilling ones—and not in the porn industry. While we have all had our share of hurdles, we have succeeded in overcoming them.

How did we do it? I can only speak for myself, but I can say it was a choice. I knew that I wanted something different for my life. It begins with a simple level of awareness, whether it is unconscious or conscious. We can all make a choice about what we want or do not want in the world around us. And once we choose, the key is to focus on what we do want instead of what we don't want. I wanted to be beautiful and thin when I grew up, so when I finally stopped looking in the mirror and reminding myself that I was fat—what I didn't want—and stopped comparing myself to pictures of women on magazines but visualized the body and beauty that I did want, I begin to create that.

That's the beauty of it. If we don't like who we were, we get to change it. We get to become exactly who we want to become as long as we don't keep allowing the past to fill up the present, because then we truly do not have a new future.

So the gift in this lies in that, if we can look at each other as divine beings, we can love. It takes having greater compassion and understanding not just for others, but for ourselves.

The present is another gift; pay attention to that, stay in the moment and look forward to the possibilities that lie ahead. We all have a story to share. Make it a good one that may have had its ups and downs, so that it gives you the courage to be who you are today. One that has given you the courage to do the things you have passion for tomorrow. Live full out. Learn from your story, and laugh as much as you can.

I think I would much rather look at myself as a resilient, brilliant diamond. And, my parents and my relationships were polishing that stone for every rough and challenging experience like the pearl in the ocean it is—the rock that grinds away at that oyster, turning it into that beautiful pearl. It is those rocks in our lives that create that diamond. The rough spots turn us into who we will become and give us the courage to look at our potential.

My mission is pretty simple. I figure that when God was handing out life missions, I really got a good deal. Besides, how much better can it get than spreading world joy? And helping people to find their J-Spot. I think I got the best job on the planet for me! I got hooked up, and I will take it! As did you, you merely have to be courageous enough to discover your purpose and live with passion.

It took a lot of courage to leave what I knew behind me and make a huge relocation to Sedona. When I moved there, I left my real estate business behind, which I had been relatively successful in and gained the notoriety of being named the "Rookie of the Year" in 2001. From there I went on to become the top producing agent in my office and then opened my own brokerage—making millions and millions of dollars and losing a lot of them too!

I knew that there was still more for me to do in my life, including writing this book. I knew that I was intended to touch the world in a positive way in this lifetime and I knew that one of the ways in which I would do that would be by becoming an author.

My family may never understand me and they may see this book as their crazy daughter going at it again. But I am perfectly okay with that. And I hope that you, too, will love and accept not only my family and my life experiences, but your own too.

What is it that you choose? What is it that you want to be in your life? Did you have a plain vanilla life or did you have a rocky road? Either way, you are right! The story is just that—a story. And from where you stand now—right here, right now—you get a chance to start anew and be the person you want to be and the person you want to become. Take your story and work with your story. Maybe you ought to even write your story. Either way, you will heal and grow if you are willing to look at it dead-on and take responsibility for your part and your interpretation of the events.

Maybe I am just like everyone else; I had traumas, just like they did. I am in touch with who I am. And, if there is something in my life that has been traumatic, then it is time to face it and release it. And, if not, that is okay too. We all have some skeletons in our closet; whatever they are, who knows what it is or isn't? That poor Johnny Larson had to deal with my cruelty.

The underlying message in all of this is that it doesn't really matter what your story is. It doesn't matter if it is real, or what you believe to be real, since everything that we experience in life is just our own reality anyway. Einstein said, "There is no reality, only perception."

So, at the end of the day, what matters is your outlook on the stories and what you choose to do with them. Do you choose to use them as character-builders and become a victor, or do you choose to be a victim your whole life and claim that life handed you a bad hand? We can all go back through our cards and ask for a new hand, or we can keep the cards that we like and throw back the ones we don't.

The beauty of life is that there are no rules to this game—only the ones we make up. Who says you can't tell your wish out loud when you blow out a birthday candle? And who says you can only celebrate once a year? Whose rules are these anyway? I make as many wishes as I want, say them out loud and celebrate my birthday every day, not just once a year. You too can write your own script.

We can throw our hand back as many times as we want and we can reuse the cards that we want. We can even look through the deck and just decide which ones we want and make them ours, regardless of whether they are at the beginning or the end or even the middle of the stack. I suggest you live dangerously and buy yourself a different deck entirely and then mix and match. They don't all have to be a four of a kind. How about adding to the stack some angel cards and fairy cards? Create your own deck of cards or use various one to create some templates.

Let down your boundaries and be creative. We have a chance to live our life's purpose right here and right now in this moment or we can keep living in the past. But you cannot move forward or as a creator until you dump the baggage. Let go of what other people do, or don't think about it, and just be okay with it either way.

Obviously, it was a colorful childhood and I have had an interesting life. I am blessed to have such a story to tell. And, rather than hate my parents for what seemed like neglectful behavior and a lack of love and follow-through on their part, I realize that they did the best they could.

Recognize that the things appearing as detriments or hindrances are actually the greatest diamonds of all. We need to say: "Oh, who cares? That is just some rock in my shoe or a pain in my ass." We can raise it to the light and see the absolute splendor and brilliance of it. Thank God; thank life. Live well and laugh hard, but above all—love others with all your heart and don't forget to love yourself too.

This is the most amazing playground that we have had the chance to play on. And I say, "Play full out! Play hard; play well; live with no regrets; and love yourself like no one else will. Dance and sing like no one else is looking, and set yourself free. And don't forget to find your J-Spot. You will be rewarded for it in so many ways!

About the Author

Cynthia Glickman

Cynthia L. Glickman, Ph.D. - Author, Joy Coach and Motivational Speaker

Cynthia Glickman is now stepping into the market with her life story, *Daughter of a Porn King*. The human being that resulted from her upbringing obtained her doctorate by age twenty-seven and became a National Figure competitor (which is the top one percent in physical fitness), was a professor for seven years, a dean of a college and business owner before the age of thirty-five.

Dr. Glickman attended the University of California at Santa Cruz, where she obtained her bachelor's degree in mathematics and minored in statistics. After teaching English in Prague and the Czech Republic, she continued her studies at the University of Nevada, Las Vegas, where she taught mathematics while earning her master's degree and doctorate. Her doctorate focused on mathematics, technology and, most importantly, how the adult mind operates and learns.

After just one year in real estate, she became the industry "Rookie of the Year," earning ten times her prior annual teaching salary and then doubling that realty income the following year.

For the last twenty years, Dr. Glickman has developed her teaching skills and understanding of the human mind via reading, researching and practicing personal development and spiritual growth. As an author and speaker, she knows how to connect with her audience and has spoken at several events throughout her life. Clients consult with her for joy coaching in both their business and personal lives. As a coach, she has integrated her readings into her life and assists others with that knowledge.

Dr. Glickman currently works full-time as a writer, speaker and Joy Coach. She has written three other books that include "Finding Your J- Spot", "Your Reality Sucks, Change It!" and "What's This World Coming to Anyway?" To reserve your copy and to <u>learn more about Dr. Glickman's</u> secrets to overcoming your own obstacles and the steps for creating the life you want, go to:

www.cynthiaglickman.com

Find Your "J" Spot
Visit www.yourjspot.com today.

Uplifting Live Events:
Join others in our community.

Tele-seminars:
Enjoy tools and inspiration from home

Free Downloads:
Download your free 101 Joy Tips and receive weekly inspiration and tips to live more joyfully and abundantly.

Visit **www.Yourjspot.com** and enter DPK for your special discount to the next live event in your area.

CHAPTER 30

Epilogue

We Are One

From the depths of hell and back again—would that be a true way to describe what I went through? I don't think so. I didn't have such an awful childhood, did I? You can be the judge but, in the end, it is up to us as individuals to judge situations for ourselves. Whatever our story, we judge it; we create the meaning out of it that we want.

While one might presume that our upbringing would lead me and my brothers to troubled lives as adults, the fact is that we are all leading fulfilling ones—and not in the porn industry. While we have all had our share of hurdles, we have succeeded in overcoming them.

How did we do it? I can only speak for myself, but I can say it was a choice. I knew that I wanted something different for my life. It begins with a simple level of awareness, whether it is unconscious or conscious. We can all make a choice about what we want or do not want in the world around us. And once we choose, the key is to focus on what we do want instead of what we don't want. I wanted to be beautiful and thin when I grew up, so when I finally stopped looking in the mirror and reminding myself that I was fat—what I didn't want—and stopped comparing myself to pictures of women on magazines but visualized the body and beauty that I did want, I begin to create that.

That's the beauty of it. If we don't like who we were, we get to change it. We get to become exactly who we want to become as long as we don't keep allowing the past to fill up the present, because then we truly do not have a new future.

So the gift in this lies in that, if we can look at each other as divine beings, we can love. It takes having greater compassion and understanding not just for others, but for ourselves.

The present is another gift; pay attention to that, stay in the moment and look forward to the possibilities that lie ahead. We all have a story to share. Make it a good one that may have had its ups and downs, so that it gives you the courage to be who you are today. One that has given you the courage to do the things you have passion for tomorrow. Live full out. Learn from your story, and laugh as much as you can.

I think I would much rather look at myself as a resilient, brilliant diamond. And, my parents and my relationships were polishing that stone for every rough and challenging experience like the pearl in the ocean it is—the rock that grinds away at that oyster, turning it into that beautiful pearl. It is those rocks in our lives that create that diamond. The rough spots turn us into who we will become and give us the courage to look at our potential.

My mission is pretty simple. I figure that when God was handing out life missions, I really got a good deal. Besides, how much better can it get than spreading world joy? And helping people to find their J-Spot. I think I got the best job on the planet for me! I got hooked up, and I will take it! As did you, you merely have to be courageous enough to discover your purpose and live with passion.

www.ingramcontent.com/pod-product-compliance
Lightning Source LLC
Chambersburg PA
CBHW060001100426
42740CB00010B/1357